MY ADVENTURE
AN ENCOUNTER WITH LIFE

MY ADVENTURE
AN ENCOUNTER WITH LIFE

A MEMOIR

WILLIAM MILLARD

ARCHWAY
PUBLISHING

Archway Publishing books may be ordered through booksellers or by contacting:

Archway Publishing
1663 Liberty Drive
Bloomington, IN 47403
www.archwaypublishing.com
1 (888) 242-5904

Williammillardauthor.com

ISBN: 978-1-4808-8616-2 (sc)
ISBN: 978-1-4808-8617-9 (hc)
ISBN: 978-1-4808-8618-6 (e)

Library of Congress Control Number: 2020901943

Print information available on the last page.

Archway Publishing rev. date: 02/26/2020

For my mother, Nancy Millard, my sister
Ann Millard Keith, and my children
Will Millard and Grace Millard.

CONTENTS

PROLOGUE
MY ADVENTURE

I begin this story with the comforting realization that I do not promise to be completely accurate about everything that happened to me. I have no intent not to be truthful or precise, but it is not my purpose to pursue complete accuracy. So much is based on my perceptions of what happened that I could not hope to recreate all that might have actually happened each day. In fact, to require more precision likely means this book would never get written. The story I present here is based on what I perceive (and usually remember quite accurately) happened to me. This book has a purpose. In writing my story, I discovered that the purpose is to share my experiences with others who may be facing a personal crisis. I am compelled to tell this story about an experience in my life that, while at one time dire, somehow had a fortunate twist of fate resulting in my survival—at least up until I write these words. Survival is not imperative in life and certainly is not assured. Survival is really just a temporary pursuit of brief existence during the vast expanse of human history. We all know we will die someday. In the scheme of all time, we are here but for a brief period of time, although, fortunately, our time feels as if it moves slowly day to day. As we age, we look back and wonder where all that time went. However, having the fortune of surviving as long as you can and trying to appreciate the existence you have is a great thing. Although my experiences described in this story really began when I was fifty-four years old, the potentially killer illness that so radically changed my life does not lead me to present answers to any particular questions, but only to share with you what I observed.

Given the proviso that I cannot be completely accurate in recounting all of my experiences, I do remember a lot about my adventure, often in vivid detail. In this book I choose to refer to my midlife battle with life-changing health problems since 2008 or so as "my adventure." Maybe I could have sought a more descriptive or tantalizing term, such as "my comeback from near death" or "my personal struggle with seemingly unyielding health problems," but those seem self-congratulating and employ too much exaggeration of my actual contributions. I was not singularly responsible for any of my fortune; at best, perhaps I had a positive influence. Besides, titles that long would never fit on the spine of the book. This is a story about my battles with acute health problems that, on more than one occasion, did nearly kill me. My problems took several years out of my anticipated normal life and forever changed the life I once knew. These changes are related to family and career ambitions, my relationship with my God, and my relationship with friends and people of all ages. My story is not unusual to any patient who has undergone a serious illness (especially those blessed to recover), but I have been lucky to learn a lot and emerge a changed man. I am no less imperfect than I ever was, but I am different in many ways. Obviously, this can happen anytime in one's life; in my case it occurred just past my anticipated midlife. I am far from unique in that sense. My story is what I remember happened (with help from the observations of outside sources) and my thoughts on what may have contributed to my recovery. I hope I might offer encouragement and some understanding to others facing difficult and seemingly dire circumstances. I hope my reader gains an appreciation of what it is like to go through something like this. It's a thing called life.

My adventure had many twists, turns, and unexpected events. The story tells of my rapidly deteriorating health and ultimate fortune to survive. It recounts times of lost consciousness, heavily prescribed drug sedation, light (legal) drug use that created frequent confusion, and even some pretty darn clear-headed awareness of what was happening to me. Latter parts of my story share moments during my slow, challenged, and by no means anticipated successful recovery. The time frame when this occurred was from 2008 through 2019, although I am blessed to still face some consequences of this experience and likely will do so for the rest of my life.

The action in this book includes times living in Dallas, Texas, the home of my family and career; in Muncie, Indiana, at my mother's house and then at the Morrison Woods Health Campus, where I spent some eighteen months after my initial seizure; in Rockford, Illinois, my sister's hometown, where I lived first for three some years at Alden Park Strathmoor Skilled Care and then at Crimson Pointe, an assisted-living facility; and, finally, beginning in February 2016, back in Dallas at The Forum at Park Lane, an assisted- and senior-living facility, where I completed this manuscript.

Because I cannot always be sure of the clarity of my mental state at the time of an experience, I admit my story may at times be a bit creative, as you will certainly see in some of my strange dreams I recount experiencing so vividly. It is, however, a good-faith combination of what I remember, what I think I remember, what a select few have told me happened, and what I perceive as having happened. Along the way, I have reviewed the comments and records of friends, family, doctors, and medical staff. I have been particularly fortunate to have access to my mother, Nancy Millard (and her extraordinary reporters journal she updated nearly every day during the initial years of the crisis); my sister, Ann Millard Keith (also sometimes referred to herein as "Missy"); her husband, physician Dr. Jack Keith; and a number of my invaluable friends who include (by no means by way of limitation), among others, Bill and Kristi Francis, Rob Topping, Kevin Smith, Lloyd Rowland, Bryan Ballowe, Jim Vanderslice, Mike Harvey, Chris Fuller, Sam Gleason, Dan Freiburger, Glenn Ballard, Ben Caswell, Tom Bateman, Jim Borgmann, and Chris Rentzel, each of whom was, in his or her own special way, at one time or another on the front lines of my collapse, rescue, and subsequent recovery. These various sources, journals, medical records, and my still fertile mind are all critical parts of the telling of my adventure.

With thanks to all and praise to the God of my very existence, here is my story.

CHAPTER 1
TURNING POINT

Nothing quite excites me like a trip into Chicago. It really does not matter the reason, as long as I get to go. I love the feel and sounds of that big, brawny American city.

This was certainly the case one brisk winter morning in February 2014. It helped that this simple trip to Chicago was a rare treat for me, as I had spent recent years as a quadriplegic unable to stand and confined to a hospital bed and wheelchair in skilled care medical facilities in Muncie, Indiana, and my now permanent home in Rockford, Illinois. Unknown to me that morning, this trip was more than just a chance to enjoy the excitement of one of America's greatest cities; this trip was to be one of the most important in my life.

Walter, whom we considered our private contract driver, arrived early in the morning at the dock loading door in the back of the Park Strathmoor E-wing building, my skilled care facility in Rockford. He drove his special handicapped person's custom van to the dock. Missy and Jack, my attentive sister and brother-in-law, had already arrived and were waiting in my room for the adventure to begin. One of the staff nursing assistants helped Jack lift my prone body from my bed and placed me into my travel wheelchair—not my beloved electric-powered wheelchair that I used to whip around the grounds of the facility, but the small, tight one that could be folded up and put in the back of the van. I had been wakened early that morning, fed, and dressed in some of my more fashionable "special occasion" clothes. Any chance to go to this big city was always a special occasion for me.

This trip, however, was not going to be ordinary. While it may not be easy to conceive of anything ordinary about taking a quadriplegic man who was living on a respirator for a two-hour drive to Chicago, I was going for medical reasons. After much creative cajoling, the magnificent Dr. Shawn Wallery, my Rockford neurologist, had secured my appointment with a doctor he described as a preeminent ALS specialist at the University of Chicago Medical Center. The scheduled appointment that day was threatened to be put off not only because I was having severe chest congestion problems but also because my skin had suffered a nasty-looking breakout of shingles. I was certainly not a pleasant sight. Park Strathmoor's executive director was concerned about letting me travel at all. Missy and Jack were, nevertheless, adamant about my need for immediate attention, as my overall condition seemed to be declining. Later I learned from Missy that this was not the only occasion when my health care facility warned them that I was close to death and any activity could greatly jeopardize my survival. Fortunately, my family's strong commitment to accepting all innovative treatment suggestions prevailed. I was wheeled into Walter's custom-fit van, fastened in place, and off we went for the over one-hundred-mile trip to University of Chicago Medical Center.

Traffic was congested that morning, which in Chicago is never a surprise. We bounced along in Walter's old van. Jack and Missy carried on conversation with Walter while I, in my somewhat drugged state, stared out at the rural countryside in the hope of spotting a deer in a distant field, as I once had done, much to my excitement. At some point, less than halfway to the city, the rural scenery became distant Chicago suburbs lined with the modern freeway, office buildings, and distribution warehouses. Approaching the city, with O'Hare Airport on my right, traffic backed up; the slow crawl to Chicago's south side meant from a time standpoint that we were only halfway there. The journey into the city was completed, and the gray gothic buildings on the University of Chicago campus began to surround us. Police in the streets directed us to the medical center building entrance, where a valet jumped up to extract me from the van. I noticed I was not the only dazed-looking wheelchair-bound person in the busy entrance area. Healthy family and medical staff were buzzing around the lobby of the enchanting facility. This was big-city busy for sure.

This trip to a leading neurological specialist was no accident, although it was far from expected. In January, I had suffered one of my severe setbacks, which had caused Missy and Jack to send me from skilled long-term care at Park Strathmoor to the SwedishAmerican hospital in Rockford. While family knew what was at risk for me, it proved to be an extremely fortunate event in my recovery.

The hospital I encountered was first-class in all respects. I soon discovered I had a gorgeous, young, Swedish-looking blonde nurse who seemed particularly kind to me in my hideous physical state. She soon had me out of the bed and sitting up in a cushioned chair. Nobody had challenged me to do that in the past few years. They had gotten me into a wheelchair maybe, but not a lounging chair. It actually was a physical challenge not to simply roll over or out of my position in the chair. I remember that this nurse seemed to provide nothing but optimism for me during my couple-week stay at SwedishAmerican. Soon she was filling Missy in on her observations about my body and some movements she claimed she saw in my feet. She wondered whether I was in fact fighting something other than ALS.

She took her concerns to the hospital neurologist, and suddenly we received some encouraging observations. I think I was primarily unhappy because this gorgeous, vivacious nurse who seemed to take such an interest in me was already married. Regardless, she sure was good to me.

After returning to Park Strathmoor, Dr. Wallery arranged my February appointment with the doctor at the University of Chicago, whom he described as a leading neurologist in America.

At the UC Med Center, we were soon ushered upstairs to a crowded neurological department office. During the wait, Jack had to attend to several of my disabilities, including my gross congestion. I could not reach a hand up to my face or touch my nose. I was pushed in my wheelchair through some surprisingly narrow hallways and doorways, and finally into a patient diagnosis room. After the usual precheck of my vitals, Dr. Kourosh Rezania made his first appearance. Dr. Rezania, I was told, was raised in Iran and came to America at about the time of the fall of the shah.

"I understand you have ALS," he said. "The records I have seen certainly suggest that."

Missy recalls that I immediately lost my composure. I began sobbing uncontrollably. I rarely had actually done that, Missy says, probably because I rarely was aware of what I was truly facing. This time, however, the bad news hit home. Missy immediately declared, "We don't choose to believe that." As a family, we had tried to maintain optimism all along. This time, prior to the doctor even running new tests, it sounded so determinative and so dreadful. This time I realized it meant I was going to die.

Dr. Rezania had his technician run various tests to see if his prognosis was correct. I remember there was a lot of testing of places on my body, including legs, arms, hands, and feet. These were not the formal complete tests I would undergo later that day but the first for the doctor to try to determine what we were facing. He took notice of the results being shown on the screen but made no early conclusions. Instead he asked that we return to his examination room later that day—3:30 p.m., as I recall.

It was a long afternoon for me to wait, as while we had not been told anything conclusive, we still had no reason to be optimistic.

Sitting in waiting areas, unable to move around or adjust my sitting position in my tight wheelchair, seemed interminable.

Finally we were called and went to the special examination room on the first floor. Dr. Rezania surprised us by personally running the tests. He seemed excited. Electrodes were applied all over my body, especially on my legs and extremities. The exam seemed to take forever. I remember the jolts I experienced as he focused on different spots. It was a weird feeling of little zaps that made me twitch with some discomfort, but not big zaps that could make me convulse. Dr. Rezania got more excited. He squirmed and made little comments—observations, really—as the test results appeared intermittently on his computer screen. His thick Iranian accent did not allow me to understand what he was thinking, but obviously he was getting excited.

My body involuntarily twitched with each zap. My feet and legs would wiggle and at least seemed to timely react. It was involuntary. He looked at us. "This is great," he said. "With true ALS, you should not be reacting this way."

More tests were run. Visible excitement continued. Then the doctor turned to us and said, "This may not be ALS … This is something else, I believe. I think you might be able to get better."

I don't recall what the doctor speculated I might be experiencing, but he was emphatic that it was not ALS. Something neuro-myopic, I believe he said. There were other confusing words in the description as well. It was something serious but not necessarily fatal. Those were the magic words to me. Certainly, they were to Missy. It did not matter to me as long as it was not the dreaded ALS. We were elated. It felt as if something major had just been lifted from me. Nothing physically was different at that moment, but at least I had hope. I could move some things, ever so slightly maybe, but I had movement nevertheless—movement that now meant something, even though it was no different from the movement I had the day before. What was it? He did not know. But after three long years of being treated for ALS in some form or another, there was at least some light shining at the end of this long, dark tunnel. What was ahead? I did not know; nor did he tell me. But suddenly optimism was back. I know I thanked God, but truly I had no reason to expect such optimism, as I had not been praying that God cure me. I prayed for strength and patience and good medical help, but I never wanted to ask my Lord to do what I assumed was impossible. God could help me face the inevitable with peace and comfort, but there was no way insignificant, unimportant me would ask for miracles that I had every reason to doubt would truly occur. My faith had not developed to the point that I could accept death as a positive alternative. I knew I was not really worthy of being spared. Too many "worthy" people have gone too early before me. I would never dream of putting God in that spot. I did not want to test him. Honestly, I probably did not have enough faith to risk finding out.

We went straight home to Rockford, but it had to be the most joyous trip ever. I sensed that only hard work and good fortune would determine my life ahead. Even then, of course, there would be no guarantees. At least for now, I did not have to start to prepare to die. Movement of any kind was huge. Maybe it was only in my toes, an ankle, or just my fingers, but now in my mind it no longer indicated bodily deterioration but improvement, gradual as it was to be. In a sense, my story was really just beginning—at least part two of my adventure.

CHAPTER 2
A PRIVILEGED START

My life has been spectacular. Privileged, really. What does privilege mean to me? Let's start with what it is not to me in this context. I do not mean great wealth, perceived class, brilliance, or superior athletic, intellectual, or artistic talents. I do not mean a special silver-spoon existence that many, in fact, are fortunate to be born into, or at least savvy enough to achieve. That understood, I mean a more generic, possibly global form of privilege—a privilege that many people experience in life no matter their personal setting, economic circumstances, intelligence, or most any other perceived factor. I am thinking that if you can look at your life and recognize good fortune, general happiness, satisfaction in personal achievement, and perhaps good health and an absence of significant personal crisis, you are privileged. I suppose this includes the fortune to not manage to screw things up beyond mild normal youthful development. Even some screw-ups don't disqualify you from being privileged. We all have challenges and periods of difficulty and uncertainty, but we also know many people who face trials and experiences far worse than many of us will ever experience. It is very fair to think your life is not privileged. Aging has helped me recognize that if we live long enough, we all will experience many traumas of one sort or another; it's called life. But for most of my life, I have been privileged, at least as I perceive it. The basics of being what I call privileged have not escaped me. I had family, health, reasonable intelligence, avoidance of poverty and violence, good friends, teachers and mentors, and a surprisingly (though maybe naively) good outlook on my life ahead. I did not experience much death around me, danger, or a lack of love. My sense of my privilege is not necessarily unique or any more special than anyone else's, but nevertheless, in my mind, I am very fortunate, inspiring, creative, and spiritually rich. I have had a life full of experiences that cumulatively make it special to me. Modest as it certainly is, it is a life I love living and always want to enhance. It is also a life that, as a result of my adventure, I at one point learned I was not afraid of losing. During my adventure, the real likelihood of imminent death was staring me in the face. Before, I was not practically prepared for that to happen. I did not want to die when I became sick, but I realize now that there was definitely a point where I was ready to accept death, or at least where death was not an unreasonable option. I do not remember feeling as if I were grasping for some bar or ledge to hang on, hoping to avoid an impending fall. I admit that when I was younger, I feared death—or at least the concept of it. It seemed unimaginable that I could die and somehow life would continue on without me—that people would still go to work the next day and ballgames would still be played. One of my favorite so-called guiding principles in my early years was Woody Allen's witty observation made many years ago: "It's not that I am afraid of dying, I just don't want to be there when it happens." My adventure has certainly clarified in my mind that, absent premature or unexpected immediate death, one actually can be comfortably prepared to die. Then I guess it just happens. I suppose even that is a form of privilege for me. More on that later.

My life that I perceive as being so privileged includes being born in Dallas, Texas (making me a certified Texan for life!) and having the inherent advantage of growing up in a modest midsize Midwestern town—Muncie, Indiana. Being a healthy child in Muncie was definitely a form of privilege, even though I had no full appreciation at the time. Most kids take that for granted. Like so many childhood experiences in America, one can look back fondly at life in their own hometown and, supposing one was otherwise reasonably fortunate, can now realize it was a great place to grow up. Surrounded by farmland, friendly and educated people, and just enough businesses to stay somewhat interesting, Muncie in the 1960s is a place one can be proud to be from. "Funcie"? That may be stretching it. No, eastern central Indiana did not have mountains or picturesque coastlines, fashionable department stores, or nearby professional sports teams (surely one cannot count the Fort Wayne Komets minor league hockey team; I never did). Muncie was not a suburb of a great American city like Chicago, with all its intriguing attractions. The nearest city was Indianapolis, some sixty miles away. At that time, Indianapolis was really only known to me for being the capital of Indiana and, more significantly, the home of the great annual five-hundred-mile race that dominated the month of May. It was also the seat of the culmination of Indiana's beloved high school basketball season in March (commonly referred to locally as "Hoosier Hysteria"). Back then, even we nearby residents sometimes referred to Indianapolis by its derogatory popular name, Nap Town—not that we residents of Muncie knew any better. For me and the friends I grew up with, Muncie was stability; it was adequate public grade schools that we were all very tribal over, the nice Ball State University and its pretty campus, and all sorts of churches, factories, franchise businesses, and predominately safe and pleasant neighborhoods. People in this town of some sixty thousand seemed to know many of each other, used the same hospital and local doctors, shopped at the same stores, and traveled the same streets. The police often knew each of us by name, knew who our parents were, and knew where we lived. While maybe not paradise by coastal standards, Muncie was stable and seemed happy.

My privileged life in Muncie included being raised in a family (parents and sister) of good health, with wonderfully involved grandparents, all of whom eventually led me in later life to experience the joys of a family of my own—a wife and two children. I had my perceived advantages of growing up with Indiana Hoosier values (you might have to be a Hoosier to recognize them), being raised in a protestant Christian faith (Presbyterian at the time, as that was where my parents thought the most inspiring minister in Muncie was preaching), attending a creative and kind of unique public grade school, being a Boy Scout (eventually earning Eagle Scout status), being a Nixon Republican at a mere twelve years of age (okay, maybe I didn't know better), and being a frustrated underachieving but determined athlete. All this greatly shaped who I am and was to become (although I acknowledge that many may question whether those were, in fact, advantages). Things didn't necessarily come easy but, looking back, I see that it never seemed hard either. I went to Burris School for all twelve years of my grade school education. Burris was proudly experimental, as it was a laboratory school for college students seeking teaching degrees at Ball State. "Will making this change improve teaching? Try it out on the Burris kids to find out."

Everything in Muncie seemed familiar. We rode our bicycles anywhere. We did everything with neighborhood friends, and organized and played baseball, touch football, tennis, and basketball wherever was possible in the neighborhood. We knew where there was fun to be had, what was safe, and where not to venture. We were Boy Scouts who cut up whenever we could get away with it, but we still recited the Pledge of Allegiance because that's what one did and we were taught to respect the flag. We had fun campouts at nearby state parks, went to Sunday school with many of our neighbors, had part-time jobs in high school (I served meals for a catering service at Ball State), mowed neighbors' yards for some spending money, tried to party (as we perceived it in Muncie, anyway), played lots of sports, and pretty much knew everyone in our world. Of course, everyone knew us too, especially our friends' parents and our teachers.

My parents were special; they were my parents. I guess we were sort of upper middle class, at least by Muncie standards at that time. My dad, William Sr. (I am a "Junior" legally), owned his own business, a small regional advertising agency that served, among others, the state's automotive parts industry and Ball Brothers Corporation, the home canning jar manufacturer. He took a reliable and sufficient salary and supported his family successfully. At the office, he had a modest-sized staff who depended on his success. He went to work before 8 a.m. Monday through Friday, and he was not expected home until about 6:00 p.m. He wore refined Brooks Brothers suits he bought in Chicago. He often traveled for work, which frequently included not only sales meetings but also golf outings with clients. On Saturdays, golf for leisure was played at 8:00 a.m. at the local Delaware Country Club with Cardle, Hazelton, Hughes, and Quinn. When the Hazeltons moved away a few years later, Cullison slipped in as the new fourth. This went on for years. The rest of Saturday was spent together with my father mowing our large yard, raking leaves, and generally cleaning up. (Actually, before long he did more of the supervising of me as I got to do the mowing and raking—my first lesson in witnessing good personnel management skills.) That yard was always a regular spot for our neighborhood sports. As I grew, my mowing duties increased to include having a number of neighbor yards to mow throughout the spring and summer. These were wonderful times of the year, but I was happiest when the rapidly growing grass finally slowed down. Unfortunately, that usually coincided with more leaf raking and a return to school.

My mother, Nancy, was (and still is), of course, a spectacular mother. She was, after all, my mother—the only mother I was ever to have. I am proudly biased. She was a well-educated Midwestern 1960s mother and was uniquely responsible for formulating the adults my younger sister, Ann, and I grew to become. Like most of my friends' mothers in Muncie, she set the daily agenda and to a great degree ran the household and our lives. She was always present, even if not necessarily always physically in the house. I grew to observe that she was a woman with endless spirit, enthusiasm, and high expectations. She set high family standards because that is what her parents instilled in her. She and my dad were educated. (She met my father, then a recent World War II veteran of what I understood to be the Battle of the Bulge European theatre, at Northwestern University, where they both attended college.) She was a natural artist and lover of arts, music, cooking, writing, and generally things constituting beauty in life. She would claim she was naturally shy, but living in Muncie she was anything but. When I was entering elementary school, she spent part of her days getting a master's degree in pottery at the Ball State Arts Department, where several of her friends were a group of pottery-making artsy-type college students. Several of those students went on to become accomplished potters and remain among her friends today. About the same time, my mother began writing a weekly feature article for the *Muncie Star,* our town's morning newspaper. "Much Ado," the column's initial name, soon became a fixture in Muncie journalism. Her writing for Muncie periodicals continued uninterrupted until 2017, some fifty years later. The Sunday articles covered whatever my mother found interesting: travel; food; art; music; Muncie residents who did unusual, admirable, and creative things; musicians; artists; architects; gardeners; professors—it did not matter. My mother, who has that zest for life, influenced my sister and me. The offshoots of my upbringing involved love of sports and exercise, whether swimming, playing tennis or basketball, and following my favorite teams: the Dodgers, Cowboys, Burris Owls high school basketball, Ball State, Texas Longhorns, and SMU Mustangs. While my mother never pretended to know much about the teams I followed, it was that enthusiasm for things she enjoyed that made me a rabid fan. In applicable years, I also was fixated on politics (not many kids wore their "Nixon's the One" button to junior high school each day during the 1968 campaign). I remember stuffing envelopes at the Delaware County GOP headquarters with my friend Tommy for some elderly congressman neither of us really understood or particularly cared for. My parents subtly made me sort of politically aggressive. I ran for student council in the seventh grade, suffering a defeat in the election to a smarter, clearly more clever student, Warren—something I remember to this day. Warren ran a brilliant counterestablishment campaign and made everyone laugh. Everyone loved my friend Warren. Later I became one of the first juniors in the high school to ever become student council president at Burris, a brazen act that temporarily earned the disapproval of several of my close friends in the senior class. Being outwardly successful, I learned, was not always a pleasant experience.

Throughout their lives, my mother and father collected several beautiful things. Their travels often resulted in acquiring unique items for the home. There were exotic pieces from Asia, New Mexican Indian art acquired in Albuquerque and Santa Fe, unique batiks and treasures from Indonesia, original midcentury contemporary furniture designed by architects, and framed paintings and prints that caught their eye. Like their own parents, my mother and father loved books. Rooms had bookshelves everywhere, including her art and cookbooks and his war novels and history books. No surprise, my sister and I, as children, became hooked on books, the favorites of which we probably still have today. The house was dignified and lovely but, reflective of her creative mind, always a bit comfortably cluttered. The formal dining room with its Baker furniture ("never write or study or pile anything on that table") also served as her writing office. Books, clippings, papers, and her typewriter dominated one half of the room. Beautifully decorated, our house was definitely a home that reflected lots of interests and creativity. It was not organized like a museum but was still full of interesting things squeezed in throughout.

In Muncie in the 1960s and 1970s, among my friends, our parents rarely supervised our fun other than to make sure we showed up for whatever lessons might be scheduled on a particular day. It was a time during which parents expected kids to organize their own fun. They did not coach or supervise our teams or referee our games. They cared that we participate, of course, but they showed it by dropping us off on time for swimming lessons at the local YMCA or the gym or the public park's tennis courts. Our parents uniformly supported our coaches and instructors, as our participating at all was a privilege for us. They had no expectations respecting our athletic talent. (Mine was never all that good.) Early on, we rode our own bicycles to school each day and in the summer to our tennis lessons at the area park. I remember walking to my piano teacher's nearby house for those dreaded lessons once or twice each week. It took a couple of years to finally convince my mother I had no musical talent; fortunately, my talented sister became the focus of that development. Missy went on to master piano and cello, which, of course, thrilled my mother. Only on the rainiest of days were Missy and I ever driven to school. Walking home from Burris across the expansive Ball State campus with my friends was an adventure in itself. On the campus, we were frequently collectively referred to as "those Burris Brats." We did not know better; the campus, its students, and its big, imposing buildings were a source of constant potential excitement and mischievous behavior for children.

My family was surrounded by friends. The Hazeltons either came over seemingly every Sunday evening for cocktails or we went to their house. Even though we children varied in age, we sat in our designated family room, watching television and otherwise learning to get along. Adults were in the living room, recounting stories, laughing, having a cocktail or three, and otherwise demonstrating how adults had a good time. Kids didn't often go into the living room; nor did any mommies hold their children while the ninety minutes passed. If a parent had to referee our conduct at all, we knew we were in trouble. Dinner for the children was served early, and only the parents typically ate in the dining room. We admired their laughing and telling stories. On other nights, adult dinner parties in the home were not uncommon. As children, we were expected to greet our parents' friends and go learn to entertain ourselves. There were no video games, movies on tape, or big-screen televisions. Board games and *Lassie* (and, in later years, a late-afternoon live broadcast football game featuring the West Coast Rams or 49ers) on television were more than enough. There just seemed to be a lot of relaxed fun.

As I grew into my teens, our lives with friends and family progressed. Basketball was played on Saturday mornings at the gym with my friends Tommy, Mark, Ted, Doug, Mike, and Kevin, among others. If you were among the least talented you became accustomed to being among the last picked for a team. If that bothered you, you could quit or learn to get better. I was usually fortunate not to be the least athletically talented, but I was certainly not among the most. Other than organized Indiana High School basketball, we were not coached by parents and played only Saturday morning intramurals or off-hour gym basketball. We called our own fouls, as there was no adult supervisor there to oversee us. Often the much-admired varsity players played with us; after all, in our small school they were our friends. Unfortunately, as exhibited by our varsity team's season record, their talent level was not a whole lot better than the rest of ours. In Indiana, boys' high school basketball was king. We did not even have high school football or any girl's teams at Burris. Back then the gals seemed content socially to be cheerleaders, members of the cheer block, or in the band at the boys' games. They also liked to date the basketball players. (Somewhat ironically, Burris later not only started offering women's sports; for many years it had a dominant high school women's volleyball team that more than once rated number one in America in *USA Today*.)

Social life for those of high school age in Muncie centered around Friday or Saturday night high school basketball games. We even loved it through those years of winning only two or maybe five games in a thirty-game season. Hey, Burris had classes of only fifty or sixty students (and half of those were girls), while the Muncie area independent schools were many times larger. Awkward (for some of us more than others) postgame dances were held back at the high school gymnasium. Popular music on 45s was played by a volunteer high school DJ, and otherwise there might be a high-school-aged local attempt at a rock band. I was never very comfortable at these dances, but showing up was necessary in my mind. I never wanted to run the risk of being forgotten as a human being in high school. Breaking down social barriers often was a developing skill that seemed to take several years or at least several more games.

During my senior year of high school, my friend Doug and I somehow discovered Schlitz Malt Liquor. I remember it was a big adventure for us to occasionally share a six-pack after a game. We might hang in a parking lot near a local liquor store and hope a college boy could be enticed to go buy us a six-pack. Looking back now, it was hilarious that we thought that was so cool and adventuresome. Schlitz Malt Liquor had a high alcohol content (much higher than conventional beers), and frankly it was nasty tasting to both of us. Seeing as how I have no recollections of either of us ever getting drunk or even in trouble, I don't think it actually played much of a role in our social life. For us it felt adventuresome. What a Friday night in Muncie!

Burris was, in many respects, a wonderful place featuring many inspiring teachers, coaches, and staff. The school prided itself on providing creative liberal and experimental education. Many of us spent our lives growing up together, K through 12. Kids were inspired in creative writing, arts, socialization, and political awareness. While Ball State was never confused as a seat of 1960s radical student protests, we were aware of Vietnam War protests. Many of my classmates wore long hair and green army jackets and came from politically liberal families. Ball State had its share of hippie students. We enjoyed pretending to participate in the occasional Ball State campus sit-in and protest rallies, such as when the college kids dug Cambodian bomb craters on the college green. I assume my "Nixon's the One" button was safely deep in my pocket. Likely we most enjoyed missing class that afternoon. Burris students all came from the district immediately surrounding Ball State. Everyone was within walking distance of Burris, and if you did not routinely walk home with others, you probably ran the risk of feeling like a social outcast. We had so many inspiring teachers, several at the full professorship level, in the teachers' college at Ball State. Teachers such as Carl Keener, Ruth Dutro, Anthony Tovatt, Nancy Mannies, Pete Carr, and Coach Bob Gordon had near rock star status for me in the 1970s. None of them looked like a rock star, but they were rock stars in my life. Indeed, Coach Gordon probably coached nearly every sport I ever played at Burris. He insisted that I swim for our high school team so this naturally pudgy boy would become a more fit tennis player. I remember that year beating only one competitor in swim meets, and he was a member of my own team. Ironically, swimming became a lifetime passion for me in later years as my times greatly improved. Sorry, Coach.

Summers in Muncie in the 1960s were spent doing summer things. Tommy and I played all day, usually throwing baseballs, shooting basketballs in his driveway, or playing our favorite board game, All-Star Baseball. Our self-made all-star game cards usually featured our current favorite Yankees and Dodgers. Funny how Bobby Richardson and Wes Parker became much better hitters in our version of the game than, say, Willie Mays and Stan Musial. Mickey Mantle and Roger Maris, our personal favorites, were off the human performance charts in our homemade cards. Whatever the field of play, games or physical sports, our competition was always fierce although always friendly, as most important of all was that we had to stay friends. We both learned the risk of not having someone to play with should we get quarrelsome. I guess that was a socialization process.

As I entered junior high school years, my parents decided it was time for me to experience summer camp—not just a one-week Boy Scout or YMCA camp, but one of those private camps that were found scattered around the upper Midwest. For a few years I went to a beautiful old camp called Camp Charlevoix for a four-week session. Located deep in the woods and on the banks of Michigan's Lake Charlevoix, the camp featured every type of sport and outdoor adventure a boy could imagine. In addition to sports like baseball and soccer, we rode horses, swam in the lake, sailed in sunfish boats, shot arrows at the archery range, and learned to row a canoe. Indeed, Charlevoix afforded me the opportunity to load up on those Boy Scout merit badges ultimately required to become an Eagle Scout. Camp Charlevoix was an old camp attracting kids from all over the Midwest. Many of the boys in my cabin were second-generation campers, and many had friends with them from their hometowns. Other than my friend Rick (whose father had also attended as a camper a generation before), I was unaware of anyone else from Muncie. I was fortunate to make new friends. Not everyone was as lucky, as several boys would go home early, usually citing homesickness. I thrived for some reason; being placed in a cabin with eight or ten other boys and a college boy who was our camp counselor was thrilling to me. The counselors were so cool for a boy my age; I can still remember Mike and Steve to this day. I appreciate now that this was my parents' plan to get me exposed to being away from home and develop some self-reliance skills. I have no doubt this made it much easier in life for me to get on that plane to Asia alone only one day after graduating from high school, go away to college, join a fraternity, function in a business organization, and expect to make new friends throughout life. Obviously, this Muncie-style socialization affected my later years as a lawyer in Dallas and in living in assisted-living facilities during my adventure. Independence just became an expected way for me to live.

In my early years of high school, my father's older sister, my Aunt Mary, married a famous World War II general, Mark Wayne Clark. General Clark led the American Fifth Army campaigns in North Africa and Italy and was particularly known for outracing Montgomery and the British troops to liberate Rome. The Fifth Army, of course, did not fight the British (it was the Nazis it was fighting) but won a publicity war by getting to newly liberated Rome first. After the war, Clark served as president of The Citadel, the military college in Charleston, South Carolina. In the low country of South Carolina, where there were great military traditions and active federal military bases, Clark was a true local celebrity. This was, of course, foreign to me, as southern traditions and strong support for the military were much different from life in Muncie, Indiana. While we certainly had many proud war veterans, Muncie had no military bases with soldiers running around in town. At my Aunt's urging, I spent three interesting summers at The Citadel Summer Camp for Boys. A Muncie buddy went with me the first summer as a camper, but overall it was a totally new experience for me. Like the military college, the summer camp was designed to expose campers to military traditions, featuring great respect for God and country, and our likely first experience with military-type discipline. Most of the campers were from military families in South Carolina or surrounding southern states. A Yankee fitting in with these southern boys was likely a big challenge. I nevertheless had a great time. While I doubt many campers had any idea what Indiana was and why my nasally Midwestern accent was so strange, I actually was able to make friends. The traditions were strange: sweet iced tea, grits for breakfast, addressing every older male as "sir," hitting a military brace and doing push-ups for the slightest transgression. No doubt it was an adjustment for me, but other than saying "sir" or "ma'am" to everyone appropriate, it was an adjustment for all my fellow campers as well.

After graduating from high school, my privileged and fortunate life seemed to accelerate. Two days after the all-night graduation party, I boarded a plane (several actually) for the long flight to Singapore in far Southeast Asia. My mother's brother, Charlie Howes (Uncle Bud to me), and his family lived in Singapore, where he operated an off-shore oil drilling rig. My cousin Danny (two years older than me) and I were to spend the summer working on his dad's rig, the Gettysburg, which was operating some one hundred miles off the coast of West Irian in Indonesia (a portion of an island formerly known as New Guinea). The experience was amazing to me. At eighteen, this Hoosier boy was to spend the next seventy-nine days traveling the world, much of the time and in many of the places on my own. My itinerary had me circle the earth, as my plans included stops in Hawaii, Hong Kong, Singapore, Bali, Jakarta, Bangkok, Athens, Rome, Amsterdam, and London. I think in some respects I grew up on that trip in ways I did not fully appreciate at the time. New cities, unfamiliar hotels and cultures, new acquaintances, and new adventures were just part of nearly every day while traveling. I arrived at my appointed destination and things just seemed to go along from there. My Uncle Bud, Aunt Ida Bess, and my four cousins were my home base in Asia, but my time in Singapore was not long. Once on the rig, I did not return to Singapore until the end of the summer. The city was totally enchanting to me. Old Singapore with its English colonial era influences, its Chinese and Asian districts, and the intriguing Arab areas were still very much alive. But Singapore under the benign dictatorship of Lee Kuan Yew was a city-nation that was rapidly modernizing, which has been borne out as the sparkling nation-state it is today.

Each stop on the trip was a new adventure for me. First I had to find my way to Waikiki Beach and my hotel in Honolulu. That first day, I managed to get too much sun on the beach, so my journey started with a sunburned stomach. Hong Kong was a bit overwhelming for me; I had never seen so many people, all of them with dark black hair and speaking another language. Just the taxi ride from the airport was an out-of-my-world experience as the driver sped along, honking his horn, weaving in and out of traffic, and dodging the ever-present bicycles and trishaws that seemed to be in every traffic lane. I was booked at the moderately luxurious Hong Kong Hotel in the center of the city, but even with such protected convenience that first full day, I was too intimidated to leave the hotel grounds and venture into the city. Instead I spent that day in the Ocean Terminal shopping mall attached to the hotel. Everyone had black hair and seemed to be short, and no faces were familiar to me. Fortunately, my father had arranged a contact for me—a nice, young American couple living in

Hong Kong. The next day, the wife took me out into the city, through the open-air city market (complete with freshly severed pig and cow heads for sale), around the blocks of dense high-rise buildings, and through the parks and squares. The evening included dinner with her husband on one of the historic dinner boats in the harbor. We traveled to the boat in a sampan, which was totally exotic to me. The following day, alone and with newfound confidence, I took a tour bus to the New Territories, the area adjacent to Hong Kong that was controlled by Red China. This was my first visit to a communist country (even though it was intentionally touristy). After a couple of days in Hong Kong, it was off to Singapore for a week with my cousins, prior to leaving for the oil rig.

The travel to the oil rig was unlike anything I had ever contemplated. My cousin Dan and I flew on an old company-operated prop plane that was filled with oil company personnel. Our first stop was at a Phillips Petroleum–owned jungle compound on the island of Borneo. Borneo? I was where? Looking out the window of my plane, all I saw was very dense jungle, some coastal beaches, and a few authentic bamboo-and-jungle-growth huts that locals actually lived in. The compound was carved out of some space in the jungle, and other than the small airstrip on which we landed, I doubt seriously there was any other means of access or egress by land for a Westerner. On we flew, over open sea and small Indonesian islands dense with dark green woods. We arrived at night at a small oil town called Sorong in West Irian (now West Papua). While it had some semblance of an airport, it was really there only to serve as a base for international oil companies operating in the region. Today I read that it is now considered a coastal town that is the gateway to Indonesia's Raja Ampat Islands. We were delivered to a small guesthouse full of oilmen. I don't really remember if there were any other Westerners present that night, but there were at least a dozen Indonesian roustabouts—the men I was to subsequently learn did the dangerous work with the drilling pipes on the rig. Dan and I shared a room that I recall was nothing

like most hotel rooms I had ever seen. In the middle of the night, I
opened our door to go into what served as the bathroom; this was my
first encounter with the water-free Indonesian hole in the floor over
which one was expected to squat or aim carefully while doing one's
business. Before I got to the bathroom, my first cultural shock (as if
the non-toilet was not enough) hit me. There in the room that served
as the living room were several Indonesian men all huddled on one
couch. What they were doing does not need much elaboration nor do
I know for sure. Fortunately I did not look very closely, but it is enough
to say that there was late-night activity among them. I am not sure I
really slept much the rest of that night, as it is hard to sleep with one
eye open and trained on the closed but unlocked door of one's room.

The next morning, Dan and I were put onto a company helicopter
for transport to the Gettysburg rig, which was sitting one hundred
miles or so off in the open sea. Again I could not take my eyes off
the dense jungles below. As we soared over the landscape, I spotted
an occasional native hut; some were deep in the woods, and others
were against barren beaches. Then, as we soared out over the vast
sea, the Gettysburg rig slowly came into view. As the pilot negoti-
ated our landing onto the small helipad on the rig, I noticed several
workers scurrying around on the deck. There was lots of excitement;
we were to discover that the fishermen had pulled up a large white
shark that one of them had caught by dangling a raw beef steak on
a crude line over the side of the rig. Fortunately for me, the shark
was dead by the time I stepped onto the deck, but the message was
clear to me: no swimming in these shark-infested waters. I still have
a tooth from that old shark that one of the roustabouts gave me that
morning years ago.

The rest of my trip during that summer of 1974 was fascinating and full of adventure. In addition to life on the oil rig, which
included living and mingling with men from all over the world (Irish,
British, German, Filipino, Indonesian and Louisiana Cajun), I worked
in the rig's equipment supply tool room, ate dinners, and shared a

four-person dorm room with strangers, all of whom were older than me. I quickly learned more about the importance of getting along. Half of the occupants on the rig were native Indonesians. The Western riggers, coming from places as exotic to me as Ireland, England, Spain, and Louisiana, had fascinating worldly experiences. Most all talked (bragged?) incessantly about their time spent off the rig deservedly after working twelve-hour shifts for a few weeks straight. Most had apartments in a small town in the Philippines where they had "kept" girlfriends of local source. The stories I heard! They were like nothing this Hoosier boy had ever imagined.

I digress and distract from my story here if I try to recount all of the fun and interesting and challenging experiences I had on the remainder of my trip—or, for that matter, my several years thereafter. This book is not meant as an autobiography of non-special me but rather as an indication of why, by my middle fifties, when I became seriously ill and faced the singular greatest challenge of my life, I believed I had lived a wonderful, loving, intelligent, and fascinating existence. In short, in my mind, I had been totally privileged. Subsequent years were filled with moderately challenging accomplishments. I loved my four years as a college student at Southern Methodist University, a private school in Dallas. I made freshman-year friends and even more as a member of the Phi Gamma Delta (Fiji) social fraternity. I did pretty well academically (magna cum laude and Phi Beta Kappa graduate), an achievement accomplished in no small part by avoiding as many strenuous math, science, and language classes as possible. I wrote about sports for the SMU campus newspaper and had a great time serving as the sports editor for two years. I became good friends with SMU football coach Ron Meyer (future coach of the NFL's Patriots and Colts), covered the team, and traveled to all its away games for two years. Postgame locker room press conferences allowed me to meet legendary coaches Woody Hayes, Darrell Royal, Bear Bryant, Hayden Fry, and Frank Broyles. The meetings were not memorable experiences for those great coaches, but they definitely were for wide-eyed me. Unsure about my future (would I spend the rest of my life in a tiny town covering high school sports if I became a sports writer?), I chose instead to go to law school at SMU. Far from being a spectacular law student (my slow reading skills and lack of an ordered mind were soon exposed), I took the bait offered by my favorite professor friend, Mike Harvey at the business school, and added an MBA to my law degree pursuit. My performance was not special in business school either, but I did graduate with two degrees, one in law and the other an MBA. I spent summers between classes first working in a small criminal law practice in downtown Dallas, at which one of my duties was opening up the office early Saturday mornings so the clients (all facing criminal charges—"Your name you go by is really Meat Hanger?") could meet with my attorney boss when he eventually arrived. "Seriously, Mr. Meat Hanger, try to be patient; your attorney will be here soon" (more likely not for two hours). My next summer was spent receiving corporate legal department experience interning at Frito-Lay headquarters during that infamous Dallas summer of 1980 when temperatures exceeded 100 degrees for over one hundred consecutive days! My yellow Camaro faded to a sickly pale color in the intense heat. The upside: I had free Pepsi, Fritos, and Lay's potato chips all summer!

I first spent my summer during college following my freshman year working as a maintenance boy in a print shop in Muncie. The second summer, I traveled and worked with my new college friend, Lloyd, in Alaska (driving the whole way up in his mother's station wagon, on which we put some eighteen thousand miles). After graduation in 1978, the two of us made a trip backpacking across Europe. The summer of my final year in law school was spent participating in one of the lucrative summer clerkship programs established law firms like to provide for potential recruits. If you do your work well and generally prove you can get along socially during your summer clerkship, you then hope to receive an offer for full-time employment as a new associate attorney who starts following your graduation the forthcoming year. I had two good firms offering me employment, one in Houston and the other in New Orleans. I had wanted and expected to get a job in Dallas, my chosen home. However, competition for SMU law students among the big firms in Dallas was tough, and opportunities usually went to those with the highest grades. I have already acknowledged that I showed no signs of being an emerging Supreme Court justice, let alone a legal scholar, so I was delighted that two good out-of-Dallas firms offered me a position. I think it was probably because they had gone to the expense of sending a lawyer to recruit at SMU in Dallas and, with it not being SMU students' first choice to go out of town, I was among the few they could bag on the hunt. I gladly accepted both offers and split the summer between them. I collected the high wages and had a great time in two magnificent cities, making new friends. Law firms expend big dollars making sure its clerks have a fun and entertaining summer experience so that maybe they will get fooled into thinking that's how real life is at the firm once fully employed. They didn't emphasize much the expectation of billing some fifty hours a week. Of course, the high salaries first-years receive makes up for any misunderstanding there. After all the fun of wining and dining in Houston and New Orleans as part of the clerkships, I returned to SMU for my final year of school. My heart was in Dallas, and I was fortunate to get hired by a small new firm offering the same high salary. That summer after graduating, I took the Texas Bar, put the worrying about passing behind me, and traveled back to Europe for another month of exploring and "finding myself"; rumor had it that vacations might be hard to come by once one was working full time. Penniless from my travels and bar-taking expenses, I started my new legal career in September at the firm in Dallas.

My concept of privilege just continued to follow me. I was sharing an inexpensive campus-owned apartment with my buddy Rob. My friends were mostly single, and when not working at our new jobs, we had a great time being young, wealthy (at least in our low-cost, cash-flow-driven minds), healthy, sports-playing, bar-hopping guys.

I really liked my job with the firm, enjoyed the lawyers, and even re-ceived word that I had passed the state bar. (Not everyone does, and we each knew the implications of failing the bar on our lucrative new jobs.) At my boss's insistence, I started planting the seeds of becoming a good corporate and real estate lawyer (especially when I abandoned the idea of being an oil and gas lawyer—that deficiency in math skills was catching up with me again). My boss, Chris Rentzel, was very tol-erant of my deficiencies, and though he could be tough and exacting, I owe most of my progress in becoming a good lawyer substantially to him. Little did we know at the time that Chris (who was four years older than me) and I would become the best of friends and practice together as partners for the next thirty years. Chris and I (and our beloved legal assistant/typist extraordinaire, Carol Van Dine) stuck together through four different law firms up to the day I was let go. What a privilege that was!

They say you can't be an irresponsible, fun-loving kid forever. I did my best to dispel that for the next six years or so after starting my practice of law by skiing, exercising, playing basketball and tennis, swimming, dating a few (lucky?) women, and taking advantage of Dallas's vibrant nightlife. I had a wider group of close friends than at any other time of my life. The DFW Airport was our gateway to good travels and winter fun. Rob and I even tried our hand at investing in a couple of houses in the Dallas area, one eventually returning us a modest profit. Life was good, and I could only be considered privi-leged in my mind.

As the years began going by, my goals and desires (and even maturity?) began changing. I fell in love with a beautiful gal who loved me. My fiancée was an elementary school teacher, and soon our friendships began expanding. I acquired a new family, her family, of very special people, and the good times really began. We were in love, and my privileged life just got better. I was four years older than my wife when I married at age thirty-three. Our immediate family grew with the birth of our two children, who were seventeen months apart. During our eighteen years of marriage, we had six different houses, several memorable pets, a couple of swimming pools, wonderful neighborhoods, and a life that in so many ways was living the American dream. Yes, I was a privileged man, and I knew it.

CHAPTER 3

COLLAPSE OF A MAN: "I DON'T UNDERSTAND WHAT YOU ARE SAYING?"

I can't be sure when it actually started to happen. I really can't point to one time when I realized a decline in my health, even though it eventually turned into a debilitating illness. My adventure started gradually, subtly, most likely in 2008, as I began experiencing unusual incidents and seemingly minor problems with my health. Of course, it was hard to understand why, as it was slowly developing at the time of some of my fondest family and professional experiences. My children were in high school, and we were enjoying some of our richest family times. Our kids were now maturing in their activities, academics, and social lives. My wife and I were active in the kids' activities. Our family attended church most every Sunday, participated in youth fellowship and sports, and in general experienced the good life associated with active, smart children. As they grew up, our travels were no longer just child-centered activities like Disney World or beach vacations but now featured adventure destinations such as the south of France, historic Boston, Philadelphia, Washington DC, and New Orleans, as well as ski trips to Colorado.

I enjoyed coaching several of my son's elementary school basketball teams, and we all had fun going to his league games as he grew older. We were frequent companions to college football and basketball games, as well as the occasional Dallas-area Cowboys, Mavs, and Stars games. My wife was a wonderfully attentive and involved mother always on top of the children's every conceivable need. The sheer joy of our sharing children's experiences and unique challenges was something only a parent could fully appreciate. My son experienced certain issues beginning shortly after birth that frequently interrupted his daily activities during his childhood (athletic as well as school). To see him get back up, take a few minutes to regain his control, and then start participating again was, of course, an inspiration. His attitude was incredible. We were actually in awe. What a brave little boy. Other children and families were so good to him, and I know he could not fully appreciate the great impact his courage had on everyone. His younger sister is a smart, pleasant, and pretty little girl, and she became her brother's biggest fan and supporter. The experiences of my son made us all better. We witnessed firsthand a true meaning of life with uncertain challenges and its necessary struggles. We all survived, even thrived, and made the best of it. Privileged? Of course, we all were.

Professionally, my life was thriving. My experience in the big law firm was improving constantly. Bracewell & Patterson, LLP, was a national law firm founded and headquartered In Houston, Texas. Later during my career there, Bracewell became known as Bracewell & Giuliani, as it partnered with the former mayor to open an office in New York City. I was fortunate to become a full-equity partner in this fine national law firm, which in itself was a great honor to me. My team of lawyers and staff could not have been better. Brock Bailey, Mason Griffin, and Chris Fuller, talented associates under my supervision, were carrying big responsibilities for the firm with important clients.

I suppose I learned by reading in history books that an effective leader surrounds himself with people smarter and more talented than himself. In this sense, I was smart (if not just lucky). Each was among the best associates in the entire firm. The client base I was credited with overseeing became the largest single revenue generator in the entire firm one year. I was totally dependent on my team's great support. The biggest revenue client, America's largest cellular telephone provider, introduced to us by a newly hired senior counsel, Jay Sullivan, was developed into a multi-office client for Bracewell. Our teams handled the rollout of its wireless cell phone technology throughout Texas and Oklahoma. The wireless telecommunications company was not the traditional type of representation with which my law firm was particularly familiar, but it was one we developed from scratch. Teams were formed in several cities to serve the client, and at one point we had up to twenty-two fee earners billing on the account. Most of the work was performed in Dallas and also San Antonio (overseen magnificently by a San Antonio partner who became a good friend). To me, wireless telephone towers scattered across Texas never looked so good. My client base responsibilities also included a premier national commercial real estate office and residential developer, the commercial contracting and corporate work for the largest advertising agency in Texas, local dispute resolution for the national office of the largest title insurance company in America, and probably my most personally satisfying client (because he taught me to love creative real estate development), local Dallas retail developer, the late Ken Hughes. I spent a lot of time with his two-person team providing the legal work for developing the innovative Mockingbird Station multiuse transportation development in Dallas. There were others too. With so many friends and such professional and wonderful family experiences, I truly knew I was privileged. Everything professionally for me seemed to be pointing straight up.

Then my life began to change. Soon into 2008, unusual things began happening to my body and my legal practice. At one point, I noticed a small amount of blood in my stool. Privately I watched for a while, hoping it would go away. As the condition continued, I prayed that this was not something serious and, more importantly, that the toilet would always flush after my use—something that could not always be guaranteed. I got scared as I put off my inevitable trip to the gastro doctor who was referred to me by my primary physician. What could it be? Blood was surely indicative of something wrong. Fortunately the Dallas gastro decided, after conducting a colonoscopy, that all I had was a case of ulcerative colitis. This was not pleasant by any means; it was fortunate to me only because this did not sound terminal. Little did I know then that this was the start of an ugly unforeseen battle for my health that would have horrible consequences, including my forthcoming suffering as a quadriplegic diagnosed with ALS for several years thereafter. Subsequently, although no parts of my colon were ever removed, I did for the next several months experience the indignities of daily medicines, self-administered enemas, and annual colonoscopies. As bad as all that was, I still think the worst was those twenty-four-hour days I spent drinking that dreadful gallon of liquid designed to clean out my system before my mandatory colonoscopy was performed. No thank you.

I also knew that my performance at work was becoming suspect. Some partners questioned my reasoning and quality of performance. Others reported concerns about my communication skills. Concurrently, a pronounced dip in the economic conditions for the Dallas commercial real estate market did not help my economic performance and workload. As team leader, I needed to be sure my senior associates had sufficient work, especially if we were to be able to stay together at the firm. As talented overachievers, it was natural for each of them to consume the hours and assume more client front-chair responsibility. I also considered it my personal mission that each be elevated from associate status and elected partner within the firm. As a partner, this required more client development so that our workloads increased in the firm. Unfortunately for me (as well as every partner), this inevitably meant fewer personal hours billed and fees personally collected. For a partner in a law firm, this could be curtains. Law firm economics require high billing of hours at the maximum possible hourly rate. Partners usually bill at the highest hourly rate. Chris Fuller and I immediately undertook trying to aggressively expand our real estate and business practices. While we were creative and had some measurable success, finding paying clients in the down Dallas economy of 2008 and 2009 was not always easy. Marketing our services meant meeting new contacts and attending real estate gatherings to expand our network of contacts and our areas of expertise. This took time, and time spent marketing meant fewer hours billed by me to a paying client. It was imperative to me that Chris make partner, as our professional relationship as lawyers had become among the most satisfying I had personally experienced.

For me that meant creeping increased pressure. Worries mounted. I assume I became less pleasant to be around. Monthly computer-generated accounting reports confirmed that my personal economic performance was down. Partner income depended on personal economic performance. As a family, we chose to live in a desired Dallas-area neighborhood with superior public schools. We had the normal pressures and joys experienced by many families trying to raise their children. Some at the firm said I was becoming unclear in my directives at work. I had always talked too much, but my use of too many words in a sentence just made things worse. Some said I slurred when I spoke. Chris was increasingly having to serve as my unofficial interpreter when I provided assignments to other attorneys. Why was I not clear to people? Chris had become maybe my closest friend—not the wisest thing when I was his supervising attorney and, frankly, his boss in a large organization. I know I was becoming more concerned about our practicing law together for as long as we could rather than enhancing my sole success as a partner at Bracewell. If that meant moving together to another firm or opening our own, I thought I was prepared for that. My optimism knew no bounds. Of course, we would succeed in such a venture. I always have. Remember? I am privileged when encountering problems; I knew that.

Each year before the accounting year ends for the firm, every partner meets with a member of the firm's elite management committee. Most of these management members were from the main office in Houston, and maybe some from Washington. Their knowledge of our performance was primarily what the accounting reports conveyed. Great economic numbers? One must be good. Ostensibly the meeting's purpose is to review where you and your practice are at that point in time and, more importantly, what you forecast for the economic year ahead. The planned meeting with management is always a big deal for many of us partners, primarily because we all know this interview will be relayed to the full management committee. Then, in its infinite wisdom, the committee sets our personal compensation for the year ahead. It is, of course, a good chance to learn where one stands in the partnership. It may come as no surprise that many of us privately started referring to the interview as "dare to be great." We knew we had to blow our own horns or we may be underappreciated. Our compensation for the next year would reflect that. At least that was the consensus of many of us in the firm's outer offices, such as mine in Dallas.

I usually spent a full month prior to the interview date preparing my written report to the management committee. Lots of thought and statistical self-analysis of my performance was necessary. I knew there were some weaknesses in my economic performance that prior year. The pressure was on. As a partner, one had to know one's facts to put the best spin on one's performance and the prognosis for the next year. If the numbers indicated that the real estate economy was getting worse, I had to show how I expected to keep my economic performance up and that my practice was growing. On top of that, all this was in the face of a constant pressure as a partner to raise my personal billing rate per hour. More hours billed and higher rates meant good things at a law firm. The pressure was on to keep the clients content with my rates while at the same time looking for more specialized opportunities so my practice could charge a higher rate. Many in the firm believed a commercial real estate practice was somewhat of a commodity; there were lots of lawyers practicing real estate in Dallas. A heavy supply of competition meant lower rates for me to charge. Client pressure was on me to lower, not increase, my rates. I had to maximize my efficiency to keep clients happy. One way to meet a client's desire was to involve more good help from associates, all of whom billed at a lower rate than me as a partner. Helping my associates meet their budget hours required that I push more work to my associates while still finding enough hours to justify my performance. Associates were not rewarded for nonbillable hours spent attracting new work. That's what partners did. I appreciated my team, so I openly favored providing my associates with prime work. I do not regret this decision, as I was always optimistic about our ability to perform, pressure or not. My goal was to keep my team together and performing well; it was up to me to keep pursuing higher-rate clients for myself. I suppose this reality caught up with me, but I am proud to say that none of my high-performing team members ever left while they were part of my team at the firm.

Unavoidably, the big day was coming. The management committee had designated one of the firm's senior-most Houston litigators to interview me and discuss my performance. The senior partner was a long-term litigator at the firm and was considered one of its finest lawyers. He was also a truly principled gentleman with whom I had a friendly professional relationship. I considered it fortunate that my meeting would be with this particular member of management. As always, I was a little nervous, but I certainly felt that I was well prepared. I knew my positions and expected a tough but good meeting. The appointed time arrived. The senior partner was ushered into my office, where he met my associate team, and we proceeded to exchange the usual pleasantries. The rest is now a fog to me. This was my one chance to look good this year before management. But not this day.

Usually I thrived on these opportunities; I was confident with my gift of gab and my ability to self-promote myself. I don't know how things fell apart. I was not glib or appearing confident. I could tell he was soon confused. Was I doing it again? Was I in my right mind? I was making no sense to him. At one point he interrupted me and said, "What are you trying to say? You are making no sense to me. I don't understand you!" I might as well have been hit by a bolt of lightning. What was I saying? I must have practiced in my mind what I wanted to say a dozen times (mostly while lying awake at night). Our interview ended. I was speechless, likely blubbering nonsense. What a disaster. I was so shaken. I remember, after it ended, going into Chris's office and breaking into tears, this in front of my associate. I think now of Nixon crying before Kissinger when he was forced to resign the presidency. What a breach of professionalism. Chris was my subordinate in the organization. I was partially scared that I had just destroyed his chances to be elected partner, as his supervising partner at the firm was now discredited. I think I had already told him about the appearance of blood in my stool. What the hell was happening to me? Was I collapsing? I assume the senior partner's report to the management committee was not good. How could it have been? I have no doubt that I was now being watched and my performance closely monitored. Nevertheless, nothing happened to me immediately for much of that new year, although I assume my reputation was already hurt. My physical problems continued. As my economic performance did not improve and other indiscretions and mistakes occurred later through that year, my inevitable dismissal was set for November 30, 2009. My career at the law firm was over, and that hurt. It was in no way Bracewell's fault or an inappropriate decision; it was just a combination of unfortunate circumstances all brought on by me. Besides, why worry? I had a nearly thirty-year respected legal career in Dallas; certainly, there were plenty of other jobs. Little did I know at that moment that the further collapse of this man was definitely underway.

In 2008 and 2009, prior to my actually leaving Bracewell, there

were indications beyond the ulcerative colitis that other areas of my
life were not normal. I sensed that weird comments were being made
even more frequently than before. Strange to me were the observations
and warnings from family and friends, and the instances of various
acquaintances asking me unusual questions. Was I lost? Confused?
Forgetful? My speech was unclear. Some questioned my driving skills.
Was I unsteady? I never thought so, but more than one person said
so. A preacher at my church thought I was disoriented when he came
upon me one morning in the hallway. The woman who was my barber for many years was openly worried about my health and physical
condition. I don't remember feeling particularly strange, but people
were talking. Of course, similar confusion and observations were
being made occasionally at the law firm. Even I grew to know that
something seemed different. I had two strange episodes involving a
type of seizure activity that sent me for a day to nearby Presbyterian
Hospital. The episodes seemed violent, as on two different mornings
I could not even get from my bed to the bathroom as I lost control
over my physical conditions. My wife called an ambulance on each
occasion. The feeling from each episode did not at the time seem to
have lasting effects, as I went to work shortly after release from the
emergency room. It was weird nevertheless.

After I was asked to leave my law firm by the end of November, I
remember what a strange experience it was to be a lame duck in that
final thirty days. Chris Fuller and I worked on one final big deal together—the purchase of a North Dallas office complex for a high-tech
client moving its headquarters from California to Dallas. Although I
did most of the work preparing for the acquisition (actually up to the
day I left), I was transitioning Chris into handling the closing. The new
client was a referral from a Dallas real estate broker we had befriended
while closing another deal. This was just the type of top-level work
we worked so hard to attract. In hindsight, I felt a little like a veteran
quarterback leading his team down the field as time in the game was
expiring, except this time the quarterback was pulled from the game

as he reached the ten-yard line. My talented associate, Chris, ably stepped in to complete the drive. I would not be able to return to the field ever again. My life was about to undergo extraordinary change. My adventure would soon be underway.

CHAPTER 4
MY STRANGE NEW EXISTENCE

December 1, 2009. My wife gets up and, as she does every Monday, takes the kids to school. Then she's off on an errand of some sort; the house is empty. I am up, but now what? The empty house is actually not empty; I am home. I have nowhere I am supposed to be. The house is not really empty, because Boomer, our mixed-breed golden retriever, is there with me. So what now? A walk with Boomer? Yeah, that's it. I take Boomer for a walk around the neighborhood. Boomer rarely gets one of these at this hour on Monday morning. Nearby I see traffic is bustling; people are leaving for work or to drop their kids at school. Me? What am I supposed to do? Now I have already taken my dog for his walk. I can bring in the newspaper. The house has that early-morning emptiness feeling. It is neat from last night, but except for some breakfast dishes in the sink, it's too early to feel lived in. I set my laptop up on the dining room table and go online. I check my Gmail mailbox—not my law firm mailbox, as it has been closed down. In Gmail there are the usual daily news bulletins and promotional offers. But no work. Nothing important. Nothing pressing. Where was I?

Boomer, my new secretary?

This was to be the pattern for me for months to come. *It is morning, what do I need to do?* My highlight of the morning might be receiving delivery of the mail, but that involved beating our dog to intercept it before it slid to the floor. Boomer was no secretary who sorted the mail and placed it on my desk in order of importance. I had to grab it before Boomer tore into it with his big, wet mouth. In time, my routine developed. In addition to getting the mail and reading parts of the *Dallas Morning News*, which I never used to have time to read, I was now actively contacting friends and former colleagues. "Hey, I am looking for a job."

They would respond, "What job?"

"You know, practicing law."

This led to some interviews and a few follow-ups. I felt optimistic. But what was the deal? They said they would get back to me soon, surely, but it never seemed to happen. Since these were meetings with contacts I had known for years, it was not a formal interview process. I did not receive applicant rejection letters, but usually just silence. There was no follow-up. *What now?* My focus changed. What did I really want to do? I joined up with a friend I knew at church who was also looking for work. We talked, we strategized, and we commiserated. I met with friends, old clients, and contacts. They were sympathetic and friendly but offered no leads. Over time, some even suggested I get help. Where was I going? My confidence waned. Did I really want to even practice law? Soon I dismissed the idea of opening my own law office. I was not one of those lawyers equipped to take whatever came in the door. I was confident about what I did; I had twice been selected as a "Texas Super Lawyer" practicing in corporate real estate law. I was a commercial real estate and business lawyer by choice, not a litigator, let alone a traffic ticket fixer. (There were already specialists in that field.) Besides, I came from an era in which lawyers were supported by a secretary, a receptionist, and a technology expert—maybe even a librarian. Boomer did not offer any of those services. While I used a computer at work, I never pretended to do everything myself or really understand why it did those unpredictable things it seemed to choose to do from time to time. That was the new generation. That's why we had computer technicians at the firm. My search for employment soon turned into signing up for career counseling classes. The classes met in hotel ballrooms. Lots of people were there, all looking for work. How do you get a job? Do you know what you best have to offer? Prepare that winning résumé. I paid for the service and went to a hotel ballroom filled with others a couple days per week. I never considered unemployment benefits. I was not really unemployed … just between jobs. Things got tougher. Nothing seemed to be coming together. I could not even make myself write a good résumé. Everything was frustrating. The kids were confused. "Why is Daddy home?" "Why is he picking us up from school?" Many days I worked out at the YMCA or spent a couple hours hitting golf balls at the country club we had joined as a family a few years before. It was strange being there on a Tuesday morning. The club was empty except for a few elderly retired men who met every week. On I drifted.

Sometime in February, Dr. Paul Greenberg, my family's longtime physician (dating back to helping my grandparents in the early 1980s) gave me the name of a psychiatrist he suggested I see. The doctor, a man named Marty, proved to be a wonderful elderly man who did lots of interesting things. I grew attached to Marty and looked forward to our once-per-week sessions. Soon he had me spilling my guts. I even cried one day as I recounted the importance of my grandfather in my life. I felt confident with Marty—even bordering on cocky, I suppose. I was not really sure why I needed to be there; I didn't see anything wrong with me. I was not aware of any friends or family who saw a shrink. Nevertheless, I was comfortable talking, and Marty listened. Over time, Marty clearly became increasingly concerned. At one point, he finally suggested I get tested by a specialist. Marty sensed some confusion on my part. Was it a type of frontal dementia he suggested? He referred me to a specialist associated with neurologists at nearby Presbyterian Hospital in Dallas. A full day's battery of mental tests was conducted. As I took the tests, I thought they were a breeze—silly, really. Oh, I made a mistake here and there, but who really cared if I could memorize four groups of fruits, animals, furniture, and games, and repeat them back five minutes later. I was pretty good at remembering the list—at least until I was inadvertently interrupted with some other memory task. Oops, I guess that meant something.

The results came back. Marty tried to comfort me as he explained that the tests showed some sort of mental issues. He suggested creeping dementia once again. Dementia meant I would fade away over time, he warned. I was to prepare myself. *Huh?* I needed to see a full neurologist. My wife and I met with the specialist at Presbyterian Hospital, and a number of follow-up tests were run, including EMGs and a spinal tap. At the same time, I was undergoing tests to analyze my continuing ulcerative colitis. It seemed as though half my time was now being spent getting diagnoses and tests for my mounting physical health problems. Then the word came from the neurologist. Not only did he think I showed signs of frontal dementia; incredibly, the doctor believed I had amyotrophic lateral sclerosis, or ALS, often referred to as Lou Gehrig's disease. *Unbelievable. How? Why? Surely that is not possible?* The little I had ever heard of ALS sounded dreadful. *Can anyone survive?* The websites said no; they said it was incurable. According to the ALS Association, ALS is a progressive neurodegenerative disease that affects nerve cells in the brain and spinal cord. "A" means "no," "myo" refers to muscle, and "trophic" means "nourishment." No muscle nourishment—that did not sound good to me.

Of course, one immediately wants to deny such a diagnosis. I did not even want to think about what it meant. My wife suggested my problem must be something that could be managed holistically. ADD seemed far more likely to her. I had always seemed easily distractible, but no one ever had diagnosed me as having ADD. I now had new massive issues to confront. Some doctors in Dallas actually suggested I not undergo the frustrating and usually unsuccessful pursuit of second and third opinions. No way was that my style at my young age. I don't really know where my head was after confronting this news. I recall I discontinued seeing my psychiatrist, and I assume this is when my frustrating attempts to find a job or new career were all but discontinued. Despite the admonition I received to just start to accept the diagnosis, my wife and I scheduled a meeting at Mayo Clinic in Scottsdale. We made the trip and met with the variety of neurospecialists, and worst of all, I spent most of that week being prepped for a final-day colonoscopy. At the time, my colitis was particularly awful. My poor, brave wife, what hell that week and experience must have been for her!

The Mayo diagnosis came back. ALS was ultimately confirmed, although one doctor initially questioned the diagnosis. I don't recall

actually suffering any specific signs, but what did I know? My driving privileges were taken away and my opportunity to see friends
undoubtedly restricted. *What now? Wait to die?* It is very strange to
have little or no memory of the second half of 2010. I know I was
receiving some holistic treatment and together with my wife began
seeing a marriage counselor referred by our church. The pressure on
her had to be horrible. I remember that the counselor was a disaster
in my mind. My perception was that he thought every problem in our
marriage was my fault and my duty to rectify. Was he correct? I just
know I did not agree. I assume that only increased our marital stress.
I do remember thinking at one point that the suggested solutions
seemed impossible to me. Nothing she asked for was unreasonable
for a married couple; I was just incapable of complying. Our finances
were now greatly challenged. No paychecks for me were coming in.
Our family still had other health issues. Of course, the country club
membership disappeared, but we still had many expenses. We lived
in a nice neighborhood, as we wanted our children to go to a superior
public school. We did not want to believe the ALS diagnosis. How
could I promise to have a full-paying job secured within six weeks?
There were other expectations. I suspect my frustrations and sense of
failure only grew. I had to be a miserable example of a husband and
father. My family was heading for a world of hurt.

I vaguely remember that the Christmas holiday that year was
strained. As her family's frustrations with me grew, I am sure things
must not have been well. Of course, I did not see my mother or sister's
family at all during that time. Christmas holidays and the start of the
New Year just seemed to come and go.

Happier days 2010, with son at the Cotton Bowl game

In the New Year, 2011, I was undergoing various medical treatments. None of them seemed to be treatment for ALS, but I may be wrong on that. I don't recall being prescribed medicine for ALS or creeping frontal dementia. My wife would drive me out to Irving, a Dallas suburb, to some clinic in a warehouse area where a nurse practitioner was giving me medicine to help my feelings. I liked the doctor, but I do not have any recollection of what impact the treatment had on me. I know things were just becoming more frustrating for my wife and children.

At some point in late winter or early spring, my wife announced that our house was on the market for sale. One of her friends was a real estate agent and would be handling the listing. By now I was in bad enough shape that I have little recollection of the terms or timing of the sale. I know I was not making anything happen with respect to our moving out. I signed some papers authorizing the sale as co-owner of the house. My home library office was a cramped mess of hundreds of books, art, and music. My closet was full of clothes. I did not seem to worry about what was happening.

The indispensable Kristi and Bill Francis.

At one point, Dr. Greenberg decided I was now suffering from a bout with pneumonia. In my physical condition at the time, this was a really big deal. I remember I was completely bedridden at home. Dr. Greenberg learned that I would be alone during the forthcoming week. He was worried about me being home alone for an extended period of time. My mother and sister each soon received an unsolicited call expressing his concern. It was apparent they were not fully aware of my condition and situation. Their concern now became heightened. Incredibly, the good doctor personally intervened and arranged for in-house nursing care to be at my side twenty-four hours per day. I vaguely remember the kind assistance. At some point, my mother learned that I would not be moving to the new house with my wife and children. What did they intend to do with me? This did not go over well for either side. My mother and sister got into action; soon a few cousins I had not seen in years descended on my house and began packing me up. My mother and sister came to town and professed to be shocked at the condition I was in. Extraordinary friends, including Bill and Kristi Francis, took time from their busy work schedules to join in packing me up. I vaguely remember the overwhelming task they faced in helping me disassemble my library office. My pack-rat style of living was nothing similar to their orderly neat house and offices. There was a true sense that the fabulous personal relationship with my life in Dallas, dating since college days at SMU, was coming to an end. Bill helped immeasurably in getting my stuff to storage. Indeed, once the decision was made that I would be going to my mother's home in Muncie, Bill insisted I spend that last night at their home. Bill said he could not envision my potentially last night ever in Dallas, the city I loved, being spent in some hotel. I remember Bill took me to the airport the next morning and made sure I was safely on the American Airlines flight to Indiana. My Dallas adventure and family life as I knew it was now over. My adventure was now effectively underway.

———

CHAPTER 5
THINGS SEEM TO GET WORSE

As I got ill, I spent a lot of time with just me—something that became more and more apparent from the advent of the first signs I was not doing well. In 2010, when I was diagnosed with possible creeping frontal dementia by the Dallas physician, I was warned that this was not going to be a pleasant experience. When the Dallas neurologist also decided I had symptoms of ALS, the road ahead looked even worse. That spring, the Mayo Clinic further confirmed the joint diagnosis. New drugs were prescribed, and my life began to lose control as time moved further into 2010 and 2011. Two years is a long time. The pain and tension it created for my family only made things increasingly worse. The burden on my wife and children was incredibly unfair. I knew that. But was I really capable of doing anything about it?

I have very few memories of my mental decline. Friends began to withdraw or distance themselves as they obviously saw changes in my mental condition. Former clients and close personal friends Jim Vanderslice and Ken Hughes stayed particularly loyal and frequently invited me for breakfast or an after-work cocktail. I am sure it was increasingly hard on them as they, too, began sensing things were not right. There were several frank discussions but little I could retain. Another friend suggested I go to a camp somewhere in rural Texas that I assume was some sort of rehabilitation facility for those needing mental help. He acknowledged that he had spent some time recovering there. I never followed up on the suggestion, I suppose because I did not take it seriously or appreciate the importance of the opportunity. Stop now? I was still looking for work. I realize today that it would not have made any difference.

I have no recollection of any specific dreams prior to my ultimate physical collapse. Certainly I had dreams—every working mind does—but I did not retain any. I think they enhanced my anxiety. I do remember a few events that were important in my collapse. I remember being told that I needed to stop driving the kids, as I was now a risky and unsafe driver. I don't remember any specific incidents, although my wife would not have insisted on this if there were not actual events of concern. I remember there were other perfectly normal requests that I simply was not capable of addressing. Little did I appreciate at the time that I would soon face marital separation, divorce, estrangement from my children, loss of career, being uprooted from my city, and potential financial ruin. While I was aware that bad things were happening to me, I just did not know what to do about it.

I remember a few strange incidents that now in hindsight certainly foreshadowed my struggle. I remember going out one day to lunch with my friend Chris Fuller, which was certainly a special treat for me. I can only imagine that what we talked about was probably filled with my naively optimistic expectations. I learned later that when Chris drove me back to my house, he paused in his car to watch me go into my front door. Apparently I headed off in the wrong direction, maybe not even aware of where I was supposed to be going. Chris made sure I got into my house. To think I was once his supervising partner at the law firm! On one particularly icy cold winter morning I remember going out the front door to our sidewalk in front of the house. I picked up the morning newspaper and started to return to the house. Our yard slanted down from the house to the sidewalk. As I started up the incline of the yard, I lost my balance on the icy grass. I fell on my back. I was not hurt, but I just lay there floundering, feeling like an upside-down turtle rolling on its shell. I could not get up. It seemed like minutes as I lay there struggling. Finally a car on our street stopped and a lady got out and helped me back on my feet. She made sure I got back into my house, but how embarrassing was that? This only confirmed for me that I was not all right. Events would accelerate from there.

CHAPTER 6

MUNCIE, MY NEW HOME

I really don't recall much about my final days in Dallas, but it's actually miraculous that I remember so well my trip to my new home at my mother's house in Muncie. This was sometime in June 2011. The whirlwind of final days is now vague for me, but I know one way or another the house my family lived in was being emptied, my wife and children were gone, and shortly someone new would be moving into our house. Arrangements were made; I was flying from Dallas to Indianapolis, and I was going alone on a direct flight. My mother and her beloved companion and longtime friend, the always reliable Dick Jaggers, would be there to meet me at the airport upon arrival.

I don't recall how sick I really was at that time, but it could not have been too bad, as I do remember having a final dinner get-together with my friends Chris Rentzel, Bob Sharp, and John Bauer at a local favorite watering hole (a.k.a. neighborhood sports bar). I know this because later I saw a picture of us smiling dudes in the restaurant. I probably had a massive cheeseburger and more than one beer. That was a couple of days before my flight out. What whirlwind happened thereafter is not clear to me now, but I managed to get my big yellow

L.L.Bean duffel bag filled with enough clothes to get by for a while during my trip to Muncie. I assumed it was going to be a temporary trip to Muncie. I don't recall being part of any mass emptying of our house or packing up my share of our stuff, other than the temporary visits of my cousins, Bill and Kristi, and my mother and sister. As many of my assorted belongings ended up in storage at a warehouse facility in Dallas, I assume my wife had to take over responsibility for splitting up our house. This must have occurred after I was shipped off to Muncie.

The day before I was scheduled to leave, as I previously recounted, my friend Bill came and got me from the house. Bill had been one of my closest friends, beginning when we first met during his freshman year at SMU. Bill took me to his house that last evening in Dallas. I assume we went out to dinner, but I mostly recall the kindness of Bill opening his spacious home to me that last night. The guest room was every bit as nice as any hotel I could have fled to. The next morning, Bill took me to DFW Airport and made sure I made it through security and onto the appropriate flight to Indianapolis. As we said goodbye, I remember sensing that my friend felt as if he were helping an old sick friend move on to the next stage of his life, uncertain how long that might be destined to be. I was that poorly off. Little did I know what plight awaited me, but Bill remained a critically valuable friend throughout my adventure. He became so important to my sister in providing moral support and handling any number of things from Dallas, including accounting and functioning as co-point person with her in what proved to be a challenging contested divorce. Words, of course, don't adequately express what friends like Bill and his wife, Kristi, meant to me. I choose to believe that God planted the seeds of our lifetime together beginning as mere teens at SMU so many years before.

My mother Nancy and her friend Dick Jagger.

My flight went without incident. I remember disembarking and finding my mother and Dick outside the gate at Indianapolis's new airport. She seemed surprised that things seemed to go so well for me. After a turkey sandwich at a fashionable restaurant in the airport, Dick drove us to Muncie. I did not, at the time, anticipate that this was going to be my new permanent home. I was sick; I was not sure just how sick, but the Mayo diagnosis of ALS and creeping dementia was hanging over me. So was my unpredictable behavior. I thought they just wanted me to get some rest. My mother's plans for me were clearly different. She was eighty-five at the time but by no means unwilling to take on this challenge. Her (and my sister's) plans were based on reality, while I only had my vague understanding of reality. Hey, I was a Texas lawyer with a family in Dallas. I had a life to get on with, and things to get done back in Dallas. My plans did not assume a long stay in Muncie.

Life in Muncie at first seemed quite understandable. I would surely only be here for a few weeks; then I could expect to return to Dallas. My mother's house was still lovely; her garden was breaking out as summer arrived, and her cute little Shih Tzu dog was always ready for walks around the park. My breakfast was on the table for me as soon I woke up, although the days of expecting a big bagel or muffin and a large ("Grande, please") Starbucks coffee were over for the time being. Breakfasts would be healthy now; I could count on a daily bowl of oatmeal and a small glass of orange juice freshly made from frozen concentrate in the freezer. "Want a banana?" my mother asked. Starbucks? "We have one of those here now, but I have never been," she explained. "Who could possibly want to pay that much for coffee?"

Returning to my mother's home initially had all the tranquility of a nice visit to my hometown. Almost all meals featured her wonderful home cooking. My mother loved to cook and for years had been writing food articles for the *Muncie Star*. "Why would you ever go out to a Muncie restaurant?" she would ask. "The food is so much better here." Of course, she was partially right, but remember, Mom, it's okay to be out in the public letting someone else cook your meal now and then.

After settling in, I realized my being in Muncie was, in fact, a well-planned arrangement. My health was clearly suspect, though I was part of walking her dog and visiting old friends now and then. Our once-a-week visit to the nearby (though just out of walking distance) Starbucks was a treat for me she was happy to provide. We spent time trying to locate a local doctor to treat my ALS. We did not have much luck, but at least I was not suffering many apparent symptoms. For exercise, Dick might join us for a vigorous walk through the Muncie Mall. My mother usually sped ahead while Dick and I paused on a bench until she returned. I was not driving, so I was totally dependent on my mother (and occasionally Dick) for rides. This soon became a mental handicap for me. Not that Muncie had all that many interesting places to go, but the lack of flexibility to pick up and go anywhere whenever I wanted did begin to wear on me. In fact, my mother was so naturally busy, she was at best fitting me into her otherwise busy life. She had articles to write and deadlines to meet for the local Muncie magazine, *M*, as well as community board meetings, volunteer work at the church, garden club, art league, and the like. And don't forget her pride and joy, that incredible garden she maintained in the backyard. There was nothing lazy about my mother. To know her was to be impressed, if not awed, by her energy. But for me that meant that I should not be expecting to get to leave the house often, and hardly never after noon.

After a few weeks, my health did show signs of deteriorating. Most conspicuous was the ongoing problem of controlling my bowels. Ulcerative colitis was back, and it was becoming steadily more inconvenient. More and more frequently, I would have to bolt to the bathroom to relieve myself. I usually had diarrhea. The challenge was merely getting to the toilet on time. This was not a pretty picture and, much to my chagrin, was a problem I might have to address for the rest of my life. Colitis, in time, made it undesirable for me to even leave the house. Despite my mother's great efforts to keep me happy, this was a significant contributor to my depression. Here I was; I had gone from a busy lawyer and family man in Dallas, Texas, to a partial invalid living under the care of my loving elderly mother in a town I had left long ago. Times seemed hard, or at least I let them become such.

I was not particularly happy as my stay extended into August of 2011, and my health was not getting any better. I could function physically, but I was not sleeping very well, and fatigue now seemed to be part of my day. The dreams I was having were weird, and I was stewing a lot about unfinished business and my children back in Dallas. I don't recall any specific events that constituted an immediate crisis as time moved into September. Then, on September 11, in the middle of the night, as my dear mother slept, it finally happened. This was the night my life was to radically change forever. If prior to that night losing my immediate family, my job and career, my city, my dog, my BMW, and my Dallas friends was not enough, now my personal tornado struck—the event. Life was never going to be what I expected again. My adventure was now going into overdrive.

CHAPTER 7

THE EVENT

I don't really remember any details of the events on that night of September 11, 2011. In fact, the relevant night might actually be September 6, 2011, as the records available to me are not absolutely clear. I have to rely on others for the rendition of what happened, as I was quickly in no position to have any idea what was going on. As best I can tell from my mother's notes, it was the night of September 11.

Sometime shortly after midnight, I am told, lying in my bed at my mother's house, my mother woke up hearing me making unusual noises in my bedroom. Earlier my mother and I had spent a nice evening having a steak dinner with Mr. Jaggers. If I remember anything about the noise I started making, I think I recall a strange dream that had me thinking I was being tricked and betrayed. I have occasionally caught myself waking up with a scream during a stressful dream. I felt I was in the middle of something I had no control over, and it involved the trust I was placing in my dear mother and Mr. Jaggers. The idea that they had ulterior motives of any sort is patently absurd, of course, as no one was being kinder and more caring to me than those two. I have recollections of lashing out, in frustration, in my bed. My mother woke up, hearing my struggle coming from my bedroom next to hers. In hindsight, I am horrified to think that my dear mother, then in her mid-eighties, would confront someone in my state late at night. She said later that I was only halfway on the bed and that I was thrashing violently when she found me. I fell to the floor. Somehow, surely keeping her self-control, she contacted 911, and an ambulance from the nearby Ball Memorial Hospital was soon on its way. I have no recollection of being treated by the medics, but I am told I was soon delivered to the emergency room at the hospital. My mother recalls she stayed with me at the hospital until 5:00 a.m. The medical staff looked very concerned at the time she left.

Records reflect that this event was the start of a very hard few weeks, both for my mother and for me. I was quickly diagnosed with having suffered a grand mal seizure arising from various ongoing medical complications. I have only the faintest, if any, memory of my stay in the ICU, my seizure, and my delivery to the hospital. Family members and possibly a few friends gathered during this time, fully expecting the worst, just as they had been warned. My mother recalls that I spent at least four days fully comatose. Not until Saturday did my eyes even flicker. Although I have no recollection of this, I am told that I was pretty much in the comatose state for a few weeks. I don't personally know the order in which things occurred, but I became a man who could not fully breathe on his own, who was now in a substantially motionless state, and who could no longer eat or drink or effectively relieve himself. Most significant to me, I was not aware what was happening. I was truly out of it. Likely that was a blessing. A doctor told me later that it is indeed a blessing that rarely can anybody remember what it is like to be in the ICU for an extended period of time.

For reasons I will not attempt to explain at this point, I did not perish. When I regained a semblance of consciousness, I was now living in a Muncie-area hospital in the intensive care unit. I can't tell you really anything that I remember of the several weeks I spent in the

ICU at Ball Hospital. I only recall being severely disoriented and that I was somewhere very different than any place I had ever been. Things just seemed to be happening outside my control, and I obviously just rolled with the treatment. No opinions were forthcoming from me— not even any resistance. I was just there. When I later was transferred to Morrison Woods, the extended care facility in Muncie in which I was to spend the next eighteen or so months, and after my stay in Ball Hospital, I do remember being awake but having a constant sense of disorientation and general confusion about my very existence. Where was I? I didn't really know. I was never sure. Sometimes I thought I was in Waco, Dallas, Milwaukee, or even Australia. Something did not seem to link my mother's presence to me being in Muncie. More on that craziness later.

My surroundings were usually strange to me, but soon I at least had recognition of my mother, Mr. Jaggers, my sister Ann, and the facility staff caring for me. Over the next few months, I was blessed to have visits by dear friends Rob Topping from Chicago, Bill Francis from Dallas, Kevin Smith from Muncie, Sam Gleason from Brazil via a visit to Houston, Mack Findley from Columbus, Lloyd Rowland from San Diego, and Bob Wright from St. Louis, among others. These were all longtime friends of mine, and their visits were thrilling to me even though I remain cloudy as to specifics. Rob and Mack even made sure my convalescence room had a new television. Bill and Rob found me in such bad shape on one visit together that they actually went off to a Ball State basketball game to pass time.

Within a day after the first seizure incident, my sister Ann arrived from Illinois. At the time we did not know that Missy would take over legal and health care responsibility of my care for the next six years and ultimately become the singular most significant person in my re-covery. She is the hero of this story. Why was I such a stereotypically difficult big brother during our childhood?

Ann Millard Keith, my sister arrives on the scene.

As I tell my story, I acknowledge that this will be based on my sense of reality as I knew it then and recall it as I write. I have not reviewed boxes of medical or legal records (and there are many!) that remain in storage somewhere. This is a story about what I went through, not a medical report. I do, however, have possession of my mother's notebook, in which she, as a lifetime newspaper reporter and journalist, made remarkable comments and observations regarding these stressful days. The notebook is incredible. Comments she entered provide the most accurate account I can possibly present here. While effort has been made to check facts, receive the input of witnesses and get dates of events reasonably accurate, the importance of telling the story of my adventure is to recall it as I do: distorted often frequently by powerful drugs—the very thing we could all go through sometime during this wonderful adventure called life. There are many events in my story that may seem (and in fact likely are) impossible—events too crazy to explain or justify. There are my impressions of the remarkable care I received from wonderful caretakers, doctors, nurses, aides, and administrators. There are recollections of adventures, vivid in my mind, which simply could not physically have happened. Many I acknowledge were prescription-drug-inspired dreams. There will also be detailed recollections of some bizarre dreams I know I had, as they seemed to last for months at a time and caused me much consternation. Some are recounted in this book. At the time, they were very vivid in my mind and memory. But for me, everything in this account is what I know and remember. At least it is what I think I know and remember.

When I finally began to awaken in the ICU, I am not sure I ever was aware of looking ahead, worrying about my future, planning my escape, or planning my recovery. Nor do I have any recollection of being bitter, frustrated, or angry about my perceived plight. Lying there in my near immobile state, I just reacted to the moment, and I am pretty sure I had no expectation that I would still be in highly skilled health care facilities some four years later, let alone the seven consecutive years (2011 to 2019) in care facilities I have experienced as of this writing.

I reference that my mother kept an extraordinary little five-by-seven-inch black notebook first dated the Monday after my massive seizure occurred. It is a remarkable collection of entries that reveals the unanticipated excitement, concern, and uncertainty she and my sister encountered as soon as that dreadful event happened. The first entry is dated September 15 but reflects the immediate chaos that naturally ensued after my seizure on September 11. My sister began adding notes to the notebook on that day also, which means she had already arrived on the scene in Muncie from her home in Rockford, Illinois. The initial entries include their need to contact our family attorney in Muncie so he could set up a legal guardianship to address my health and financial issues. There are notes concerning the uncertainty of insurance coverage: What insurance do I have? Whom do they contact? What pays for what? How is the government involved? Where do my mother and Missy start? Is Texas insurance involved? The notes reflect many contacts and phone numbers to be pursued. Uncertainty was natural, as no one is usually in a position to address the totally unexpected emergency—especially when it involves immediate critical medical care. My sister and mother had no reason to be aware of my financial situation in Dallas. Fortunately the hospital emergency room and medical staff were available to help, as all the important payment, insurance, and legal issues had to be addressed promptly. (How do they approve the procedures recommended without my court-appointed guardian becoming personally liable for the expensive costs incurred?) The first-day entries reflect this. It must have been terribly stressful for my mother and sister.

My mother's notebook covers entries that go through February 21, 2012. Among these are comments on her near daily visits to my skilled care facility, not only to cheer me up and take me for long wheelchair walks outside but also to oversee my treatment, my physical awareness, and my attention from medical staff (we learned that you need a constant advocate for attentive care), and to ascertain any changes in conditions I was showing. Critical treatment decisions had to be made that required the consent (and authorization) of my mother and sister. These included life-threatening procedures, many of which carried up-front risks that could have resulted in my death. As her notes reflect, this included breathing and swallowing impairments, colitis at its worst, the eventual need to feed me through a stomach tube, approved use of heavy steroidal drugs to keep me alive, and even unforeseen problems, such as my unanticipated bout with sepsis. My body was facing immediate challenges requiring powerful drugs. Sepsis, I read now, is itself life threatening and is triggered when the chemicals in the life-saving drugs I was being given are released in the bloodstream and cause inflammatory responses throughout one's body. Multiple organ systems in my weakened body were under immediate threat of failure. My mother and sister were, fortunately, greatly supported by Ann's husband, Jack Keith, an anesthesiologist by training (and a darn brilliant one at that), who took on guiding the family through these great and difficult medical decisions. Without Jack, of course, this story would not be told by me.

Perusal of my mother's notebook entries begins with September 15, 2011, in which she and Ann note many desperate legal issues to be addressed immediately, including estate planning and long-term health care coverage. There is also a notation confirming that I had suffered a "severe seizure." Notes on the next day indicate follow-up scrambling to ascertain what coverage I had, what alternatives might be available in Indiana, as well as comments on several doctor visits to get assessments about my condition. Numerous phone calls and meetings were noted, and much basic information about my life was being gathered. There was a notation confirming that a divorce petition was now pending against me, filed a month or so previously, and my designated attorney in Dallas had been contacted to make him aware of my seizure. On Saturday, September 17, there is the first notation as to my actual condition; I had begun to awaken from my coma. This indicates that I was completely comatose for the first six days following the seizure. Apparently as my eyes fluttered, I tried to talk but could not. The notation reported that I was agitated. That's a big surprise. I could not move my body, and I had been unconscious for six days. If I was aware of that, I am sure it agitated me. Sunday notations on September 18 show active preparation of a to-do list created by Ann and my mother to undertake. The list was extensive. There is no way they could they have expected this prior to my seizure. What an undertaking they now faced; it was certainly not one they had anticipated or cleared their respective personal schedules to face. The task ahead was massive in scope and full of uncertainties. For me to have a mother and sister like this just further confirmed, even in my then present state, that I was indeed a privileged man.

One issue that had to be confronted immediately was that the hospital would soon be discharging me after my time spent in intensive care. Although a date was not set, it was necessary to begin addressing my qualification for a transitional care unit (TCU). Typically, we were told, I would be in the TCU for maybe ten days and thereafter would be sent to a longer-term skilled-care facility. All this had to be arranged quickly, so both Ann and my mother were visiting area facilities. Fortunately, a TCU operating independently on another floor of the hospital was available, so finding one was not a big problem. Temporary guardianship was established by court order for me for ninety days, pursuant to Indiana law, and Ann and my mother became the guardian trustees. In time, my sister and mother selected a local long-term skilled-care facility, Morrison Woods, to which I would be transferred after my time in the TCU.

An interesting entry to the notebook was made on September 21: "Bill awakes, turns his head, looks at who is talking. Follows the conversation. His color is better … his eyes are alert." Missy was reading to me from the sports pages of the *Wall Street Journal*. At 3:00 p.m., my mother reports, my eyes were moving actively, although I was still unable to speak. I was no longer a vegetable, I guess, but I was barely mentally present nevertheless. The entry on September 23 reports that early in the morning I was trying to speak but was still groggy, as I apparently had not been sleeping for the previous three nights. Further progress the next day was recorded, as they had me sitting up in bed and I was still trying to talk. Further breathing treatments were undertaken, but they caused me such anxiety that I was given a strong drug that, as noted, I "was not able to tolerate." Whether I remained on that drug is not clear, but there are frequent observations as to my appearing hungover and otherwise not mentally responsive. The next day, my tenure in the ICU ended and I was moved upstairs to room 15 in the TCU, which was operated by a company called Integra. This meant I was now in a more traditional hospital room with new medical staff attendants. I don't recall much difference other than that I could now watch the starlings descending on the building roof outside my small window. My mother and Ann were now actively visiting Muncie-area skilled-care facilities so as to find a more permanent place for my long-term convalescence. The largest in the area was considered very efficient but nevertheless was rejected by mother as "not cheerful enough and smelling like sauerkraut." Morrison Woods seemed to fit the bill.

The focus in the TCU turned to concerns about my swallowing, which was greatly impaired as a result of the seizure. In fact, this was to turn into a critical problem for me over the next few years. The speech therapist took on the obvious swallowing problems, and the first of many types of swallowing tests was performed. A notation indicates that I was given applesauce to try to get something down my throat but that there were still big issues. One problem, which was to continue for the next few years, was that I was having terrible secretions in my throat. Unable to effectively move, I was encouraged initially to just swallow whatever came up. The frequently employed alternative was simply to drool constantly all over the front of my flimsy hospital gown. These secretions seemed to happen constantly. X-rays were ordered to try to discover the extent of the swallowing issues. The results were never good for the next several years, and it was the primary reason a hole was cut in my stomach on October 10 so I could thereafter be fed by tubes from a bottle hanging above my head. Day and night, nurses would check that bottle and dicker around with replacing it or its brown liquid contents, always waking me up or otherwise creating some interruptions. Little did I know that such was to become standard operating procedure, as it was soon apparent that I was in no condition to be doing any swallowing of any kind through my throat for the foreseeable future. The condition actually worsened later on during my stay at my skilled-care facilities, as all swallowing became impossible. My throat was severely impaired to such a degree that aspiration in my lungs was a strong likelihood. Liquids and food could go directly into my lungs. As a result, at some point all swallowing of liquids of every kind, including water and ice and all foodstuffs, was strictly prohibited. Shockingly to me, it was several years before I could even advance to pureed food and ice cream. That was a condition I never anticipated. Fortunately my throat did get stronger, and I no longer have swallowing issues. It all just seemed to take a very long time to heal.

Another big problem that developed as a result of my seizure was an inability to breathe. Early on I was put on a respirator that required a tube in my nose. Not being particularly cognizant, it was common for me to try to pull the tubes out of my nose. Maybe the good news here was that one of my hands and arms must have been moving somewhat, as that is the only logical means by which I could possibly pull the tube out. The bad news, of course, is that doing so placed my life in further peril, as obviously I had to be able to breathe. My personal recollection is that tubes in my throat and nose were extremely annoying and sedatives were required to keep me under control. The notes indicate that I was put on a drug called Ativan, administered every four to six hours, which is used to treat anxiety. Apparently my discomfort was causing me to thrash around, which also jeopardized my tubes. Feeling something plastic in my nasal passages and down my throat was very upsetting whenever I woke up. I was constantly on oxygen, which was fed from somewhere behind my bed. Advanced respiratory care became an important issue in my treatment and ultimately was a primary reason I was moved some eighteen months later, when my condition worsened, from the Muncie facility to Alden Park Strathmoor in Rockford. Park Strathmoor not only offered more sophisticated respiratory care, it was conveniently located in the same geographic area in which my sister and her family lived.

Notations from late September into October include some

entries that must have been devastating for my mother and sister. On September 30, my Muncie PCP and another doctor (whom my mother described as "very on the ball") both confirmed to my mother that, based on review of my prior Mayo Clinic reports, I did indeed have ALS. My Muncie PCP apparently told my mother that the ALS confirmation seemed "odd" to him. It was accepted by all nevertheless. My weight was only 132 pounds, obviously well below my normal weight of 180 pounds that I carried around prior to my illness. Another note that day has the doctors confirming that I was now on "full code" alert, which meant that my mother would be notified immediately when I was deemed to be dying.

Apparently I did not die, as the story of my adventure here would not be going anywhere if I had; I would have nothing else to share, let alone write, and much of the excitement is still ahead. Things did not immediately get better for me, but it was important that I be prepared to be moved to a long-term skilled-care health facility. During this final week at the ICU, there was an increasingly panicky drive to confirm how this future care would all be paid for. Notes indicate that Ann spent full days seeking insurance information by talking to our lawyers, agents, and the provider representatives. Of course, everything had to be legal, and this was all new to Ann and my mother. Court orders were obtained. The stress they were under is shown from the various notations in the notebook. Calls were being made all over, and information provided as required by the prospective health care facilities. This was when my forever friend (at least since college days) and Dallas accountant, Bill Francis, reemerged on the scene. He was to become such a great source of strength and understanding for my sister throughout the whole of my adventure. We have no idea how so many issues would have been satisfactorily resolved without his constant involvement on so many fronts, especially with respect to my life in Dallas. For my family, Bill was a magic man.

On October 11, safely now in Morrison Woods, my mother made several observations about my physical well-being. She found it significant enough to note that I was showing some movement in my wrists and hands. Additionally, I was holding my head up while sitting in the wheelchair, which I had now advanced to being able to tolerate. This is significant because by noting that I was showing movement in my hands, it was actually improvement from my initial paralysis. My body was malleable but not something I could control. I could be placed in a wheelchair but had to be strapped into my seat to prevent my rolling out. My condition soon worsened. Additional seizure activity was noted from time to time, at least into January, although none as significant as the first back on September 11. While maybe not as drastic, these seizures were to cause some setbacks. After a few seizures I was reported to have suffered, I did not always show this much flexibility. I remember that those months at Morrison Woods involved a lot of controversy about my ability to hold my head up. Frequently it dropped to my side or I stared at the floor. Drooling usually accompanied this problem. I know it looked terrible, and it was certainly indicative of my lack of muscular control. I remember it was a near daily controversy as I was being urged to hold my head up and look alive. There was no harm in requesting, but my complying was really difficult. At various times, I was given a brace to hold up my head, but I really hated to use it. I guess I had quick muscular fatigue and often got irritated. The natural alternative of returning to bed so I could lie down was not always permitted, as I needed to be up and out of bed as much as possible. Physically for me, that was very hard to endure.

CHAPTER 8

REMEMBRANCES FROM MORRISON WOODS

My many months at the Morrison Woods facility in Muncie featured significant time under the impairment of heavy drugs, prednisone being the most obvious, even though I had periods with some meaningfully active mental awareness. My mother's notes reflect that during the first few weeks at Morrison Woods, I was often mentally out of it. There were portions of days where I remember talking with family, friends, staff, and other patients. I know there were lots of times during which I had friendly banter with nurses and staff assistants. Several actually seemed to like me—at least when I was not being a nuisance or requiring attention at inconvenient times. I also remember visits with doctors who were coming into my room and sharing with me assessments of my current condition and explaining possible effects of the forthcoming next treatment. I am not sure I was really aware of the purpose of a proposed action, but I don't remember feeling anxious about anything as my mother and sister were making the decisions. My mother's notebook recounts everything discussed or prescribed. Looking back, I find that notebook indispensable in appreciating my condition at the time. It even reflects descriptions of the faces of the doctors as they explained the risks involved.

Big health decisions were frequently being made. I, of course, have no idea what was going on during my occasional comatose sessions. I understand that there were life-and-death decisions. My dear mother received extraordinary support from Ann and Jack. This had to be reassuring for her. No one wants to ever be in the position of making life-and-death decisions alone, although we all know loved ones who frequently are in such situations. I consider this to have been yet another sign of privilege in my life.

Morrison Woods Healthcare, Muncie, Indiana.

My memories of my mother's visits to Morrison Woods are still vivid to me. Fortunately the facility was within a few miles of her house, but she still chose to make the trek, rain, snow, or shine. While her notebook reflects that there were many occasions when I was either unconscious or asleep during her visit, I do recall other times

when I was fully aware and anxious to see her. Her visits meant I
might be getting out of bed and leaving my room all with her assistance. We explored the hallways and even the world outside the
facility. My mother was a great walker; our near daily time outside
was spent with her pushing my wheelchair around the whole facility.
We watched the ducks at the small ponds in the fields nearby, we
counted the blooming flowers along the walkways, and I studied the
action at the houses across the street. These were real people doing
real things, such as washing their cars and mowing the lawn. Inside
the facility, that was all foreign to my world. Would it be foreign to
me forever? Sometimes mornings seemed interminable for me, as her
standard practice was usually to come in the late afternoon. I felt like
the elementary schoolkid I once was, just waiting for the wall clock in
the classroom to move toward the end of the day. The clock moved so
slowly. It was not as if my mother had nothing to do; her days included
serving on community boards, going to woman's club meetings (garden, art, conversational), tending to her little dog, and writing her
frequent articles for the local Muncie magazine. When she finally
showed up in my room, it was usually after she had checked with a
nurse or an aide on duty. More than a few times she might find me,
in her opinion, unattended, unbathed, in dirty clothes, or abandoned
in my wheelchair. She was, each day, my biggest advocate, which is
actually what every invalid patient absolutely needs. Care facilities
mean well, I know, but at even the finest of facilities there are times
when a patient is unattended, feels neglected, or is subject to an aide's
attention necessarily being elsewhere. This was no one's fault, as I was
not paying for twenty-four-hour in-room attention; nevertheless, my
gown was sometimes half off, my diaper dirty, or my head drooping
to my side. I know her arrival caused some tension with the staff, and
eyeballs probably rolled as my mother came down the hall, but what
we learned is that you do not for a minute, to the extent possible, fail
to keep your eye on things for your loved one. A squeaky wheel from
family is a godsend for patients in a nursing facility. My mother, while

always kind, was quite demanding—much to my good fortune. None of these comments are intended to allege institutional neglect, but just the realities of not having personalized and very costly twenty-four-hour on-site care. There are wealthy patients who, in fact, pay to receive such care, but it is not mainstream for most of us.

I remember being aware enough to begin listening for signs that my mother was coming. Not infrequently, it was common to hear my mother stopping to visit one or more of the elderly and disabled patients. Soon she knew most all of them by name. She easily was more popular with patients of the facility than I ever was. Many were her older aged friends or parents of one of her friends. The joy I would hear from these people was pronounced. She often shared her freshly baked brownies or zinnias and marigolds cut from her beloved garden. I realize now that my mother was probably older than many of the people she stopped to visit, but it was simply her nature to be so kind to those who were suffering or alone. I wondered if a bit of this might have been her realizing "But for the grace of God, there go I." There is nothing wrong with feeling that; dealing with limited time left on this earth is just part of the necessary psyche in places like Morrison Woods. Very few resident patients had any realistic expectations of actually getting out. I don't think many even cared about that. Who among us was really going to get physically better? Where was there to go? It's a mindset common to all but still very personal to the patient. In my case, it did not seem to be disappointing or a reason to be depressed, as my physical condition and heavily drugged fuzzy mind never even contemplated getting out. I was simply a new wheelchair-bound soul who had no reason to expect to ever walk or stand again. Before many more weeks, I would find that the issue was not just walking but even surviving at all. Some said I showed great patience. Patience implies waiting for something good to happen—being cognizant that you are waiting. For me it was not so much being patient as dealing with what faced me that very minute on that particular day. Today was, for me, plenty far enough in advance.

My mother's visits grew to include reading me the sports pages. She kept me up to date with scores and team results. Was I always able to appreciate the importance of the information? Most likely not, as I must admit I have no recollection of my hometown Texas Rangers nearly beating the St. Louis Cardinals in the World Series. All those years of suffering as a Rangers fan back in Dallas and I did not even appreciate that they were now finally playing in a World Series. The TV was on in my room for the whole Series, but I did not realize the significance. I do remember my mother growing to like reading me the *Wall Street Journal* sports columns by Jason Gay. "What a witty and clever writer he is," she would proclaim. Whether she understood the game he was writing about is another issue.

Depression is a natural issue in long-term care facilities. I think it is naturally worse when a patient sees life descending with illness or inevitable old age. But facing the realization that you may never walk or see again has every bit the same implications. I saw that those who initially move into an independent-living or, especially, an assisted-living facility have a naturally difficult time, as they are living change and are aware of its limitations. In a highly skilled care facility, such as the one I was at Morrison Woods, it is less of an issue because chances are you are in such bad shape that you are not really aware of what you are going through or otherwise missing. Getting your diaper changed or avoiding the next shower was far more relevant for me as a skilled care patient. I tended to live by the moment, concerned only by what was happening next. Depression was nevertheless seen as an expected problem for me. I was put on a strong antidepressant drug, which I see from my mother's notes she thought was soon knocking me out for much of a day, if not several days. My being depressed was alleviated by the squelching of my ability to even think. My mother was frequently alarmed on finding me unresponsive to her or visitors. At some point after a few weeks, I was declared allergic to the drug because I slept too much and was switched to Prozac in the hope that I would not be so loopy. I soon declared my daily Prozac "my happy pill." I can't say it really made an ounce of difference, but no one thought I was very depressed anymore, so thank you Prozac.

Some of my favorite memories are visits from my friends. As mentioned, several good friends made the trip to Muncie to see me. I don't know if this was motivated by their intent to pay their respects to a dying old pal, but since I did not think I was dying, I just loved the visits. I have recollections of apparently being asleep (more likely, momentarily dozing), waking up, and then seeing a great and unexpected friend. I am sure there was shock on their faces, but they usually hid it well. It's scary walking in on an old buddy who seems lifeless, or at least extremely different. For me it was better than any dream (and I had many vivid ones); my great friend was there, standing at the foot of my bed or sitting in the chair beside me. What joy; instant memories of times together came to life for me. Those were better times, yes, but my pal was here! Sometimes I really could not talk clearly. Sometimes I just listened. I felt frustrated but not defeated. I hated for our visits to end, but unless I dozed off in their presence (very common, as I understand), I was totally invigorated. I would feel a new joy, if only temporary. Firsthand I can tell you that visits from friends were so appreciated, even if I was not in my right mind and looked like hell. (Interesting thought: is a facility designed to encourage maximum pleasant visits from family and friends?)

I must mention how special my visits were from my old Muncie pal Kevin Smith. We were high school tennis teammates at Burris and actually such close friends we stayed in contact whenever I returned to visit Muncie. Kevin made a habit of visiting me nearly every week during my stay at Morrison Woods. Unfortunately, his father was in a facility nearby, but I never expected him to visit me so frequently. We would talk about college football (he loved Notre Dame and Purdue) and his frequent road trips to games. *Oh, to have such freedom*, I thought. Poor Kevin, I know the visits with me were often hard. Some days I was mentally not there or even unable to wake up. During many visits, I could not even talk. It had to be so boring for him. Ever patient, Kevin would go on talking away, telling me about sports, his trips, or his family updates. The visits were never long, but they were so special to me. Later I asked Kevin why he did it so regularly. He said, "You'd have done it for me." Really? I don't really want to reply to that. What a special guy Kevin is.

The hallway and sitting room outside my room were usually filled with very elderly and quiet people. Some moaned or babbled, and others just sat silently. A nurses' station overlooked the patients, but times were never very lively. I do recall the room had a television set, but it always seemed to be on a channel broadcasting old black-and-white westerns or musicals—never a game or the current news. Sitting in my wheelchair in the hallway could be a very boring experience. I soon was trying to roll away farther down the long hallway—the place where different faces seemed to come from. At the end of the hall was a big room into which several different hallways seemed to converge. There was no television, but there was a small refreshments area where, miraculously, cookies seemed to appear. Cookies! Man did I want one! I often wheeled my way over to the counter. Could I sneak just one? My efforts were always in vain. Try as I might, my arms would not reach upward to the top of that counter. The cookies were always just out of reach. Never mind that I was prohibited from eating solid foods; my recollection is that I tried every chance I got.

In my mind, the hallway to freedom was actually more like a mountain, or at least a tall hill. Many times I could not seem to get up the hill. Up a hill? That likely meant I was too physically weak to proceed on what was actually a flat hallway. Little did I appreciate that sometimes the aide on duty locked the brakes on my wheelchair so I could not move it. Keeping tabs on several patients all with a little bit of mobility must have been like herding cats for a busy nurse. I was confused; my wheelchair had moved just minutes ago. Why not now? In my mind, I was convinced that my chair was chained to the floor. I often had objections to how, in my fuzzy mind, I was occasionally treated. Some could have been legitimate, but were they realistic? I wanted to believe some aides were too physical in their treatment of me. Their moving me to the shower that doubled as my toilet was particularly dreadful. CNAs (referred to at Park Strathmoor more clinically as "Certified Nursing Assistants") had to lift me from my bed, which was never pleasant for me. Once placed on the toilet (something I was rarely provided to relieve myself, because of legitimate physical impairment), I was then sprayed with the shower water by the aide. I swear the water was always cold; it probably was not. I hated being lifted up and vigorously dried off. I am sure I squirmed and tried to resist. The aides had their responsibility, and that was to get me dry, clothed in my gown, and back in my bed. I never liked any of it, but what did I know? I appreciated later that the facility was acting in my best interests.

I had some very dear people among the aides helping me at Morrison Woods. There was Sheen, the kindly day nurse my mother favored so much. Sheen was so good to my mother and me. She was encouraging during times when encouragement may not have been entirely in order. My mother's notebook has several entries from during my time at the facility when Sheen took it upon herself to call my mother at off hours to update her on my condition. More than once, my mother intimated to me what a wonderful spouse Sheen would make for me. Poor Sheen! Just what she needed—a twenty-four-hour-per-day invalid! Several others on the staff were also good to me. Karen Reichle was activity director and actually a jack-of-all-trades at the facility. Karen went to Burris while I did and had known us most of her life. She loved talking and planting gardens at the facility with my mother and even took on the harrowing task of driving us in the aging facility-owned van to my important neurologist appointment in Indianapolis. Whether harrowing to Karen or not, the ride was for me, as I was all strapped into my wheelchair in the back of the bus. The hour-plus ride featured endless encounters with potholes on Indiana roads. Karen's natural good attitude more than made the ride tolerable, although the doctor's assessments from the visit really did not change anything for me.

Many of the younger employees at the facility were particularly good to me. My memories of the staff assistants are of nice and competent people. There were a couple I believed were being too rough on me, but considering my condition at the time, who can be sure? My primary issue with them was only how long it took for them to respond to my calls for assistance. Were they told to ignore me? Sounds a bit conspiratorial in my fuzzy mind. Was I pushing my nurse call button too often? Likely. Never mind how many other patients also needed help; that certainly was not my primary concern. I guess my patience was not so good in a micro sense. On a number of occasions, when I was exhausted from sitting in my wheelchair (and failing to hold my head up), I remember wheeling up to the edge of my bed and trying to generate the strength to throw myself on the bed. If I could just get there, my head could rest on my pillow. I had a brief history of falling out of my wheelchair or off my bed, so I was never supposed to do so alone. But if no staff would come for me, I felt I had no choice but to do it myself. Several times I sat by the edge of the bed and tried to get up my nerve to make the two-foot leap. I don't think I ever tried; whether because of a lack of physical strength or more likely the belt that secured me in my seat, I never made the actual leap. What a frustration that was for me.

I remember in particular a personable college boy from Ball State who was interning at the facility. His goal was to go to nursing school someday. As the staff took him and his fellow interns around on in-room patient visits, he particularly stood out to me because we could talk sports. I felt he treated me as a person and not just an object to be observed. I enjoyed hearing what was going on in his world. Was it a world to which I would ever be able to return? The athletic-looking young man was working to put himself through undergraduate school. I recall him describing a very popular fried chicken restaurant his family owned in southern Indiana. He said he drove home each weekend to wait tables and take advantage of the big crowds that filled the restaurant on weekends. "Best fried chicken in Indiana," he liked to proclaim. How I wanted to taste a piece. That, of course, was prohibited for me. But what an impressive kid; he was working hard for his future ahead. I was trying not to think much about my future.

My life surrounding my meals never seemed pleasant to me. Much of my time at Morrison Woods was spent being fed from a feeding tube to my stomach while in my room. Before I experienced some subsequent seizures, which I previously described in detail, eating certain foods was still an option. I remember being taken to the dining room at Morrison Woods several hallways away and seeing patients eating together and conversing. A good-smelling soup greeted me as I was wheeled in. Was that lentil soup today? But wait, that was not for me. The dining room was for the healthy and independent residents who functioned without assistance at the table. Where was my dining room? It was that small, crowded room in the back on the other side of that door. There the menu was different, the food far more mundane. Nothing was meant to be challenging or enticing to one's taste buds. Very ill-seeming folk were wheeled into crowded tables—I among them. The menu choices were far more limited. Jell-O, macaroni, hot dogs—why do those seem to standout? Even while I felt stronger, I was prohibited from doing much by the staff. I thought the food was terrible. The people at my table rarely spoke, and if they could, nothing they said seemed to make sense. I dreaded going there for meals, but it was the only way I could expect to eat at a designated time. (Remember: this was before the subsequent seizure activity in early 2012 forced me to use the feeding tube and to stay in my room to eat.) My table mates in that dining room often seemed to just disappear. "What happened to that old fellow, Tom?" Time moved on; Tom no longer was there. New faces appeared. I don't remember any of them today. I do not really remember how long I ate in that depressing dining room in Morrison Woods, but I do know my eating conditions changed radically when I was moved to Park Strathmoor in Rockford. That would prove not always to be for the better.

CHAPTER 9

THINGS TURN DARK AT MORRISON WOODS

My initial few months in Morrison Woods following my grand mal seizure were full of challenges, but as depicted in my mother's notebook, they included some obvious improvements in my health. Little victories were being obtained even though I was terribly incapacitated. I was now sitting in a wheelchair, trying to talk, eating ice cream and those beloved frozen magic cups, dining in that dreadful small side room, receiving visitors, and being taken outside on pretty days. Events such as being given a PEG tube in my stomach and a catheter to address relief issues were forms of progress. I had my good days, but obviously there were many tough days when I was not very coherent or aware. The sheer volume of financial, insurance, and legal issues that my mother and sister had to address seemed overwhelming. What medical coverage? Social security benefits? A legal guardianship for me? I was deemed mentally incompetent (for legal standards) by my new Muncie Primary Care Physician. That meant an Indiana judicial court had to get involved and designate a legal guardian. Somehow my mother and family prevailed. All that has been covered in pages before this.

On Tuesday, December 6, 2011, I took a big step backward. My mother's notes record that at 12:30 a.m. I suffered a significant seizure at Morrison Woods. It is not stated when I was discovered in such condition, but Sheen called my mother at about 8:00 a.m. the next morning to report that she had found me with a contorted face, clenched teeth, and heavy wheezing from my lungs. After she had performed some undescribed procedure on my chest, my eyes fluttered and opened, though they did not focus on her. I was promptly transferred to the Ball Hospital emergency room. In a sense, I suppose I was once again back where it all started in September. Whatever progress I had made since my early September seizure was no longer very relevant.

I remained in Ball Hospital for a week, being sent back to Morrison Woods on Tuesday, December 13 (coincidently, what would have been my deceased father's ninety-sixth birthday). Sporadic notes show that during my week in the hospital I was soon trying to talk again. "Where is my son?" she recorded I asked several times. I had a small (one-minute?) seizure on Thursday at night. Additional antiseizure drugs were being given, some of them newly prescribed. Minor seizure activity was occurring on that Friday as well. The nurses and doctors caring for me said to my mother that I was "very out of it" that whole day.

My mother mentions that when I returned to Morrison Woods, I received a warm welcome back from staff and several patients on my wing. At best, I was merely whispering any sort of response. Even the nurse my mother had the most problems with greeted us both with a nice, welcoming hug. It probably helped that my mother noted it was the nurse's birthday and had brought her a poinsettia as a gift. Friday, December 16, was a tough day for my mother. Although I was sitting in my wheelchair once again, my head was drooping and I was responding poorly. A visit from Kevin and a good high school buddy, Ted, did not go well. I have no recollection of Ted being there, and with his having once been such a good friend, I know I would have been excited to see him. My mother says that later that day we did wrap some Christmas presents to send to my two children, but that did not seem to cheer me up. She records that I was very depressed—sounding hopeless, in fact. I complained of being physically mistreated by some staff. I am confident today that such a complaint was nothing more than the perception of a very fuzzy mind and sick body merely responding to basic good care. Moving me at all was not necessarily my first choice. My sleeping was disturbed at night, and staff became conditioned to my dozing off unexpectedly at various times during the day. My mother noted that I did look peaceful when she saw me sleeping that afternoon. The list of drugs I was being given at the time seems staggering.

The medical attention I now required after this new December series of seizures was alarmingly expensive. An hour of physical training on-site cost as much as $200. My family was upset. Money to pay for these unforeseen expenditures was obviously a huge concern. Ann and my mother spent a lot of their day once again addressing payments. Add that to the depressing visits one or both had with me most every day, and I cannot imagine the stress they were both under.

During this time, and up to about Christmas Day, it was noted that I could no longer be on even a semblance of a normal diet. Several types of swallow tests were undertaken, and real problems quickly became apparent. It was called a neurological problem, but regardless of the cause, it was soon to become an ongoing issue for me. Ice cream and liquids, including water, were no longer to be consumed through my mouth. In other words, I was not to drink water or eat ice cream at all! Any solid foods were, of course, out of the question. This deprivation was to continue for the next several years, indeed in both of my skilled-care facilities. The alternative, I was told, was aspiration, which meant choking to death. Little did I know I was going to hear this dire warning time and again every time I wanted to eat, drink, or dampen my throat.

Christmas came about the time I was put on the antiseizure drug

Keppra and the antidepressant drug Prozac. The doses of Keppra initially were huge but were deemed to be in an acceptable range. My mother noted that my weight was now so far down ("he is so thin") that she worried what my body could handle. Ann reports a few days later that the Keppra was appearing to prevent further seizures. I find it interesting that these two drugs are still prescribed drugs I take as of this writing today, albeit in much smaller doses. It is impressive that my Muncie doctors got this all underway for me and that their treatment was, in effect, endorsed later at the University of Chicago Medical Center and UT Southwestern Medical Center in Dallas.

The New Year, 2012, has some early January entries which indicate that my sister and my mother both saw some improvements in my condition. They were gradual but still apparent. I expressed concerns about my financial circumstances and investments. My friend and financial advisor, Rob, was even called in Hawaii to see if he had any idea what I was trying to say about my finances. The only reported good news was that Rob would be coming to Muncie to visit me during the forthcoming weekend. This may have been the weekend my old friend Mack Findley in Ohio joined Rob in visiting and buying me a television. I was cognizant enough to be in light physical therapy at the facility. However, I was dismissed from therapy at one stage for not trying hard enough. I know this upset my mother. I was asked several times to try harder, but I can't imagine that had much effect on my actual performance. That failure put my Medicare coverage for therapy in jeopardy. My December 6, 2011, seizure was acknowledged as causing a real setback in my condition, even though I was at least showing some renewed progress.

As hard as it may seem, things actually turned for the worse for me in later January 2012. I was sent to Ball Hospital on January 22, early in the morning at 5:45 a.m., reportedly because of some disturbing presence of blood in my stool. That darn colitis—an issue once again. Then, on January 24, while still at the hospital I suffered what was labeled a "massive seizure" at 10:45 a.m. This one was considered particularly significant, and my mother reported that "blue codes" were being alerted. I was unconscious, which later was acknowledged to be in a comatose state. My breathing was an immediate issue. I was not doing any natural breathing now. The ventilator became my only hope for survival. Several tubes were hooked up and sticking in me now. I was once again on what was called life support. I was to remain in Ball Hospital until I was sent back to Morrison Woods five days later, my condition reportedly stabilizing. That date, February 6, ironically happened to be my mother's birthday. Quite the birthday party guy I proved to be. The fun did not last long, however, as once again, this time on Monday, February 13, I was rushed to the Ball Hospital emergency room because of some scary problems with my right arm. The notes indicate that I was given a Doppler examination to determine whether the PEG tube in my right arm was causing the arm to turn a shade of blue and my wrist to swell badly. Fortunately, the conclusion was that I only had a bad bruise. The cause of the bad bruise on my arm was not noted.

There are only a few more entries in my mother's incredible notebook. In later February, the issues seemed to be centered on my inability to swallow. Speech therapists were treating me daily, and updates were being given. Nothing was very good, but at least there was a reference to trying to give me some frozen liquid treats. I remember that my favorite was Luigi's lemon ice. I think it reminded me of those great Italian frozen ice treats I once had as a child walking the Freedom Trail in Boston. I complained that, try as I might, I could not really talk above a whisper. Whatever I managed to whisper never seemed to make much sense anyway, as I was aware of the listeners' confused looks and gentle nods as if to say they agreed. The best news was that X-rays showed that my throat was not irreparably messed up and I could move my tongue—some of the time, anyway.

My mother's final entry in her notebook near the end of February says I was very alert on that Sunday afternoon. I spoke up well but primarily was concerned about our plans for my ongoing care. She learned that I had discussed plans for my inevitable funeral. I had not discussed death with my mother. She wrote, "He seems to protect me." No more entries appear in the notebook after February 27. My adventure, however, was far from complete.

CHAPTER 10

DREAMS—A POTENT PART OF MY EXISTENCE

During the course of my adventure, I spent a lot of time with just me. If you ever wondered what it would be like to have time to do nothing but exist and be free of normal earthly concerns, such as family, work, finances, eating, having fun, cleaning house, catching a game or a concert, etc., I can tell you about it. I used to wonder what it would be like to be able to just lie in a bed and not need or want to do anything. Looking back, I find it surprising that I spent a great deal of time after my initial seizures, through the point where I felt truly conscious again, not really caring what I did. People turned on the television for me, my mother read to me, visitors visited me, and I dozed off often for long periods of many days. For a number of months, I had no computers or telephone, no email or social media, and not even the need to listen to my favorite music to help occupy my day. While I obviously recall being serviced by the facility staff (nurses and CNAs) each day, the one thing that really strikes me is how vividly I remember a number of my dreams. In a strange way, dreams became my daily life. I was obviously being administered high dosages of powerful drugs, some of which were described as steroidal, but the one particular effect on me was some powerful, vivid dreams. My sense of reality was way out of kilter. Dreams affected my emotions and seemed to stay with me on a daily basis.

I never imagined that dreams were destined to become such an important part of my existence during my adventure. Throughout my illness, I experienced some of the most bizarre and ridiculous distortions of reality. I definitely remember these dreams, as in fact, at some point or another, I lived them. These dreams were so real to me and, like a long-running television series, in most cases seemed to last for months at a time. I always understood that when one had a dream, maybe even a nightmare, it tended to actually be only for a brief period of time and almost always only for no more than one night. Usually when I sensed I had experienced a crazy dream, I could not even recount it the next morning. That occurs even today. Crazy? Yes. Of course, some dreams recur for all of us from time to time, but they had never before done so for me as though they were my daily reality. Recurring topics for me today include the frustration of not being able to get to my gate in time to catch an airplane or failing to buy the necessary textbook for a college class in which I have a final exam coming up the following week. I think most of us have some variation of those silly but frustratingly stressful dreams.

The dreams I recall experiencing while at Morrison Woods and Park Strathmoor were much more potent and vivid to me. They seemed to last for months at a time as I lived and experienced some crazy adventures that had an active impact on me day-to-day. Undoubtedly these were caused by the assortment of powerful drugs being prescribed just to save my life. I will not try to recount what specific drugs caused what but, at the time, I was being administered heavy doses of drugs such as prednisone, among others, which probably contributed to my complete distortion of reality. My distortions were amazing and so vivid that I was able to live in this mindset day and night. Remember: my sleep habits were reported as very inconsistent, with me not sleeping through the night (frequently being awakened by CNAs for medical attention) and often sleeping during the daylight hours. Regardless, I sensed I was living in that distorted world, usually for several weeks, centered on a particular dream or adventure.

I mention that these dreams were very vivid to me. In fact, I can remember many specifics to this day as if I was actually there. More importantly, I was able to recall them while I was still very ill and bedridden, and also within the year or so after experiencing some and after, when I had my first access to an iPad and Acer Chromebook. While many dreams occurred while I was in Morrison Woods, I did not actually get my iPad and Chromebook until I was at Park Strathmoor. In the entries that follow, I reconstruct several of the specific dreams from actual accounts I began writing while bedridden at Park Strathmoor. I know the dreams occurred, but I also know that even these, which sometimes read as an adventure story, were not among the three I consider the most vivid and disturbing.

The first dream that I recall so specifically was tied to my work and family. Bizarre as it may seem, none of them ever seemed to recognize that I was in a quadriplegic state or even in my skilled-care facility at Morrison Woods. In this first one, I was for some reason in Milwaukee, Wisconsin. I was helping my deceased father's brother (or some undefined Millard relative) with his failing business. In reality I had been to Milwaukee only once, and that was many years ago. I never had a relative living there, let alone my father's brother. Yet, there I was helping Paul, my father's relative, deal with problems in his failing business. (My father's only brother was Bob, a deceased older brother who lived in Nevada, not Wisconsin.) In the dream, I was lucky to have this opportunity because I had lost my partnership position at the law firm back in Dallas and had no source of earnings. I don't remember what business service Paul was providing, but I tried to help him save it. Paul died, unfortunately, and I apparently gave up trying to keep the business open. That alone is not such an interesting dream, but it continued for seemingly months thereafter. It seems that Paul was under some significant debt for his Millard family ventures. Although I knew nothing about it, I was soon being looked to as Paul's successor-in-interest to resolve these debts, particularly to a bank whose name shall remain undisclosed. As a lawyer, I represented both banks and borrowers, so I knew a lot about collecting on debts gone bad. Anyway, this bank decided I was liable for some hard-to-fathom Millard-related debt that allegedly arose in the early 1900s, nearly a century ago. I, of course, told the bank that I knew nothing about it, but the bank just would not go away. I knew something about foreclosure sales, as I had conducted many over the years as a lawyer for unpaid creditors in Texas. You conduct a public sale and take away the property (usually land) that the debtor pledged as collateral for the loan. But I had no property now, nor had I assumed this debt and had certainly not pledged any property to secure the debt. I was a lawyer; I understood all of this. Why couldn't the bank? Foreclosure notices came in the mail, and my skilled-care facility passed them on to me. What was I to do? The first thing to do in such a situation is identify the property the bank has its lien against and seeks to take from you. There it was; the bank sought to foreclose on my right leg. After the sale, my leg was to be cut off and delivered to the bank (or other highest bidder) as satisfaction for the Millard debt. That was crazy, and I knew it! That's not what banks foreclose on; they foreclose on real estate or stock or some sort of personal property that has been pledged for repayment of the loan—not my leg! Even if they could foreclose on a leg, I had not ever pledged mine; nor had I even assumed a debt to this bank. Yes, it was crazy, yet these computer-generated foreclosure notices just kept coming. "Pay up or we take your leg." Well, I knew I had no money to pay any debt, let alone this one. I recall trying to handle the situation in a mature manner. I contacted the appropriate loan officers in the bank's collections department and gradually seemed to convince them that there had been a terrible mistake in their records, or at least a glitch in the computer system. We were all very friendly, and they agreed that all this silliness would soon go away. I remember a great sense of relief. In my mind, my roommate at Morrison Woods, Lyle, had recently had his foot removed for unspecified reasons, and I knew that was all very painful and disconcerting. I certainly did not want that to happen to me. What a relief! But alas, it was a disaster. I soon kept receiving these computer-generated foreclosure notices and, despite assurances from the loan officers to disregard them, a specific foreclosure date was set. My leg would be cut off that day, this time for sure. I was a mess. As so often happens just prior to a foreclosure sale, the creditor would not talk to me. The computer would not respond. The appointed day approached! What the hell! No one but me seemed concerned; no one helped! I could not even get to the bank, me being in a quadriplegic state, to pay them the money! What now? Well, fortunately nothing actually happened to my leg. I guess the date came and went. Maybe in my highly drugged state, I slept through it all. Maybe that damn computer just forgot. Whatever the reason, this very scary and prolonged event in my life just seemed to go away. Maybe those anxiety drugs that the facility was giving me finally took full effect. I've still got my right leg.

The second recurring dream I will attempt to summarize for you involved a bizarre episode in Australia. I remember it well, and I know it seemed to last for a long time. Was I there all summer? More than a year? I can't really remember. Trust me; I was there a long time. What spurred all this, I don't know. I have never been to Australia, nor did I ever really have a "must go" urge to do so. My cousins once lived in Perth in far western Australia, but that was a long time ago. Why Australia entered my drugged-up goofy mind I simply do not know. I think one day I was particularly bored being in my skilled-care facility there in Waco, Texas. Yes, Waco. Why? Don't ask. I just know I was there and that playing golf at the course adjacent to my facility was not an option. That was boring. So I gathered up some clothes, got my bag, and headed to DFW airport, up there some ninety miles away, north of Dallas and Fort Worth. I don't remember many specifics, but despite my not having a passport or other known identification with me, I boarded a plane bound for a place I knew only as Perth, Australia.

I don't know how I truly got to Perth, but strangely, I thought, I was welcomed. Surely I was not seeking political asylum, but I do remember asking for assistance from a local Methodist church. I guess I kept trying to get to a church because it seemed like a safe place to spend my first few nights. Money is not relevant to this story—not because I either lacked it or had too much; it simply is not a factor in what happened. I suppose I had adequate funds, because most significantly my first distinct memories of my time in Perth involved moving into a nursing facility where they could, I hoped, address my then current significant medical needs. I remember very clearly that this nursing facility, which I assumed was only temporary for me, was a modest-sized ship. It was not, mind you, some big ocean liner decked out for Indian Ocean pleasure cruises, but more of a sailors' dormer, complete with small private berths, an eating area, and a nice, dark wood interior. It was once intended for a crew to occupy while rendering some unspecified services in the Perth harbor. But its intended purpose is not really important to this dream. What is important is that I now was being provided a warm place to live with adequate skilled nursing care. This seemed to go on for weeks, or at least that's how I perceived my stay. I remember that I was treated nicely, and the nursing staff seemed attentive to my needs. How they understood my medical situation, I really don't know. Was someone making them aware of my problems, condition, and records back in Waco, where I thought I last lived? That does not matter, I suppose, because the important thing is that it did not seem of concern to me or in any event prove stressful in my dream.

One day after several months of satisfactory existence on the ship, something stressful did arise. I was told that particular morning by one of my nurses that soon the ship would be leaving the port in Perth and begin commencing on a journey. For whatever reason, my fellow patients and I were going to be transferred to a regional care facility located on some island in Antarctica. *Antarctica? What?* I did not know who was in charge of Antarctica, but I was pretty certain it was not these Australians who I found so kind. Who would take care of me? Who would even know where I was? This was indeed stressful, and my mind was a soon abuzz with new concerns. The reason, it was explained, was that neither I nor my fellow patients had been paying for our care. In other words, I had a big debt now owed to the nursing home provider. They knew I could not pay off the debt, so it was determined that the smartest thing to do was ship us off to another place—preferably Antarctica, I suppose. Now I was desperate to get off this vessel. I soon learned that was hard to do when you could not walk, and especially when you did not know anyone in Perth. I did not even know where these Methodists were, nor whether anyone would help me. This all built up in my dreams over the next few days. I was a nervous, frustrated mess, so I thought. But just as in my foreclosure story, I soon woke up relieved and very aware I was back in my room at Morrison Woods in Muncie. What happened to Waco?

A third of the recurring dreams involved bizarre travels I undertook from time to time. I remember escaping from my Muncie facility on a number of occasions, but why and how seemed irrelevant. Sometimes these involved strange free trips to Hawaii. I specifically remember finding myself in Philadelphia one time. I don't know why I went there, but most of my stress involved getting home. The same thing seemed to happen to me in Baltimore. Both were cities I had visited only on one occasion, and neither had any ties to my family or job. It was really strange, but the episodes seemed very real to me.

What follows are more specific encounters I remembered and wrote about while I was lying in my bed at Park Strathmoor in Rockford. I swear these were not one-night dreams but things I encountered for at least a week, if not longer. I wrestled with these dreams, though I have no clue whether I mentioned any of them to family or staff. In my drugged and groggy mental state, the dreams were real indeed.

CHAPTER 11

I THINK I KNOW WHEN ALL THIS FIRST HAPPENED: MY ADVENTURE STARTS

Like so much that I experienced in the early weeks of my adventure, that period after my grand mal seizure through the days I either was in the ICU or vaguely aware in the Morrison Woods assisted-living facility, I have a cloudy recollection of when this mess really began. Although things were not seeming right with my physical condition that day (was it the colitis or the strange drugs that practical nurse in Irving had prescribed?), I remember being excited I was going out that day with some of my work buddies. Who were they? I really can't remember, but I think they were a few of my younger associates I worked with at the law firm. This was all very exciting to me, because these young guys were among the ones I had been part of recruiting out of law school. These hotshots from Texas schools were fun and liked to party and they seemed particularly to like me, a boss some fifteen or twenty years older than them. I enjoyed them because they were not yet tired and jaded from the drain of big-firm legal practice and, as I said, we often had fun together. A few even took to referring to me as the Thrill—more specifically, Bill the Thrill. Not bad for a guy approaching middle age balancing my now strenuous law practice with the cherished responsibilities of providing for my family, the wife, two kids, and a few dogs.

I remember we went out that evening somewhere in Dallas at one of the cool restaurants where we had cocktails and a nice dinner. I don't remember how many vodka tonics I may have had, but I am sure we were all getting pretty loosened up. After this initial stop, one of these single guys had the great idea that we needed to have a nightcap at one of Dallas's hot men's clubs. That is "men's club" in the sense of a place with scantily clad female strippers dancing on tables. My recollection seems to be that this was one of those dark, smoke-filled joints full of thumping loud music, bright lights, and way too many obnoxious men watching the dancers. As may come as no surprise, this was still big business in corporate Dallas at that time, and as long as us married guys did no more than lightly window shop and certainly refrain from becoming familiar with anyone who worked there, male culture still tolerated such rare nights out. Definitely, however, we were not to enjoy it too much. That did not mean my buddies were not susceptible to wanting to get the boss liquored up and make sure he was having fun too. Knowingly or not, I of course went along and kept letting the liquor flow. Now oblivious to being concerned about how liquor would interact with new drugs, I had another and probably another after that. I don't remember any specifics of how it happened, but I seem to remember falling to the floor. My guys had me up, and soon I was passed out on some couch. I have no idea who got me out of that club, but I woke up in some strange old facility on an old Dallas street called Lemmon Avenue. I think the building was an old place I had passed many times, usually on the way to work. I thought it was either a very low-cost apartment building or maybe even a halfway house. I had been checked into a room, and there I was left. When I finally woke up, I was alone and very hungover. In time my friend Justin, one of the perpetrators from the night before, appeared and told me what had happened. For some reason family had not inquired or come to get me (probably a very good thing at that moment). Justin explained that this was where I would be living now, and everyone agreed that would be a good thing. If I proved to conform and behave, I could *expect in time to get a job at the front desk checking new arrivals in. There I lay ... what the hell?*

I was glad to see my Morrison Woods room now. There was my room-mate, the fellow with his foot cut off, over there in his bed. *Good, back to normal.* I was alive, and even though the dream I had just experi-enced had been frightful and disconcerting, I no longer had any effects of that dang hangover. I am happy to say now that even with all my drugs, this is not how things really happened.

CHAPTER 12
OLYMPIAN EFFORT

I don't have a great history of winning competitions, but for some reason this time I just cleaned up. The word went out around Morrison Woods one day that the annual patient competition was coming up shortly. I am pretty sure this occurred soon after my tenure began in my new facility. I think I was in Muncie, but my mind did not allow me to be concerned with that. I know my room was near an outer nurses' station and television lounge that sick people used to sit in, usually dozing while their day passed. For whatever reason, I was aware that I had been nominated to compete.

The scope of the competition is no longer clear in my mind. I remember thinking it had a Harry Potter aspect to it. Certain residents, usually new arrivals—one of which I was—were drafted by staff to compete in a very physical but mystical Olympic-type competition. I know the competition was quite active and seemed to be held somewhere exotic and mystical, although that may have been just down the hall from my room. Only a few of us had been drafted by the organizers. The competition went on for several days. It seemed to involve both strenuous physical activities as well as intellectual challenges. Initially I did not seem to stand out. Each night after the day's event ended, we received a status update. In the first few rounds, probably after only one or two nights, I remember being concerned as to why I was not doing better. The next evening, the competition was much more strenuous. I had to be doing something that required real physical skill and the eventual approval of my fellow patients and competitors. The quadriplegic physical state I was in during this period did not seem particularly relevant, at least in my mind. I seem to recall that this physical portion of the competition required some flying around and completing some undefined obstacle course. My time was good. Indeed, I don't recall which of my other competitors—all of whom I believe were quite elderly, as was nearly every resident of the Morrison Woods facility—actually pushed me to do my best. I know I competed hard and was really proud when I was declared the winner. Lying in my bed, I gratefully accepted the congratulations of the staff assistants. I had won on my first attempt since arriving at my new home in the facility. While I am not sure what I really did to win, I just know I was very proud. Millard was a winner once again.

Yes, I know I did, in fact, eventually wake up. I realize there was no such competition; nor did I really win anything. Yet this was so vivid in my mind that I remembered it fondly and even later was able to report it here as an important memory for me. This and other dreams seemed to linger for several days, even weeks. I was heavily drugged but thought it was reality all the same.

CHAPTER 13

RANDOM ENCOUNTERS—WACO

Waco did not seem to be all that bad of a place. My facility there was comfortable, and there was that nice fellow who prided himself as quite the golfer. He really liked the course my health care facility looked out over. When my mother would take me for walks out on the parking lot, he would stop and tell us about his day. I wanted to play with him, but on reflection, that does not seem logical, as I was in my wheelchair, quadriplegic, and being pushed by my mother.

I remember being approached by some locals who were representing a church out in the country somewhere nearby. They were very friendly and said they were Baptists. I had never been a Baptist, but I had heard that they could be very nice but a little different now and then. I was aware there was some reason I was raised a Methodist, and it was not just because my dad liked beer. The Baptist folk who approached me were nice and invited me to try out their small country church some Sunday. I could join them for lunch in the activity room too. That sounded good to me; I liked chicken and cheese casserole. I never actually went, which made sense because I was not living in or near Waco; nor did I know any Baptists there other than through some legal work I think I once was asked to do for Baylor University.

I remember that after I lost my job at Bracewell, that big law firm in Dallas, I had been approached by some Jewish people. If I agreed to become Jewish, they told me, I had a chance to move to offices in an office development they occupied near my Bracewell office, and better yet, I could continue practicing real estate law. This was initially intriguing to me because I needed a new job and I would be right downtown near my old office at Bracewell, which was in Fountain Place, a gorgeous forty-five-story modern office building that I think is the true jewel on the Dallas skyline. I agreed to a few meetings with my new Jewish friends. Man, I soon discovered that there was a lot involved in converting from being a Methodist to a Jew. I don't remember many of the specific requirements involved, but I was expected to attend a number of Saturday meetings. I think I was supposed to bring some food. I, of course, agreed to come as soon as I could feel settled. For whatever reason, I skipped that first Saturday event. When they contacted me the next week, I promised to make it this time. I remember being a little concerned about leaving Jesus, as I had been raised to have faith in him and I don't think anyone really knew for sure what the consequences would be to change my faith. For whatever reason, I ended up skipping that next meeting with my Jewish friends as well. I think I did so because I was getting cold feet and neither wanted to give up my free Saturdays nor move into what looked like somewhat dingy offices. Besides, I was living in Waco.

I remember the day that my old college roommate, Bob, drove in from St Louis specifically to visit me in my patient room at the facility. I thought it was fun that he had come, but I was not at all clear as to why he had driven so far to visit me in Waco. He never really gave me an answer, but I figured out later that the trip from St. Louis was to Muncie, which was actually much closer. That made his trip easier. I am glad I was actually in Muncie; otherwise, he may never have come.

What I thought I liked about being in that health facility in Waco was my assumption that I was pretty free to get out. I am sure it was from

Waco that I somehow got to DFW Airport in northwest Dallas one day and around. I have no idea how I got there, but I do remember being allowed to board that plane going to Perth in Western Australia. I thought it odd that I was able to board without a passport, a driver's license, or any money. Fortunately I made the flight, and the rest turned into my Australian adventure, which I described previously.

My time spent in Waco seemed pretty good. It was full of pleasant, if not dull, memories. I don't quite remember how my time in Waco ended, but I suspect I was very relieved to wake up one day and recognize my room in Muncie at Morrison Woods. My mother was there, while a few Muncie and Midwestern friends got to come visit me. There was no way they could be seeing me if I were in Waco. I even was safely back in time to go to a Ball State football game.

CHAPTER 14
FOOTBALL IS JUST TOO TOUGH FOR ME

I have no idea who was the brain that thought I needed to try out for a football team, but I sure wish I knew. It was maybe the worst week I had spent since getting sick. I am pretty sure I did not want to try out, but for some reason I do not recall, I went along with the idea. I think someone on staff thought I would enjoy it, for a little exercise maybe? The next thing I remember, I was checking into some old college dorm the football team had found to house its players for the one-week tryout. The dorm was an old gray stone structure, and I suppose it was at some small Midwestern college—or so I believed. I have no idea how I got out of Morrison Woods and to this place, but arrangements were made, and here I was. Normally my facility does not let patients go except with family. The check-in at the dorm's front desk went smoothly as I was greeted by a couple of middle-aged women I was to subsequently discover were wives of two of the team's assistant coaches. I was given some gray and dark blue workout clothes that seemed to have a sort of 1970s look. Russell Athletic wear? Why no cool Nike stuff?

I guess I had been attracted to the opportunity because whoever was on the Morrison Woods staff who knew of the team seemed so positive about my chances. I know I was frustrated lying in bed all day, or at best being stuck in my wheelchair. Sure, I could hardly move, but certainly my health care attendant would not be suggesting I try out if I physically could not do it. Besides, what she told me sounded so cool. This was described as a team in a sub-NFL league that featured players who weren't quite good enough to stick with an actual NFL team yet knew how to play football nevertheless. She said that her friend could get me a tryout. I was subsequently to learn that these teams were formed based on an innovative plan. The teams were owned by actual NFL team owners who formed them primarily for offshore gambling. Each team would play on some exotic island, though I was never really clear where these islands were. The league was apparently secret, I learned, because of gambling laws, but big-timers, I heard, loved betting on the results. Best of all, if you played for a team, you could make a lot of money betting on (or against) your team. That sounded great to me, because it had been several years since I had earned any money and I really longed for some island living. The fact that I never actually identified my team, who owned it, or where we played did not seem unusual to me. I just never thought to address that.

The training camp schedule I found that first day on my dorm bed indicated that I was to report by 10:00 a.m. to the school's practice field, which I had noticed across the street. I remember wondering if sheets and a pillow would magically appear for the plastic mattress in my room. Nobody had told me to bring any to the football camp. Well, I could worry about that later. I stripped down and pulled the gray T-shirt on over my head. There was a jock strap (man, I didn't know you could still buy those); a pair of dark blue cotton shorts to slip on; a pair of long, white cotton athletic socks; and my old Converse high-top shoes my mother must have sent with me. After I dressed, I relieved myself and headed down the stairs and out the front dorm door. A group of young men were assembling before me. As I arrived, I sensed the eyes looking me over. In return, I felt small, as I was shocked to see how young, big, and strong these guys looked. These were real college football players. They all had tried out for NFL teams the prior fall. I was an old guy, seemingly half their size and twice their age. Yet here

I was with the guys assigned to the offensive and defensive line. Maybe I was mistaken. Surely at worst I could try out for punter?

Soon we were divided into groups. What the hell? *My group had about ten of the biggest men I had ever been around. The fat, balding coach welcomed us to his "new offensive line." We were soon lined up to run sprints, touching some yellow cone about fifty yards away. Worse, we then were expected to run back to our starting line after touching the cone. The whistle blew; we were off. Man, that hurt … several of the fat guys seemed to blow by me even as their big bellies rolled this way and that. Although I finished last, I did not miss the next slowest guy by much. As we got back, I grabbed my hips as I leaned toward the dirt field below. Just then the whistle blew. "Go again, you fat butts!" shouted the coach. My rest was not as long as the others had, because I finished last in the run. I bravely turned around and headed back toward the cone some fifty yards away. This time I was not gaining on anyone. Even though sweaty bellies and breasts were shaking as the big guys made their turn at the cone, they were obviously getting farther ahead. I can't imagine how red my face must have looked. I recall struggling back to the start line, gasping. Just as I reached the line, I heard the whistle blow and coach holler, "Again, you out-of-shape big butts!" With no time to rest, I nevertheless turned around and bent over—and then it all happened. There was a nasty rush from my gut, and I blew my breakfast onto the field in front of me. "What the hell?" the coach hollered. "That's my field, you old SOB. Who is going to clean that mess up?" Well, obviously me, as two towels came flying at my face. Shortly I was on my knees, trying to scoop the mess up into the towels. I was hot and miserable. I stumbled off the field and watched as the other guys struggled on with their run. This was awful. What was happening? Why was I even here? I could not work this out in my mind; my mind made no sense. After a short break, the coach called us together and announced we were going to do some hitting—five on five, pushing into each other, one time blocking and the next time rushing. Oh my God! I managed to pair off against one of the smaller guys, who was maybe just 6'2" and 245 pounds, a burly pimple-faced farm boy who said he had played at Mississippi State.*

Turns out he was a walk-on who never actually got to play much, but his daddy knew the head coach of this team and he had agreed to let the boy try out. My experience was a disaster. The only blocking I knew anything about was what I had seen on ESPN. I could not remember ever having played football that included a real line protecting the quarterback, let alone physically hitting anyone. Now maybe since my prednisone was so prevalent in my system, maybe I just forgot. Anyway, the experience was a disaster. As I set up to block, the whistle blew, and I received an immediate blast to my head and chest. I flew back, lifted into the air, and then landed flat on my back. The coach just shook his head. Again we lined up; this time I was the rusher. Big boy got set across from me, and the whistle sounded. I thrust forward from my set position. I plowed into a wall. Rather than moving forward, I was immediately driven down into the dirt. Big boy was smashed on top of me. Everything hurt. I sensed being helped to a kneeling position; then I was dragged off the field. Lying there, I could not fathom what was happening to me. The whistle blew, and the coach hollered, "Do it again!" Then something bizarre happened. The shrill sound of the whistle jolted me awake. I stared up at what had been the hot, shining sun. But it was not there; there were just white ceiling tiles. I turned my head to see the yellow cinder-block walls, the familiar chair—my room at Morrison Woods.

I was awake in my room. There would be no football nightmare anymore. I was as stiff as a board and probably needing to be changed, but I had no football injuries.

CHAPTER 15

DREAM: THE VACANT HOSPITAL

The Dallas International Hospital developer group was an unusual legal client for me to pursue. The man trying to put the project together had been referred to me by one of my favorite clients, a man whom I had helped corporately form his advertising agency. The client ran in popular circles with entrepreneurial types like his friend who was attempting to open a new hospital. Though my recollection is a bit cloudy as to all the specifics of the services I was asked to provide, I recall that this newly referred client, a man named Paul, was primarily in the business of operating management services for existing private hospitals. I do remember that Paul was very energetic and had all sorts of creative ideas as to how to turn nonprofitable hospital operations into money makers for the owners. This by no means meant Paul worked for nonprofits; quite to the contrary, he worked for hospital owners who very much wanted to make profits.

I believe I spent about a year helping Paul in developing various programs that he put into place for the hospitals. Besides the obvious plans that included minimizing the actual cost of providing medical services to patients, Paul seemed to have endless suggestions. I am sure physicians and medical staffs were often concerned with Paul's reorganization plans, as his team would try to extend hours worked, and let go of more experienced (thus expensive) staff and replace them with young newcomers to the profession. Paul had creative plans for obtaining drugs and medical supplies, which I suspected could have resulted in lower-quality treatment and items for patients. Losing access to things like two-ply toilet paper, quality cotton bed sheets, thick bath towels, and patient gowns large enough to cover one's butt were just a few of the things Paul introduced for the patients in their now more profitable hospital. I suspect the live plants in the patient gathering areas soon were replaced by plastic potted displays that required no water or trimming.

Most important to Paul was setting up financial schemes to get patients into the hospitals. I never really knew or was privy to how the programs worked; nor did I pretend to be an expert in health care law. Health care is a heavily regulated industry subject to all sorts of federal and state laws. Many lawyers specialize in this area, and I assume that Paul had access to some whenever needed. My more recent role for Paul seemed to involve not creating his plans and programs but, more often, obtaining my law firm's legal help in enforcing his service contracts with his client hospitals. Whether patients were unhappy with their hospital, thus causing discomfort for management, did not really seem to matter as long as Paul managed to keep his client hospitals profitable.

Over time, I became increasingly aware that Paul's programs were probably just questionable schemes. There were all sorts of programs that I soon realized were not really in the patients' best interests. Most alarming was whether there were questionable choices of generic drugs or treatments. I soon became disillusioned with my client's corporate practices. Before long I suspect this showed in our relationship, and neither I nor my law firm had any more dealings with Paul.

My new nightmare was not surprising. At some point after I lost my partnership position in the law firm, I realized I had no source of income or any meaningful prospect of paying basic living expenses. I have no idea why returning to my house and living with my family was not an option, but my mind must have settled with the fact that my wife and I were now effectively split up. Being unemployed would only make matters worse. For whatever reason, going home was not even a consideration. I recall spending the first night after losing my job having to find a place to sleep. I cannot explain why I did not call on one of my many perceived friends or former colleagues; I only knew that was not an option. Maybe I never even thought of it. I felt alone. Never mind that I still owned my house (the one with my family in it and a pool out back with deck chairs to lounge on) and had healthy savings and checking accounts. Those simply were not a factor in my new very real dilemma. I remember feeling panicky because I needed a safe place to lie down and try to sleep before the evening turned dark. I soon found myself walking around an old blighted area of Dallas, hoping to not be confronted by any homeless people in the area. Wandering, I found a vacant parking garage next to an old large and empty hospital struc-ture. For whatever reason, the hospital facility had avoided the wrecking ball, which was so prevalent in Dallas at the time. The usual trash, empty bottles, dirty pieces of blankets, and other evidence of homeless vagrants was scattered around the grounds. Things were not horribly dirty but just had that appearance of owner-abandoned neglect. I remember quietly entering the garage before the night turned dark and guardedly walking up the paved parking incline to the third, or maybe fourth, floor. The garage was gray, deserted, and dark. No one appeared to be there, although a few paper cups and empty liquor bottles showed evidence that I might expect a visitor. There were no parked cars. I remember finding a corner of the garage that allowed a view of the quiet alley below. I did not dare settle near one of the closed stairwells, as who knows what I might find behind one of the heavy closed doors or if, God forbid, a door should unexpectedly be opened. I found a spot on the gray concrete to place my black leather Coach briefcase that I had taken with me when I left the office. It would serve as my pillow that evening. Somehow, after about an hour of listening to activity on the street below, I succumbed to the inevitable and fell asleep.

I slept without apparent incident. Emerging sunlight and the distant sound of a siren woke me up. I looked around but saw nothing particularly different in my third-floor garage surroundings. I got up and walked over to an opposite corner and undid the fly on my gray Brooks Brothers slacks. Piddling never felt so good as I sprinkled the corner before me. I remember wondering where I would go if or when I would have to crap. Then I remembered the downtown YMCA, at which I was still a member. A shower and a private place to go sounded appealing. But first I needed to take a better look at the vacant hospital structure adjacent to my garage.

After wandering around the outer grounds for a while, I soon discovered some activity at the far side of the building. Something was going on up on the third floor of the main building. A few construction workers were moving materials in the outer side door. I spotted a large blue sign posted outside the construction site. "Future Home: Dallas International Hospital Center." Below the wording in smaller letters was "a project of the Dallas International Hospital Group," and below that was the name of a bank financing the project. How incredible, I thought. This was my client doing a new project. I approached a portly short man wearing a white construction helmet and a blue uniform standing just outside the open door. He told me that indeed a new health care facility was being developed on the third floor. In fact he said, there were some medical operations already underway. While he could not provide me with many details, he said that the owner would likely be by soon if I wanted to wait around and learn more. After about an hour hanging around on what was an old patio, I recognized my former client Paul climbing out of his black pickup. Paul saw me and waved me over. After greeting me warmly, he asked what the heck I was doing over here. Gradually, I explained my bizarre set of circumstances. I sensed I appeared a pathetic sort, but Paul was alarmingly kind and receptive. We sat, and I further explained my situation. Rather than call the police on me for trespassing, for whatever reason, Paul seemed genuinely concerned. As I explained that I really was just reacting without a plan for even the rest of the day, let alone week, Paul declared that he had a temporary solution to suggest. "Bill, I haven't even told you about my latest project; it's right here! I am developing this new facility to serve people who need medical help and a place to live. We aren't finished with our build-out; nor do I have much staff. But I will tell you what—I've got some rooms completed and running water. I need someone staying here to keep an eye on the facility when we aren't around. Mainly this means nights and weekends. I have had some trouble with homeless breaking in and trying to sleep here. You could be a big help if you want to stay here." I accepted his offer.

My immediate problem seemed to be solved. Here was tricky Paul offering me a lifeline for at least the immediate future. I did not relish the thought of spending the night with vagrants or possible burglars breaking in, but Paul said the threat was exaggerated. I would likely never have to confront anyone unless I went out on the streets.

Paul took me up an old flight of stairs. As we came to the third floor, he opened a heavy steel door, and we were in a dark and slightly dirty hallway. He beckoned me to follow, and we walked some thirty feet to a flimsy temporary door that marked the end of the dark, deserted hallway. As we stepped into the bright light of the newly renovated hall, I saw construction workers up and down the corridor. Paul showed me the first room on the right, which was in the process of being painted. "This is the only room nearly completed, but you are welcome to it until you figure out what you want to do. I can have a bed, side table and lamp delivered today if you are willing to take it. Only thing is, I need you to stay by this temporary door and can't have you walking farther up the hall with all this construction going on." That sounded good to me. I was not in the mode of solving long-term problems, but just the immediate ones. I now had a roof over my head and soon would have a bed to sleep on. While it crossed my mind who I might encounter in the middle of the night, I accepted Paul's proposal with much appreciation. Life had changed in the last few hours, but at least it had changed for the good.

Later that afternoon, a cot was wheeled in. It was delivered by some service and not anyone I knew. My lamp and end table arrived, so at least I would not be spending the whole night in the dark. My thoughts turned to food, so I asked the contractor still on site how to return to the building in the evening after venturing out for dinner. He showed me the now pitch-black hallway on the other side of the temporary door. I remember venturing out, leaving the building, crossing the dark road, and consciously weighing whether to choose to go into the Jack-in-the-Box or the Whataburger, which sat side by side. Whataburger seemed to have a few less unsavory types out front and fewer young males hanging around. I chose the Whataburger, not only because of its bacon burger but also because I liked my chances of getting safely in and out. With my burger and fries in my paper bag, I hustled back across the street and approached my dark building. I glanced around; no one seemed to have followed me or even paid me much attention. I slipped into the big door I had left ajar. I pushed the door shut behind me. Back in my dark staircase, I gingerly found my way up the three floors. There were no rats or critters, and no unexpected guests. I found my way down the dark hallway and to the temporary door. It took no effort to push it open; nor did it require a key. Wow, I thought, not much protection should anyone want in. The lamp in my room gave off a low glow that I followed to my bed. After eating, I remember shedding my clothes and collapsing on the hard cot. I pulled the blue blanket over me and rested my head at the top of the bed. I don't know how long I stayed awake, but I remember listening intently to every creak in the building, every sound of a tree branch rubbing a window, and more than a few sounds of activity on the street below. Most of all, I concentrated on being sure I did not hear any sound of steps being taken or doors opening. As I recall, I heard none.

Paul said I was welcome to stay for a few more nights. I could see him briefly in the mornings and tell him that I had no unexpected visitors I was aware of during the night. He did tell me that there was a room farther up the hall that now had a functioning shower, which I could use. I guess I was smelling pretty bad. That night after the building emptied and all was dark, I stripped my off my clothes and made my way down the hall. I found the unfinished room and the shower in the corner. The water did work, but it seemed to take forever to get warm. Standing there naked, I shivered briefly in the dark room. What was that? A sound? Steps? No, surely not. When the water was starting to feel warm, I stepped into the open shower. The water streamed over my head and down my body. God, how awesome it was. When had I last bathed? It seemed like weeks ago. While it was actually only a couple of days since my last morning shower at home, the feeling in the dark was mesmerizing. I washed the water vigorously over all parts of my body, working as if I had soap and shampoo. Although I had nothing, I felt certain that the harder I washed, the cleaner I would feel. After about another minute, the water began to noticeably cool. My hands worked more vigorously around my body as I pushed forth every last warm moment I could muster. Then cold. I shivered and shut off the flow. Standing there wet, I began wiping my shoulders and torso with my hands. I had no towel, but I did not want to get the only skimpy blanket I had on my bed in the other room all wet. I squeezed the water accumulated in my hair in an attempt to dry myself. I figured that standing there in the dark, I would eventually start to dry. My hands shoved the remaining water drops off my body and down my legs. I stepped out of the shower stall and tried to shake off like a dog just out of a creek. It seemed to be working.

"What was that?" I gasped, and then I went silent. That sound? It was not from the street, surely. I froze, listening. There it was again. This time, I heard steps—a shuffling of feet. No way, I thought. Naked, I stepped back, away from the window, shining a bit of light in the room. Standing in a dark corner, I thought whatever it was might not spot me.

I am not sure I took a breath. I just listened. Then came the creak of the light temporary door. There was no question someone was there. He (surely not a she?) would see the dim light from my empty room and notice my empty bed. He would also surely spot my clothes I had left in a heap as I took them off to shower. Would he find my shower room?

Now I was scared. I knelt down in my dark corner. What would happen? Was he violent? Drunk? Would he even speak English and be able to understand me? How would he react to discovering a naked man up in this place? How long would I have to stay hidden here before he went away? Should I try to go out and confront him? Would he shoot me or, worse yet, slash me with the knife he likely carried to survive on these rough streets?

More sound. He moved. He must have sensed the bit of steam lingering *in the air from my shower. There was no question he was coming. Should I scream?*

I remember I sat up with a jolt. It was dark as I looked around. No one was there. I pressed the button that turned on the small light on the table next to the bed here in my room at Morrison Woods. I looked at my yellow painted walls. My bedding was familiar. I had my plastic-covered pillow. The magazine I had been reading before I went to sleep was on the floor. I was in Morrison Woods, in my bed in Muncie. What the hell? What had I been dreaming? My last thought was that I must remember to speak to my nurse tomorrow about the strength of these pills.

CHAPTER 16

THE NIGHT OF THE TRANSPORT TO ROCKFORD

I was told it would be next Tuesday at four-thirty in the afternoon. I wasn't sure what date that was; nor do I remember being particularly excited or anxious. Lying there in my usual drugged and quadriplegic state, it was just one more thing I was being told to anticipate or to be forewarned that something was going to happen. However, this was not a routine warning from my CNA that I should expect a shower, another swallowing test, or a blood test—something I likely would have let slip into oblivion until they arrived to carry out the event. This time even I knew this had significance, though I recall taking it as if with a grain of salt. Benign patience and my heavy dose of drugs just did that to me.

This time was different. I was told that next Tuesday I was being sent from my room at Morrison Woods by a special plane to my sister and her husband's hometown of Rockford, Illinois, for placement in a highly skilled health care facility. There I could expect long-term care from specialists who dealt with debilitated patients such as myself.

This was a place where they offered respiratory care and some real physical therapy and regular attention. I remember thinking the most significant thing was that I would no longer be allowed to wallow all day in my bed and gown. I was going someplace where I could expect to get up promptly in the morning and sit up in a wheelchair for much of my day. I remember my mother even prepared for me a bag of new Gap clothes and a pair of tennis shoes so I would look nice at my new place. I thought that was exciting.

As the days passed until that Tuesday afternoon, I am not sure I was filled with any particular anxiety. As usual, I was being given my medicine and had the feeding tube regularly connected as the brown liquid flowed slowly into my stomach. I was being changed and cleaned up on a familiar basis. Things seemed pretty normal even though I was going to be leaving the facility in Muncie where I had spent my last eighteen or so months. As the day approached, several nurses and CNAs said their goodbyes, gave me hugs, and wished me luck. I am sure most were guarded in their enthusiasm because they expected or knew I would not survive long. Even the nice evening CNA who had in a moment of apparent pity for me declared, "Isn't it time to just give up?" hugged me goodbye. I remember her disconcerting words; I just don't remember having any particular reaction. This was not one of those heroic situations where I rose up and declared, "Never, I shall battle on!" Quite to the contrary, I assume my response may have been "We will see" or, more likely, "Whatever."

Tuesday afternoon came, and I remember thinking, *Wow, I am getting out of this place.* At approximately 4:30 p.m., paramedics arrived, and I soon was lifted onto a gurney, wrapped in sheets with a blanket, and my head placed on a pillow. Little did I appreciate that this was to be my bed for the next several hours. Without any fanfare, I was wheeled out of my familiar surroundings and promptly taken down the long hall. I whizzed past familiar faces, gave a nod and slight wave goodbye, at least to the extent my fingers would move. I remember a few of my favorite attendants walked beside me as I was delivered to the loading dock. The paramedics guided me into the ambulance, the doors were shut, and we were on our way. Would I see Muncie, my childhood hometown, ever again? One of my favorite nurses at Morrison Woods sat beside me in the ambulance, trying to make me feel more comfortable I am sure, as I left my familiar surroundings.

I remember the ambulance pulling up to the tarmac at Muncie Municipal Airport. It was a sunny fall afternoon. We entered a hangar that contained a few planes. Muncie does not have commercial airline service, so only a few people were present. However, there was this beautiful propeller plane sitting there being refueled and waiting for me. The ambulance doors were opened, the sunlight came in, and I was wheeled out to be transferred to another gurney. Much to my delight, though I won't say complete surprise, there was an immediate gathering of familiar faces. There in front of me was my mother, standing proud with the support of her loyal companion, Dick Jaggers. Kind Dick, a former marine, had been a type of surrogate father to my sister and me since my father's death some twelve years before. Most of all, he and my mother depended on each other and thrived off their mutual companionship. My sister and I knew my mother and Dick would never be alone in Muncie as long as each survived. There was a small crowd. My best Muncie friend, Kevin Smith, left work early to be there. As previously described, Kevin had visited me nearly every week while I was at the Morrison Woods facility. He saw my ups and (mostly) downs and struggles to communicate. There were several others I recognized, a few CNAs and administrators from Morrison Woods, all of whom had been so kind to me. Some of my mother's friends were there too, including somebody representing our local Presbyterian church.

Shortly this airport sendoff would be over. I was smiling and waving goodbye as I was moved into the back of the specially equipped medical plane. As I was put on a new gurney, I viewed my friends through the small windows of the plane. It was more than I could take. I remember bursting into tears, my face contorting as I realized, maybe for the first time, the depth of my new adventure ahead. As the pilot backed the plane up and steered out of the hangar, I realized I had a small side window to peer out of at the scene below. I strained to catch sight of my friends and family. I remember the sensation of the plane lifting off as I left my now familiar places, faces, and friends behind. My tears stopped as I settled back for my forty-minute flight to my new and possibly permanent world in Illinois.

The air service that transported me to Rockford was a remarkable service that Missy somehow discovered. "Grace on Wings" is a beneficial nonprofit Christian service that transports severely ill patients throughout the Midwest. I recall we had to apply to receive the flight assistance, but if accepted it would arrange to fly me to my destination. The service specialized in serving nonambulatory patients who required medical monitoring and whose trips were within one thousand miles of Indianapolis. Amazingly the service was free (except for fuel costs), including my ambulance ride to the airport, and really exceptional. In addition to excellent equipment (today a Mitsubishi MU-2 plane), the experienced pilot and his wife, a fully licensed nurse, took care of me during the entire flight. As we crossed over the northern Indiana cornfields, I gazed out my little side window at the scenery below. The engine had an intoxicating purr, and the attentive nurse monitored my progress as time passed. Even on the flight, I was all hooked up to my medical devices. I remember the thrill of passing south of Chicago, seeing the beautiful familiar skyline against the backdrop of the blue Lake Michigan. I never fell asleep during the flight, as seeing the landscape outside inspired me. Would I ever experience it again?

As we approached Chicago-Rockford International Airport, I remember wondering what plane must have landed once or twice from Canada that permitted the "international" designation. There did not appear to be much activity around the airport, which is located some ninety miles from the world's busiest airport, Chicago's

O'Hare International. My sister tells the story of the thrill she and her family claimed to have as my plane popped out of the clouds and descended toward the Rockford runway. I have vague memories of her family's warm greeting as I was removed from the plane. We were presented with a small wooden cross I still have in my window and additional information on Grace on Wings. I was to learn later that the husband-and-wife team had started the day with an early-morning pickup in Tulsa, Oklahoma and had transported several other patients to other Midwestern cities. I was just one part of a very blessed full day.

I remember being loaded into another ambulance, and we made the slow drive from the airport to my new home at the Alden Park Strathmoor Skilled Care Facility in Rockford. I had no view from the ambulance, as it was no tour bus, but I remember the trip being slow, long and very bumpy. We seemed to be making turns constantly but never arriving anywhere. Of course, we finally did. Missy and Jack were already there waiting for me. The evening sky had turned to darkness as I was wheeled up to the back of the one-story facility—my new home. As we waited at the back door, bells were sounded to get someone's attention inside. Within minutes a small middle-aged woman opened the door and directed the paramedics to my designated room. That's how it was to happen time and again—no fanfare, just silent delivery of the new patient into a vacant room. No greetings, no sign-in; I was just moved from the gurney to my new bed. I did notice the next day that a nameplate had been placed on my door, so I did have some known presence.

Soon I was alone in my new empty room. The kindly lady who opened the door I soon learned was Linda Mueller. She hooked me up to a breathing machine and the now familiar drip food tube attached to my belly. Linda was to become my primary respiratory nurse and one of the most encouraging people I have ever known. She had a no-nonsense attitude, but it was always delivered with a confident smile and glint in her eye. She was to become my special attendant who did not hesitate to correct things others did that were not up to her standards for taking care of me. She was to become one of my biggest advocates at Park Strathmoor.

Backdoor entrance at Park Strathmoor and to my new world.

I don't know how long it was to be before I dozed off after arriving that first night in Rockford, probably shortly after my latest infusion of drugs. I do recall looking around my modest room, inspecting its concrete block walls and green tile. Missy and a few friends had decorated the room with some get well cards and floating balloons reaching for the ceiling. Little did I know that night whether this room, number 116 on E-Unit, would be the last place I would ever live.

CHAPTER 17

RANDOM OBSERVATIONS WHILE I WAS SLOWLY TRYING TO RECOVER

I remember a day when I felt as if my mind suddenly woke up. For some reason, I think of it occurring some eighteen months after my September 2011 grand mal seizure event, which was all before my move to Rockford. I have no idea if this is completely true or not, but I definitely remember an event of some sort when I just seemed to feel in control of my mind and thoughts once again. Practically, this is of course a great exaggeration of what likely occurred, as I assume no one really noticed a significant change in my behavior and communication skills, but in my mind I now felt different.

I was thinking; I now felt aware of things going on around me in a way I had not sensed before. I guessed eighteen months because I have a memory of my mother proclaiming with great joy, "This is the first time I have heard your real voice in at least eighteen months!"

When my mind woke up, I was still a quadriplegic, in my bed usually, still with bad colitis problems and awaiting further physical deterioration as more ALS symptoms were anticipated to inevitably set in.

I must now have felt more rationally aware. I don't recall this meaning I was getting more depressed (I was still on an antidepressant drug), but I could now want to do things. No longer was I just taken for walks outside by mother; I now fully appreciated the joy of getting to go outside. Previously I stared at the ducks in the patio garden, and now I wanted to lure them over to me so I could play with them. I felt joy but was also aware of what made me mad. I had a more rational sense of emotions—good and bad. This was all very exciting. ESPN sports on television once again meant something to me. I realized now that I never had really had an appreciation for my Texas Rangers playing the St Louis Cardinals in the World Series, because even though the TV was likely on in my bedroom, I did not seem to grasp what I was watching. I just missed it. I guess I heard but did not listen; I looked but did not see. Now I cared about football games, principally the Cowboys, SMU, and Northwestern. I had not realized up until now that SMU had hired the great Larry Brown as its basketball coach. I had been a season ticket holder at SMU games for over twenty years. If I had been aware, I would have been excited. This was a big deal.

I do remember a special milestone soon after I felt I was alert once again. I could not wait to read a book. To the shock of the CNA staff at Park Strathmoor, Ann let me have a new, very big biography of Lord Horatio Nelson, my hero whom I thought so often about. This was not just any old biography of Nelson (of which I had over one hundred in my possession in storage someplace), but John Sugden's volume one, his comprehensive life of Nelson, which was a mere nine hundred pages long. I know I dived into it, encountering and loving the story of my lifetime historical hero, the great British sea admiral and victor of the battle of Trafalgar. The fact that I had read many Nelson biographies through the years had no dampening effect on my enthusiasm. This was no ordinary encounter for me. Sugden had spent years researching and reading correspondence connected with Nelson's extraordinary life. Every detail imaginable in Nelson's life was in that new book, and yet those nine hundred pages covered only the first half of his life! Sugden subsequently wrote a second volume (which of course I now have), adding another nine hundred pages to Nelson's story. No Nelson biographer had ever written such a long biography of his life. Read I did, with a vengeance. Poor Ann tried to read me an occasional chapter, but I assume she found it so boring I did not encourage her to continue. A nine-hundred-page book is no easy thing to physically hold. Frankly, I could not even lift the big thing. Staff would lodge it in between my fingers, resting it on my chest or stomach, as I tried to hold it and read what I could. The important thing is that after several long months, I could finally once again read a book. Even though it took weeks, maybe months, for me to complete, it was a great badge of pride for me to be seen working my way, page by page, through that long book. Staff seemed bewildered seeing me, day after day, reading the same book.

This actually signaled for me the start of many more pleasant experiences. Soon I was reading newspapers and magazines, and following sports and politics with renewed interest. I had something now to occupy my mind, and my spirits picked up greatly. Sometime not long thereafter, I was provided my first iPad, and finally even a cell phone. The access to the internet on the small computer changed my life. Suddenly I was communicating with friends, discovering contacts I had not spoken to in years, and even exchanging ideas and thoughts. I was a person again. The feeling was extraordinary, as I was no longer solely dependent on my mother, sister, and a few visitors for connection to the world. My world and interests expanded greatly. I know my attitude changed for the better.

Possibly the most blessed result of getting the iPad, and later a Chromebook, was that I could begin writing about my experiences. I have always fancied myself as a creative writer but rarely made the time to pursue this interest. My life seemed too busy to expend energy on things other than writing legal documents, exercise, and family. In this situation, lying there most of the day on my back in my bed, I had newfound time and desire to put my brain to work. I started writing, usually about things in my day or observations I had while undergoing treatment and recovery. The result is set forth in the chapters and pages in this book, which I have rather randomly assembled in the entries that follow of my observations from living in the facilities. I intend these to give the reader the feel of experiencing being in a situation of intense and prolonged illness and recovery. I hope it helps one prepare for the patience required to accept treatment and optimistically pursue recovery. For those who may not be living in a facility, I hope it will sensitize you to what your loved one or friend in a facility may be facing or which you may expect someday to encounter. The experience, fortunately, is far from being all bad, though maybe not entirely pleasant. Nevertheless, patience and a good optimistic attitude are essential, I believe, to a good overall experience in a facility.

CHAPTER 18

DIGNITY? CHECK IT AT THE DOOR

One of the first things I learned during my adventure as a critically ill patient is that you must stop worrying about your personal dignity. This probably sounds insensitive, but the last thing you need to care about is the horrific or embarrassing or even disgusting situations you will find yourself in. They will happen, and they will continue to happen for the duration of your stay. They certainly happened to me. Frankly, I began to feel better about my situation when I began to think of my body as not much different than a car in for service. Like my car, there I was, being lifted up on the racks so mechanics could start poking around wherever they chose. When you realize that your basic sense of dignity has been violated, as you will be treated throughout the day, my strong suggestion is to go ahead and give in. Your body will be poked, prodded, moved, wiped, and cleaned whenever they feel it's time. Worrying about what you may be wearing, how your hair looks (bedhead is to be expected), and who touches what probably is not a good use of your time. When in such a situation, the caretakers will win—not because they disrespect you, but because they have a job to do. My suggestion? Check your dignity at the door.

For a patient like me, in my quadriplegic state, I was not aware of how I even ended up in that silly little hospital gown. Somewhere in the blur of it all, I was just in it. We all know these gowns if we have spent even one night in a medical facility. They are often light green and coarse from overwashing, and they tend to only cover one's front. They tie in back, but your bottom frequently seems too exposed. Dignity? Most everyone who comes into your room, from family to friends to the hospital janitor, all sooner or later will know you by the face of your bottom. Welcome to the rest of your existence.

Lacking dignity in an ALS situation is just a part of your life. Unfortunate bodily discharges, throwing up, and untimely bed baths are to be anticipated. Avoiding having it happen too often before family and friends is your only realistic goal. I noticed that once that happens, family and friends don't need to be encouraged to leave. They are pretty good about seeing themselves to the door.

Losing your dignity arises in many ways. My recollection of being given a shower on a flimsy plastic bed after being wheeled through the lobby of fellow patients is not fun. I started to hate showers even though I knew they were overdue. Dignity is checked early when you don't have any say in which nurse's aide conducts the bathing. Girls, seemingly young enough to be your daughter, that male assistant who works your floor, or just those women you see working in the halls but don't really know all become veterans of knowing stuff about you only intimates ever would know (and probably wish they did not). Should you worry about it? I say just check your dignity at the door.

Dignity, or more specifically a lack thereof, hits any long-term hospital patient in many forms. The liquid food, delivered as a strange beige milky substance administered through the newfound feeding tube protruding from my stomach, was not to be confused with my grandmother's cooking. Where's anything I ever ate or drank? What, no water? What goes in must come out, of course. While quadriplegic, having my diaper changed and that catheter bottle applied and emptied was just part of my day. I spent several years during my adventure breathing with the help of oxygen apparently bypassing my mouth through some plastic trachea. I piddled with the help of a catheter, much to my contentment. Yes, you don't even know it is happening if working correctly. How and when did that bottle get there and become so filled? At this point, does it matter?

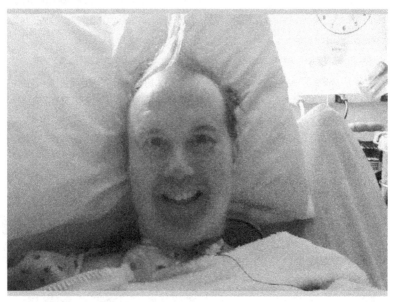

Dignity? I loved being part of the staff laughs! My first mohawk.

Your dignity is challenged when you don't control when you go to bed, get up, get changed or get cleaned up, and certainly when you are not sure what's happening and when. The key to checking it all at the door is, I think, being patient and trying not to care. Stay patient and, I found, you have a chance of feeling liked by staff. Feeling appreciated truly reduces your frustrations. Necessary treatment and physical assistance from staff may often not be pleasant, but it is tolerable when you face a long-haul recovery as I did. There are countless ways your dignity may feel violated. The key is not getting hung up on your ordinary perceptions of dignity. Check that notion of personal dignity at the door; you will be better for it.

CHAPTER 19
LONELINESS, THOUGHTS ON COMBATTING

Being alone is a natural and necessary part of life. It is a part of every day for all of us, even if at times merely momentary. While the term may insinuate a negative feeling, being alone sometimes is also a craving and a necessity for me and practically everyone I have ever known. When else can you possibly assemble your thoughts, process your issues, or simply assess your place in life? When else is it simply better to veg out or sleep? Having time alone is just that—time when no other person is interfering with your need to just be you. Let's face it; if awake, you are the only living species you actually confer with during every waking moment of the day. My mind talks to me all day; that same mind responds all day. Your innermost thoughts and assessments are with you at every given moment. A light turns on, and you notice—good, bad, too bright, too dim? A person appears in our presence; we are going to react. Cute pets and children, nurses and health care patient handlers—they are all there to affect our momentary ability to be alone. Obviously, so are bad things: bad news, sight of a car wreck, realization of financial distress. The list is endless.

Patients in a nursing facility, just as I assume is the case with a prisoner in a solitary cell, are going to experience lots of time being alone. Even with a roommate or maybe your spouse in your room, you will have plenty of time to just drift off in thought, whether mindless or not. Even with a television creating background noise, it's a small part of the day that I find I am really tuned in. A movie or a fourth-down play in a football game may get my attention, but such does not necessarily maintain my undivided attention very long. This was especially the case in the highly drugged state I was usually in while lying in bed or stationed in my wheelchair. You can't be concentrating all the time.

Being alone is different from feeling lonely. I often felt lonely when I was not getting all the personal attention that I conjured up the need for during a long day in my room. Dutiful visits by my mother or my sister were highlights of a day for me. The visits might be only for an hour or so, and a visit was often not substantially different from the one the day before. We could expect to discuss how I was feeling and important things like when my mother might be going to the grocery or conversation club. This is normal, even though my mother went to extraordinary lengths to keep things lively. When she arrived, I could expect her to insist that an assistant get me out of bed and into my wheelchair. I rarely recall having enough strength to go very far on my own at Morrison Woods, as my arms would not work. I remember I could paddle along in my chair by moving my feet so very slowly, and then, if successful at reaching the hall, I would try to grasp the railing along the wall. This was usually futile. Pulling myself was not very effective (remember, my arms could barely move), and the carpet was annoyingly resistant to my efforts. I decided the carpet was probably designed to deter patient mobility; are they really that clever? I also believed that the hallway was really a hill that was taxing for me to climb. Ironically, that hill seemed to me to go in both directions, but always upward! I was often bored when alone. I might get a disapproving look from the nurse at the desk. "Where do you think you are going?" Where was I going? "I am going where I am always going, the only place I can go—down the hall to the lobby." The surly nurse (maybe the only one I did not like) might then get up and turn me around. I soon figured out she could lock the brakes on my chair. In my screwy state of mind, I remember often not being able to understand that or why, try as I might, my wheelchair would not move. I would complain to my mother that I had a latch on my chair that they would use to chain me to the floor. I really hated that. I got bored sitting there looking back at my room or otherwise facing some elderly person sitting in some adjacent chair who was likely sleeping or coughing. Usually the TV in this area was set to an old soap or a black-and-white movie. The dread of sitting there—in my screwy mind, locked to the floor—was inescapable. I could not even get back to my bed. "You don't need to be in your bed now," the grumpy one might say. "Just stay there until I can get to you; I am busy now; can't you see? You are not my only patient here." I could see, and I knew I was not the only patient there. (What is it that author Robert Fulghum once taught us? "Everything you need to know you probably learned in Kindergarten"?) That does not mean I was happy. Frankly, I had more fun in kindergarten. The nurse was at her imposing station, filling out forms—a seemingly endless task the person on duty would do at all hours of the day. Paperwork? What? "Where does all that paper go anyway? Surely no one reads it." That comment never seemed to make her more pleasant to be with. Morrison Woods back then seemed heavy on the paperwork. It was not until I moved to Park Strathmoor in Rockford that I saw nurses with laptop computers that they could update in your room, thus providing me with some temporary human interaction. "What are you writing about me in that computer?" Park Strathmoor nurses had many more patients, so the personal attention probably had the same practical effect on me. I decided (without merit) that the Morrison Woods staffers used the paperwork as an excuse to avoid having to move at that very moment. In any event, I felt lonely being fastened in my chair even when surrounded by dozing patients, old movies on TV, and a surly nurse at the desk. My frustration level could get very high.

My poor, dear mother. She would usually come to visit sometime midafternoon almost every day. Her arrival seemed to me to take forever. When she would finally arrive, I felt a breath of fresh air. Her attitude was amazingly cheerful. Other patients would notice the frequency of her visits, and I almost felt guilty. Most days she would insist on taking me for a walk outside. "Walk" is not actually the correct term. It was she who was doing all the walking as she pushed me in my chair down the hall (or was it up?) and out the front door into the parking lot. She was so kind to everyone, including the elderly patients and staffers she would see nearly every visit. The residents naturally liked her. I knew they admired her incredible devotion in visiting pathetic old me each day. Only the woman staffer doing her paperwork did not seem to like my mother, as my mother was never above asking, "How long has he been sitting here? Why can't you do something to keep his head up? That can't be good letting his head dangle like that." A little bit of holding the staff's feet to the fire was all right with me. I am not at all sure my struggle to keep my head up was not exacerbated just as my mother arrived. I think the daily sight of her son sitting there with his head at his chest properly wore her down. I was not doing it intentionally; I had only a few muscles working in my neck. That throat was a mess. I think it heightened her awareness of the hopelessness of my situation. Adding to the frustration, I could not stop drooling when my head sank, and my mother would immediately ask for a towel from the nurse, forcing the woman to get up and raid the linen closet, thereby pulling her from her paperwork. Scorn was usually noticeable as my mother inquired whether I had been sitting like that all day (which, of course, was never the case). My wet gown was good evidence that there had been a lot of drooling.

My Mother, Nancy Millard. Christmas in Rockford.

My mother liked to take me for long walks around the grounds of the facility as often as possible. She is a big proponent of fresh air. It was always the same walk, but it was long, and occasionally we might see ducks in the adjacent field or catch a glimpse of the guy with the big red pickup truck across the street. He seemed to come home early from his day job so he could work on his yard or the exterior of his house. Work on that house never seemed to get finished, but his come-and-go freedom seemed enchanting to me. I never got to come and go, as that did not happen at Morrison Woods. Of course, visitors and staff got to go, but not us patients. Along the walk, my mother would stop so we could inspect the plants outside the building. Raising flowers was a constant in my mother's life, and she would tell me about her gorgeous garden at home. Popa (as I called my grandfather), her father, had diligently worked in his garden back in Dallas each morning well into his late eighties, noting that this was simply getting his morning chores completed before coming in for breakfast. Soon my mother was planting flowers around the grounds, often helping the senior staffer, Karen, fill out the gardens. On nice days we would sit outside in the patio in the garden. My mother often planted flowers with seeds she brought from her own garden while I sat there trying to lure the duck family to come let me touch them. As part of our daily ritual, my mother read me news highlights and interesting travel, arts, and sports stories from the *Wall Street Journal*. That was part of her morning—finding the stories she would share. When not gardening in the morning, she could be found at home, probably working on an article for the Muncie magazine, something she had been doing without interruption for the *Muncie Star* (our local newspaper and publisher of the magazine) since the 1960s. It was priority number one; I could expect no visits until her daily work was done.

Loneliness to me was a just a self-imposed issue. I could usually count on seeing my mother a minimum of five days per week. I also had Kevin Smith, my high school buddy and tennis teammate at Burris School, who would stop by nearly every week. Occasionally others might stop in, but chances were, being at my worst, I was not even aware. These of course were not daily occurrences, so it was easy for me to feel lonely. A great deal of it was due to the limitations on my physical ability to do anything. I was not strong enough to transfer myself from my bed to my wheelchair (nor back to my bed again), so that did not happen unless a nurse's aide came in. Instead I just sat. Fortunately, loneliness does not necessarily last forever. I seem to have managed to survive.

CHAPTER 20
THE BEDROOM EFFECT

I used to believe it was very important to have a great place to sleep. A part of being healthy and reasonably fit is getting plenty of good rest (at least Mike the pillow guy on television seems to tell us that). New houses feature a big master bedroom and bath (only to be matched today by the massive his-and-hers walk-in closets) because comfortable, peaceful sleeping is the primary goal. Selection of the best possible bed is, of course, at least as important, as that is where sleep and much of the fun tends to occur. Hotels, resorts, and mattress and furniture stores thrive off the concept of sleeping well.

My experience during my adventure changed my perspective on the need for a palatial bedroom experience. As I became ill, I left my nice, big bed shared with an enchanting wife, too often shared with my kids or our dogs, and a view from which I could see the pool in the urban oasis that was our backyard. I likely spent my last days in my master bed at our Amherst house with Boomer, our golden retriever mutt who stayed beside me while I suffered from my first bout of pneumonia. Little did I appreciate that, when I was soon put on a plane to my mother's house in Muncie, it would be my last night for nearly six years in a big bed, complete with comforter, hound dog, and view of our swimming pool. While ill, I was sleeping in institutional beds that were never intended to be palatial king-sized love thrones. My bed at my mother's was a nice old-style twin bed squeezed into her home office space. She was a hard worker who needed a home office, not big guest rooms. I remembered staying in the same bed as a child when I visited my grandparents in Dallas. Other than the loud 2:00 a.m. whistle of the freight train passing through Muncie each night, it certainly qualified as a comfortable single and was still good for a full night's sleep.

After suffering the grand mal seizure that night in September 2011, the next several years of beds in my life were all provided by my hospitals and nursing facilities. I cannot recall what my bed was like while in the ICU, but I am pretty certain great comfort was not the primary concern. When I was transferred to permanent skilled-care facilities at Morrison Woods and Park Strathmoor, I found that plastic-covered narrow twin-sized singles were all I could expect. Not surprisingly, this was the ever-present hospital bed. Of course, nobody asked if I had a preference for size or style. At least the sheets were not plastic (nor, by the way, satin), but everything else associated with the bed was access and safety. Unfortunately, I decided that the pillow-cases, sheets, and bed padding were often uncomfortably coarse and often felt hot. Waking up sweating on your pillow or finding my thighs wet was not unexpected. My beds had lots of buttons to play with; this one raised my head up, that one called a nurse, another turned on my TV. Sometimes, if I hit the wrong button, my bed seemed to want to fold up in a *V* formation; fortunately, my stiff body and quick finger action on the remote avoided any disasters. My bed was to permit easy access for my overhead tubes and the shifting of my position. All I required was easy access for the aides, not fluffy comforters or space for Boomer. Flexibility and fun were not important for those several years.

Closely associated with my bed comfort were the rooms I lived in. These rooms in skilled care were usually all the same, made of cinder-block walls (the nicer ones painted in some bland color, attempting to appear cheerful). One night while I was watching one of those "life in the penitentiary" shows that MSNBC runs late at night, I noticed that the stark prison rooms were remarkably similar to my room. I might not have had the open steel toilet sitting in a corner of the room, but otherwise our rooms were much the same. The only noticeable difference was that the prisoner usually did not have the bars my bed had sticking up on the side of his bed to prevent a fall. I, as a quadriplegic, did not require the bars he had instead on his cell door and window.

During the first couple of years, I shared my room with another patient. Lyle, my first roommate at Morrison Woods, was an accomplished man in his early seventies who had lived his entire life in Muncie. In my mind, I was pretty sure his right foot had been removed. He was, unsurprisingly, infirm and in frequent pain—at least that was my impression (thanks probably to my prednisone-induced state). Lyle's wife Beverley was caring and sweet. I found her every bit as thoughtful and kind to me as she was to Lyle. I think we could actually communicate with each other, although that does not make a lot of sense since my own mother said I could hardly speak for the first eighteen months or so. Then again, if they had never heard me speaking before, this new voice was all they knew. Lyle and Beverley would go on to become frequent participants in my dreams, including the one where I was trying to sleep in the back room of a hospice facility that, in my twisted mind, I soon decided was a Muncie brothel. I was really relieved to find them there; they prevented other guests in the brothel from robbing me. It was good to have friends in tight places. Lyle, as I recall, was the best roommate I was to have, as in addition to being a nice man, he liked to listen to PBS tapes covering great moments in American history. Before falling asleep, I learned from listening to his tapes about things like the Work Project Authority, art projects, and civil rights demonstrations. Otherwise, if we both happened to be awake, we got to talk (whisper?) about things like our nurses' aides who we hoped might visit that day. A few months into my stay, Lyle was moved to another room down the hall so he could live with his wife. It was no suite at the Ritz, but at least they were together again.

For much of my time at Morrison Woods, I had a single room. I don't know if it was something my mother arranged, but it was private. In afternoons, my mother would bring the *Wall Street Journal*, which she read daily at home, and then read me the highlights. We particularly enjoyed the work of Jason Gay, whose witty writing appeared on the sports page. My mother knew a good writer when she saw one, so her sports expertise advanced exponentially as she read to me. Guests such as my high school tennis buddy, Kevin, were so kind to drop by my room. Kevin told me stories of his latest adventures. His sensitivity knew no bounds. I think I also liked the freedom of being able to do whatever I wanted in my single room—no more television showing old black-and-white movies.

I had only one room at Park Strathmoor during the two plus years I lived there, and fortunately it was private. Missy and some friends had fixed it up prior to my arrival. It still had those cold cinder-block walls found in many facilities, but it seemed warmer, being freshly painted yellow and having a balloon hanging above my bed. The window was larger than I was accustomed to and looked out over brushy bushes. The only thing I could see outside my Muncie hospital window was a rooftop of the parking structure, most of which was below my line of sight.

I soon concluded that rooms were just rooms. I needed a bathroom nearby, plenty of space for staff to clean me up, and some occasional perceived feeling of privacy. In any event, feeling as though I was living in a master bedroom or nice hotel suite was just not important in my condition.

I recall that I had several different rooms during my six-week stay at the Rehabilitation Institute in Chicago (RIC). The old downtown

Chicago building had been rehabilitated, in a sense. Inside, its modern crisp and colorful hallways and fitness equipment were an inspiration. Televisions seemed to line the hallways, though I believe they were intended to just promote the virtues of the place. We were reminded every few feet or so that *US News & World Report* magazine had rated RIC the finest physical rehabilitation center in the world for each of the past twenty-three years. I was not even aware the publication still existed. Nevertheless, the rating made me feel first class.

Most of the patients in RIC were noticeably in worse shape physically than me. I had never experienced that since being quadriplegic. While they had been deemed well enough to try real rehabilitation, it was disconcerting to share mats and equipment with people who had no legs or otherwise were in very bad shape. Not all were happy, but they were there, trying hard to become mobile once again. I remember one young man whose mother often accompanied him to rehab sessions. The fellow was a strong athletic sort who had lost both legs in a construction accident. I don't know how long he had been recovering from his glaring wounds, but only now was he being given some hope of limited mobility. My heart went out to him as he struggled during rehab. He was shy, much younger than most other patients, and his mother tended to keep him away from others. I offered words of encouragement when I did see him out in the halls, but usually he spent most of his day behind his closed bedroom door. It made me feel that my situation was not nearly as daunting. I wondered if he could ever expect normal relationships again. I could tell he was a handsome boy, but his disfigured body would certainly make things challenging in the years ahead.

I had several roommates while at RIC. The changes were of my own doing, but I never actually had a single room. One of my roommates was an older man, likely in his early eighties. He really could not walk, though I gave him credit for trying. While we shared the same room, we rarely saw each other. We heard each other's snores, body noises, phone calls, and visits from staff and family. A thick plastic curtain separated us, and staff usually pulled it tight while one of us was being attended to. The sounds and discussions he had with family were easy to hear, which was soon to become an irritation for me. While in Chicago, I had no nearby family other than my old Dallas friend Rob, who lived and had his office in Evanston, a northern suburb. Rob came into the city frequently and often stopped to check on me (occasionally bringing guests or my old friends who also happened to be in town). Rob could hardly be expected to show up more than once or twice a week. This was way beyond his duty, I knew, but you can't always explain loyalty between best friends. On the other hand, the elderly man who shared my room had a diligent wife who was loyally by his side day and night—too loyally, in fact. Visitation hours at the facility were supposed to end each night at 9:00 p.m. Somehow, through sheer grit if not outright deception, she managed to get around this. Often no more than six feet away from me, she would spend the night on the room's only daybed chair. She tended to talk all the time. I am not at all sure the couple liked each other, but she was loyal. While she was kind to me, she still was a constant presence. When staff came in to attend to me (I did not have bathroom access) it was bad enough to know my roommate was on the other side of the curtain sharing our mutual necessary inconveniences, but even worse knowing his wife was there! It was not as if I could control my bodily behavior, but neither could he. His wife claimed to be a doctor, though I am not sure whether she was a medical doctor. Regardless, she questioned him as to his condition constantly and gave him unsolicited advice we often could both live without. She would question every grunt or sneeze he made, whether during the day or in the middle of the night. At times, I was sort of entertained by their constant banter. I learned all about their life in a small Illinois town, a nice nearby community long favored by well-to-do Chicagoans. She had constantly been haranguing the RIC attendants and nurses about her husband needing better attention. I soon heard (time and again) that they just did not understand. "Can't you appreciate that my husband was born a prince in a big mansion somewhere in Eastern Europe? He is not accustomed to this treatment. He is royalty, I tell you." Then she would complain about something or another he needed, none of which I could expect to receive, nor the staff to deliver. I did hold out some hope that this prince was really a monarch who would choose to show mercy on me and take his poor roomie along as he received this special treatment. She was certainly angling for it. A funny thing began to develop. One of their constant topics was the business they operated. Clearly, they had rarely been away from the business very often, as he or she was constantly on the phone to the employees holding down the fort back home. Through overhearing numerous phone calls, I was able to put together that my prince and his princess were actually running a small corner convenience store back in their town. In fact, they lived in an apartment over the store. They bantered constantly with their son, daughter, and store employees about inventory, the cash register, and who was showing up on time. Now, I admire hardworking folk who own their own businesses and tend to them night and day, but this was my prince, European royalty—a man whose wife, presumably his princess, demanded special treatment and bickered constantly over how the little store was being operated. I appreciated now why some revolutionary regime must have sent this royal family packing off to America. Learning this, I went into overdrive, turning on my personal charm with all staffers. I was able to become the room's only good-attitude friendly and cooperative patient, whom staff soon grew to favor. Before long (and primarily because I was not getting much sleep), I was moved to a much larger room down the hall away from the nagging monarchs. I was even alone for a few nights before RIC found another patient to bring in. Fortunately for me, he did not have many visitors, and he seemed to sleep all the time. I am not sure we ever even spoke. My single bed was the same bed, but this new home was much better for me.

My final Rockford bed experience was my move from Park Strathmoor to my new home at Crimson Pointe, an assisted-living center. Here I got a one-room apartment. Instead of cinder-block walls and linoleum floors, I now had white-painted dry walls, a real carpet, and even a real bathroom! I had my first little refrigerator and a microwave. I even had a sink with running water in the kitchenette and a walk-in closet. Ironically, I was now so used to my previous hospital beds that I rented another similar one from a local provider. Plastic bedding or not, I bought new thick cotton sheets and even down pillows. Although still a familiar single bed, I felt closer than ever to my desired fancy hotel suite.

When I moved to Dallas in February 2016, I moved into the assisted-living center at The Forum at Park Lane. This time I moved into a two-and-a-half-room apartment complete with two baths. Once again, my single bed was plastic-covered, hospital-style; but this time, following a visit to IKEA, I had new sheets; two big, fluffy pillows; and a down comforter. I felt as if I had moved into a place as big as a gymnasium. Bedtime had never seemed so good.

CHAPTER 21

"YOU ARE GETTING A SHOWER, BILL."

Oh, those dreaded words. Brad Hayes would, with noted confidence, enter my room at Park Strathmoor and, without asking or engaging in usual morning pleasantries, simply assert in his special-for-the-circumstances authoritative voice that, no issue, no dispute, I was getting a shower this morning. It was not an issue as to whether I liked the idea or not. I had a moment to groan and shake my head, but I soon knew it was all for naught. Usually this meant I stunk and the CNAs and Brad must have been noticing. Perhaps Missy had noticed and complained. I was only permitted "so many" bed baths (being washed down by a CNA with soap and water while still in bed) before protests were registered or, perhaps, the State of Illinois might notice my stench in Rockford and charge that some regulation regarding sanitation was being violated. Lying in my bed in my quadriplegic state, I was not in any position to resist or refuse. I would be gently seized by Brad and one or two strong CNAs, lifted up, deprived of my loose little gown, and placed naked on a big, cold, plastic table. A sheet would be placed over my lower body and shortly I would be wheeled out the door, into the E-Unit hallway, down through the lobby and to the so-called shower room.

Brad usually did not have to give showers. Brad is an athletic twenty-five-year-old post-college-aged boy who, when dressed casually in his fashionably torn jeans and bandana, looked to me like a young Bruce Springsteen. He even had a big Harley-Davidson that he proudly rode all over Rockford. At Park Strathmoor, while on duty, he wore a white male nurse's uniform (complete with a physician's white coat embroidered with his name on it) and could have passed for a young doctor. Brad was friendly, pleasant appearing, and immediately engaging. His position at Park Strathmoor made him something between a nurse (he oversaw dispensing my drugs) and a CNA. CNA's, in their capacity, had to do all the real dirty work of caring for patients.

In this instance, however, Brad clearly was forced onto the front line. I must have been, once again, misbehaving as an irritable patient, since a mere CNA was not going to likely solve this problem. It took someone with real presence to make me toe the line. As a mature-beyond-his-years authority in the facility, Brad knew he had to step up. I later learned that my attentive sister, Missy, asked Brad to solve the problem because she doubted anyone else had the cooperative full respect that I had for Brad. In other words, she knew I would obey him.

If it was not bad enough that I was to be wheeled scantily clad down the hall under that thin sheet, past several visitors and patients, and then through an active lobby full of patients who specialized in just looking around, actually being given the so-called shower itself was, to me, a form of mild torture. I suspect I know how one's dog feels being given his first bath in a "human" bathtub. Unlike a dog, however, my paralyzed physical state did not allow me to squirm or jump up or even shake my wet body as all my dogs managed to do before getting toweled off. The shower room at Park Strathmoor made me feel as if I were in a locker room scene in the movie *Hoosiers*. It was naturally humid and had a peculiar smell—sort of like a mixture of sweat and rotting fruit with a touch of Clorox tile cleaner spray. I was not sure the room received fresh air except when the door was open briefly for entry of a bather. It looked hauntingly like my old high school gymnasium's boys' locker room; the walls were clad in aged green and blue tile that seemed to unavoidably attract persistent signs of mold. The room was small, cramped, and hardly felt accommodating. A strange little breeze seemed to come over my body as if a window was ajar in the winter. Brad tossed off my sheet and steered the shower bed with my now bare body into a dark closet-like room just big enough for only me. The poor guy then had to grab the shower head, pull it from the wall, and run it over his hands until the water was deemed warm enough for my body. Often, I would discover, the water temperature did not correlate to "hot" as I was used to at home or in my high school locker room. Mildly warm was deemed acceptable if that was even possible in an old facility where outside temperatures were occasionally below zero. I am certain, although I don't really remember in this instance, that my body was able to generate a real shiver.

By now I had already learned to check my dignity at the door. A few years of ulcerative colitis in a motionless quadriplegic state will help you get there. But I do remember thinking, *Poor Brad.* I was lying there butt naked (as we used to call it in the locker room), likely irritable, waiting for him to spray the water all over me. This was a guy I enjoyed immensely and had truly grown to feel was one of my favorite people in Rockford. Now he was having to do this. How I ultimately got soaped down, washed, and rinsed everywhere is not something I prefer to recount, but washcloths helped. I know my arms could not move very much, but I do know I had to be cleaned thoroughly and somehow completely dried and toweled off. I was returned to one of those icky facility gowns, given a light blanket, and wheeled fresh and clean back through the lobby and down the hall. If I was lucky, I would be able to resist and put off another such shower experience for several days, or at least until I stunk again.

Fortunately for Brad, he would not have to break the ice and give me my "first" shower at Park Strathmoor ever again. Others took on the role after my resistance tempered. However, my admiration for this fine young professional, doing what had to be done, only helped me appreciate how much of a dedicated and patient health care worker he truly was. A skilled care facility is full of these dedicated people working hard for often rather minimal wages. Brad was truly among the best. With this kind of experience and dedication behind him, I am confident that Brad will go on to big things in life.

CHAPTER 22
BLACK TOES

"Oh my God, what is wrong with your toes? Those are the grossest I have ever seen." So proclaimed my sister, Missy. She had most kindly but unexpectedly just popped into my room at Park Strathmoor that early morning.

"What's so gross?" I asked. "Haven't you ever seen an invalid's toes before?" The temperature in my room was hot at that moment despite the onslaught of the Rockford winter outside. I was lying on top of my sheets and blanket on my bed and, as I was not expecting an early visitor, my feet were exposed. I was likely in my thin green gown and that morning had no socks on. To Missy's apparent shock, she only now was seeing one of my normally hidden parts, my toes, not covered by socks.

Yes, my toes were gross—or maybe more appropriately, disgusting. They were essentially attached to feet that no longer served much purpose in my quadriplegic state. Unfortunately, my extended paralysis or, perhaps, medicine had apparently turned my lifeless toenails an unsightly shade of dark gray, if not black. My CNAs were aware of the condition and had been applying crème on each toe and nail. I could sense when they were doing it and usually considered it a pleasant form of massage. At the time, I was not much in tune with my toes, as I had not been able to see them, let alone touch them, for the last several years. How disgusting had they become? Well, not so bad that doctors and nurses recoiled in terror, but certainly not pleasant to the layman paying a patient visit. I now had better appreciation for why I and likely most everyone else tend to look straight ahead coming down a hallway of a patient ward. What you don't see does not have to be undone in your mind after the glance into a patient room. On one occasion, a foot doctor did pay me a visit to see the condition of my toes. While he may well have been appalled by what he discovered, he did carry out his professional responsibility to cut my toenails. Shocking to me, he told me that they were nearly a quarter of an inch too long and, not surprisingly, had curled under and imbedded into my toes. Some three years without a clipping will do that to you. Yes, that was truly gross and disgusting, but fortunately, with closer attention and good medicine, my toes substantially recovered. I now can bear the thought of wearing my sandals in public once again.

Other such rough and gross things happened to me while I was in the skilled care facility in Rockford. None of us patients ever wanted to look too closely at each other. Checking one's sense of dignity did not need to extend to being afraid of seeing other patients and visitors in the hall. The professionalism of the medical staff in confronting our very human conditions cannot be praised enough. They are truly unsung heroes to me.

CHAPTER 23

I AM NOT ALONE IN MY EXPERIENCE

Throughout my adventure, I was always surrounded by people who were frankly just as bad as or, in many cases, worse off than me. I may have been in a situation that sounded dreadful to some (and certainly most who visited me from the outside), but as miserable as I may have seemed, I was distinctly aware that others were in awful, even worse situations. Those patients with dementia likely were never to experience life again as they once knew it. Fortunately, I suppose in a cruel but comforting sort of way, those most affected probably did not know it or remember much about their past. Of course, I was not aware of what they were thinking, but I witnessed many at Park Strathmoor as, several times each day, residents of B Unit, those behind locked hallway doors, were allowed out into the outdoor patio area to smoke a cigarette. After my mind had returned and doctors began assuring me that I did not have any signs of creeping dementia (as had been previously diagnosed by Dallas neurologists), I was able to observe these patients stream out under the careful watch of a supervising CNA. I noticed how several would immediately migrate to one or two of the clustered table areas and begin to light up their craved cigarettes. A few others would find seats away from anyone else, preferring to stay alone in apparent contemplation. Only a few did not choose to smoke. One man, somewhat younger than the others but also showing no expression, would quickly begin walking a makeshift trail along the outside fence of the patio area. Around and around he would walk, never smoking but also never speaking. The image of a wildcat in a zoo walking the perimeter of its cage came to mind. The silent man would do it for the full fifteen- or twenty-minute period that the smokers were allowed outside. The smokers, gathered in their little groups, passed around a lighter and helped each other get the cigarettes lit. I would hear some conversation between them, but rarely anything of much apparent substance. I don't know if it was because they were not capable of carrying on a conversation or simply because they met so often that they just did not have much to say to each other. This was simply a part of the routine of their daily lives; three or four times each day they got a smoking break outside the facility. I did find it interesting that the same patients would often sit together as a group. Talk much or not, they sought the comfort of familiarity. As their break came to an end, the CNA on watch would announce that it was time to come back inside. Quietly and without objection they would immediately line up and pass through the heavy door the CNA held open, leaving the few of us not afflicted by dementia to enjoy ourselves on the patio.

Other patients—often those with no signs of dementia, I realized—had physical situations that could not possibly be meaningfully improved. Several of the elderly would sit and moan and even holler in the hallways of Park Strathmoor. I soon assumed that sedation was the only likely solution for these people, at least for temporary relief. Some of my resident friends were missing an arm, a leg, or a foot. One middle-aged lady, younger than me, had such tiny legs and feet that she could not possibly stand and support her weight. She was always in her bed. I noticed that some days the staff rolled her bed out into the E-wing hallway, perhaps so she could look at something besides her bedroom walls. How long had she been at Park Strathmoor? While wheelchairs offered mobility, I fear these patients knew their lives would never be the lives they may have once known.

I was most struck by the young man I met at RIC who lost both legs in a construction accident, whose story I recounted earlier. I often shared a wide physical therapy mat with him during our 10:00 a.m. stretching session. Though his pain may have subsided, I feared his depression about his appearance would likely take much longer to address. Praying for these people was not necessarily enough. The most I could ask was for God to grant these people the strength to patiently face the situation as they slowly healed to their destined extent. For those there for the long run, that was the most I knew to offer. By the time I went to RIC, I know believed I could get better and someday walk again.

I don't recall why I began thinking of one of my old college friends, as we literally had not spoken in some thirty-five years. We met in a sophomore-year history class at SMU. He was obviously a smart guy, and we began to develop a friendship that started sort of slowly, as we saw each other only in a class that met only a few times each week. I soon learned that he had just transferred to SMU after a year at a prestigious eastern school. How exotic that was to me; I did not know anyone I assumed was smart enough to go to that place. I remember that my friend had an illness I did not fully understand that had caused him to leave and move back to Texas, where he would be closer to home. My buddy was probably a natural athlete but at the time was a bit frail in appearance. Over time, he developed into a close friend, among the many I had at SMU. Later in that semester, he pledged our fraternity on campus, and our friendship grew. After graduation, my friend moved away from Dallas and went to a famous law school. I remained in Dallas, attending the SMU law school, and gradually we lost touch. The intensity of law study worked against our distantly situated friendship. After law school, my friend became an associate at a large law firm in Texas. Not surprisingly, he was always a hard worker, and our careers and social lives just never seemed to interconnect. Our friendship drifted away. While I had joined a small startup firm in Dallas, my buddy soon emerged as one of the nation's top business lawyers in his field and spent his entire career as a significant partner at his firm. Only much later in our careers, by which time I had become a partner in the Dallas office of another large Texas law firm, did I even become aware of his great success. While our two firms ran in some of the same big-time corporate legal crowds, I was not engaged in his particular area of practice. We never actually had the occasion to meet, but with all my newfound free time at least I had reason to try to connect with him again. I don't recall exactly if it was through LinkedIn connections or finding his email address on a group correspondence, but it did lead me one day, lying in my bed at Park Strathmoor while playing with my new iPad, to reach out to my friend. He remembered me. We exchanged a few email pleasantries, and eventually he gave me his phone number. I had given him a heads up on my ALS and quadriplegia situation. He expressed some surprise and concern but invited me to give him a call. I called him. When he answered, he sounded cheerful though a bit tired. I had not reached him at home, but shockingly to me, he relayed that he was lying in bed in a well-known hospital far from his home. He told me he was undergoing certain neurological tests that required a specialist. He feared that something might be wrong. He was dizzy, and he could not concentrate. His said his body was not working properly. I was stunned. Soon we were comparing notes as to the health problems we both were undergoing. Here were two old college friends with parallel careers both unexpectedly discovering we were suffering illnesses after years of successful legal careers. My quadriplegia and ALS soon had him insisting I was the worse off, but as I heard about the awful things he was experiencing, I was insistent that he was the worse off. He was having mysterious neurological problems that were affecting his ability to concentrate and maintain his balance. Bad as I may have thought I was, I believed I was at least improving. Much to my horror, he felt he was getting worse. His neurologists did not seem to have an answer, and here he was now, lying in a bed at this faraway hospital. I tried to be encouraging, but I knew he was trying to be strong. Of course, it did not matter who was worse off; the important thing was that here were two old friends, both in our late fifties, going through truly earth-shattering health difficulties. We both experienced the disappointment of losing our ability to practice law (nearly simultaneously) and now faced real uncertainties about our respective futures. We soon became frequent email and phone pals and remain so to this day. I think it brought newfound joy and feelings of support to each other. I know it did to me, and given his apparent enjoyment in initiating calls to me, I believe it did to him as well. To this day, neither of us has fully recovered, but our renewed friendship is very special. We can discuss physical health stuff people rarely share with others. We are in a unique fraternity now, albeit it one neither of us sought to join.

CHAPTER 24

IMMOBILIZATION: WHY IS EVERYTHING JUST OUT OF REACH?

Without a doubt, I believe the most frustrating thing I faced during my adventure was being physically immobile. This was an impairment I never imagined. I know everyone has experienced something awful in life, as we probably have all have been sick or hurt or been in an accident or otherwise undergone some sort of surgery. The reasons for discomfort are endless, and I don't mean to disrespect whatever experience someone has had. I don't pretend to begin to equate my immobilization to the horrors I witnessed for so many other patients in my facilities. I am aware of the incredible challenges, sacrifices, and suffering unlimited numbers of people have faced since time immemorial. Victims of war, earthquakes, plagues, viruses, diseases, and violence are the human experience. But for me, this being immobilized, unable to move, was an unimaginable experience. I had spent years of my life as a tennis player, swimmer, skier, and cyclist. Now this? Whether and to what degree you spend your life immobilized is not really the point of what I want to share, as my intent here is sharing what it was like to be physically immobile, possibly permanently, for the first time in my life.

During what was likely the worst part of my adventure, I was unable to move my body even though I was mentally aware of my circumstances. When I woke up and found myself as what was labeled a quadriplegic, I did not initially think about what I could or could not do. Obviously, over time I began to worry. You can have all the faith, best wishes, and maybe slightly optimistic doctors' reports you can muster, but it does not change the situation you are living in then and now. I simply could not move most parts of my body. It seemed like eternity that I would be in this position. For several months at Morrison Woods, the right side of my body was mostly frozen in place, and I had only slight movement on my left side. I can't completely recall, but if I had even a little movement in my fingers, it certainly was not enough to hold or grip anything. My left side was not quite as bad my right. I could maybe lift my left arm an inch or two and hold a magazine or a get-well card. I believe it was the toes on my left foot that initially showed some reaction when therapists tried to massage or prick them for signs of movement. This soon changed for the worse after I suffered those additional smaller seizures at the end of 2011.

I don't recall my immobilization as being painful. Pain is, of course, to be expected when you break or severely strain something, whether hands, fingers, arms, knees, ankles, ribs, or shoulders. It's funny; I have managed to suffer almost all of those injuries, whether breakage or muscle strain, at different times in my life, none of which was pleasant, and all were especially painful a day or so later. Other than the time at Park Strathmoor when I ran my electric wheelchair into a big door (and severely sprained my right foot, which caused my ankle to hurt), I did not feel any pain when trying to move in bed. What I felt was a weird sensation of accomplishing nothing. I had a goal to move, but struggle as I might, I could not make it happen. The arm would not reach more than an inch or so, and my knees would not bend. I realize that I was not completely paralyzed, because I could be moved slightly by staff. I could be pulled upward, and I could be placed in a wheelchair or occasionally on a toilet. In other words, I was bendable or malleable to some limited degree. It did not hurt to be bent or moved, but when I was dropped or bumped my head, I was aware of some pain. Paralysis was nowhere near the sharp pain I was to experience later in Dallas, late in 2016, when I fractured my right shoulder slipping off a curb.

The bizarre sensation I experienced being immobilized was the simple failure of being able to make anything happen. No matter how much I tried to raise that hand, arm, or leg, it simply did not happen. I could try to squirm or wriggle in some direction, but to little avail. The feeling was weird. Nothing seemed to respond in my body. The more I strained or tried to lift, the more I would be fatigued, but I did not feel pain. Maybe my observation is not completely accurate, because I was occasionally on a pain pill, but pain pills were usually only for when they cut on me, such as when they created the hole in my stomach for the food tube and the hole in my throat for the tracheal tube.

I suppose it is telling of something that I do not recall experiencing severe emotional frustrations or disappointment about being unable to move. It would be natural to be frustrated that my arms would not lift, let alone hold something. I assume that I must have been frustrated at times. Indeed, I was put on Prozac at some point, as doctors were concerned that I would be depressed. I recall thinking of the governor of Texas (then lieutenant governor), Greg Abbott, spending much of his life in a wheelchair. The governor had been a partner of mine at the law firm Bracewell & Patterson. I remembered being impressed with how this friendly man got around and conducted himself with such dignity. The story I heard was that Greg had become partially paralyzed as a young man after a tree had fallen on him while he was jogging in a Houston park. While this sounds horrifying, the only remembrance I had in thinking of Greg was how successfully he seemed to get around and perform his work. I envisioned being on a stage when I got better, just like Greg, but of course being in my wheelchair. Strangely, I don't recall being frightened or anxious over the situation. I think I was just beginning to realize it was now a fact of my life. I was physically disabled but expecting to see improvements during those early months was not an emotional issue. I don't recall being overly frustrated or feeling self-pity. I don't remember being upset or crying over what I could no longer expect to do. Maybe I am forgetting something; maybe the antidepressant drug was working. I came to call my Prozac my happy pill, and maybe it was. I don't even remember being upset that I would never ski or play tennis again. I just don't recall the emotion of being mad or desperate. Like the death of a loved one, possibly time was healing those emotions, causing me to forget those frustrations. Maybe my mind could not focus on worrying about my future.

I was not completely void of any frustrations, of course. Being quadriplegic, the most frustrating experience was physically trying to reach for things. This was an emotion of the moment. Everything seemed to be, and actually was, just out of my reach. At times the call light or bell I had with me in my bed was only a few inches away. I could see it, but I could not reach it. I tried squirming towards it, but usually with no success. If I touched it, I usually had no chance of gripping it or pulling it closer. This was so frustrating. I likely wanted the call button to call an aide for help. That book or TV remote might be on my stomach, but that did not mean I could reach it. It was disturbing; I could not change a channel because I could not reach the button to get someone to help. All of this was physically within inches but might be an hour or two away depending on whether staff had reason to check on me. That is frustration; that is knowing and experiencing real immobilization.

One day I read in the *Wall Street Journal* an article about the great American architect Michael Graves living in a skilled-care or assisted-living facility during the last years of his life. Graves was a postmodern contemporary architect who seemed to specialize in fun. His famous buildings were found in cities across the world, and especially at Disney World in Orlando, where his hotel structures seemed to set the tone for a magical experience. In addition to his many buildings, Graves had also become popular with us ordinary folk by designing consumer products for Alessi and, later, Target. Many people craved his innovative teapots, toasters, and signature wall clocks. Now here was the elderly Graves living out what were to be the last few years of his life, essentially immobilized. As a creative genius often does, Graves made the most of what he was experiencing. He soon turned his nose for good design on what surrounded him in the nursing facility. For me it was all obvious. What often frustrated me most was likely some antiquated illogical design feature that permeated nearly every facility I was in. Graves was experiencing the same thing. With the noted exception of RIC, which was attuned to good design, why did everything have to be so mundane or just out of reach?

I read about some of the health care facilities Graves designed shortly before his death, some of which are in Nebraska and near DC. Without knowing many of the specifics, no matter what the exterior of a facility might look like, his design complaints were all very obvious to me. Good patient design was nearly always an interior issue. Why were things so consistently out of reach? Why was it so hard for a person in a wheelchair to maneuver through tight doorways? Why do some doors have handles that rather easily might catch on a walker or wheelchair? Maybe it was a cost issue. I was not living in a Four Seasons or Ritz resort-type facility that likely had this covered. My facilities were late twentieth century structures that were updated in part owing to government-required Americans with Disabilities Act regulations or some minimal advances in affordable physical therapy equipment. I half expected to see old-time boxing punching bags and hear concerns expressed for "one's constitution." Helpful as it may be, the ADA does not necessarily command common sense. Why are counters in patient rooms too high, and bathroom toilets uncomfortably too low? (When you cannot stand up under your own power, you can imagine the frustration of knowing you will be dropping onto a low toilet.) Mirrors sometimes did not line up for wheelchair occupants as they would for someone standing. I even had a bathroom that had no space for a wheelchair. Why couldn't I see anything but sky outside that small window in my room? Most facilities were good about having wide enough halls and doorways and a television mounted where I could actually see it, but there were many other interior issues that made no sense, especially for the immobilized patient.

Graves offered many logical changes that, through common sense and a special architect's eye for detail, would help the patient. Too many facilities seemed to be designed as if for some ordinary postmodern box-shaped motel next to an interstate. These facilities are passable and comfortable for a few nights at most, but they are not designed with an awareness of a patient's complete physical needs in mind. Among my favorites I encountered was a toilet with the flush handle around the backside corner of the water bowl, just out of my reach. There goes your dignity when you can't reach to flush. I had a problem with faucets that required two hands to balance the desired temperature. Rather than provide the faucet often found in airports, nice hotels and modern bathrooms today, the kind you push down to get water, wash your hands, and then see gradually turn off on its own, I saw patients neglecting to physically turn off one side or the other. Water ran until someone finally noticed, sometimes finding his or her feet wet from the flooding on the floor or noticing water in a cabinet from the floor above. It is not as if all patients in assisted living have good hearing and realize the water is still running. I loved those light switches in rooms that any standing adult could reach but were just beyond my ability to stretch up and touch while in my wheelchair. There were also showers with heads just low enough that I had to bend down (always risky for one with balance problems) to let the water flow on my head.

Many so-called impediments were clearly by intentional design. Carpet thickness prevented the weak wheelchair occupant from fleeing down a hall, so I thought. The counter offering cookies and coffee to guests was intentionally just high enough to make sure I did not reach anything I was not authorized to eat. I swear some of my hallways seemed to elevate as I approached the outer lobby. No, I was not strong enough to handle the incline, and more than a few patients described traversing the halls as climbing a mountain. My frustration was necessary, because whatever my desires might have been, my immobilized state was not intended to allow me free reign. Staff did not have to look up from their paperwork every few minutes to see what mischievous behavior I was up to. This all made institutional sense, whether I found it customer friendly or not.

CHAPTER 25

"LET HIM DO IT; DON'T BE BABYING THE MAN-CHILD."

"Let him do it; don't be babying the man-child." Oh, how significant those words were to become. I was to hear them much more often than once. They were first used by the lady who was to have as great an influence on my recovery as any staffer at Park Strathmoor. I had spent the past few years on my back, showing no real improvement as the ALS diagnosis seemed to take its natural effect. I was not happy about it, but after a few years in bed I was certainly accustomed to it. The CNAs would check on me to see if I needed attention. Usually this consisted of shifting my position in bed, emptying my catheter bottle hanging off the side of my bed, or, worse, changing my diaper. When nearing empty, they refilled the bottles of light brown liquids dangling over my head. I did need to eat. Knowing that nothing was going to change throughout the course of a day, it was easy to just accept the service as a sort of social break. Discomfort and boredom made me want the attention.

During the course of my adventure, I received attention in various forms many times each day from CNAs assigned to my floor. I soon became familiar with the same ones. Usually I was able to develop pleasant relations with these well-meaning (usually, but not exclusively) women. We bantered about most anything. The friendly ones laughed and gave it back to me; the grumpy ones ignored me. It became a game for this self-deluded patient to receive this constant kindness and attention despite the unpleasant matter to which they were attending. I would ring the emergency call bell that was on my bed (but barely within my reach), and an attentive CNA would come into my room to see what I needed. The problem would be addressed, assuming I actually had something that needed to be addressed. If I rang my bell or pressed my call light unnecessarily, I would soon hear about it. I learned that if I rang it too often, it was like crying "wolf" and I would be promptly ignored. I don't think I usually rang it too often, but when I did, the CNAs were nowhere to be found. Though I recall some run-ins with assistants at Morrison Woods in Muncie, CNAs at Park Strathmoor were particularly attentive and helpful. Maybe I was no longer so starved for attention.

Then I met my CNA, Angela Shaw. Was it to be my most fortunate day at Park Strathmoor? Angela was a veteran CNA with some twenty-five years of experience working at Park Strathmoor. She was an outspoken, confident woman who clearly had seen it all. I would, fortunately, prove no match for Angela. If she thought I needed it, she would not hesitate to lift me out of bed and plop me in my wheelchair, as she seemed unusually dedicated to seeing that I did not spend all day in my bed. Angela introduced me to the concept that maybe the feet on my weak legs were still there for a purpose. Sometimes she'd pull me up out of bed but then insist I stand on my own until I was lowered into my wheelchair. I wasn't always excited to see Angela enter my room, because this meant I was expected to exert some energy. Something challenging was coming to this weak and lazy body, and Angela was going to make it happen. Thank you, God.

Over time, I quit being scared of Angela, or so I like to think.

While she pretended not to respond to my usual banter, the lady had a great sense of humor. I would half-heartedly resist her demands or complain like a toddler, but Angela had seen it all and quickly seemed to no longer fall for my carrying on. Angela was the first to recognize that I needed to be pushed. I think she thought my apparent ALS condition was an excuse for being lazy. Angela was very clear; I needed to do more for myself. Soon my resistance to instructions or simple requests became a challenge for Angela. She seemed to relish in my protests and with pure goodwill insisted I take on the latest challenge on my own. As irritating as I found her sometimes becoming, this lady clearly had something else in mind for me. It was not long before she developed a name for this pampered patient of hers; from now on I was to be called the "man-child."

Before long, all the CNAs knew I was now the man-child. Few chose to say it to my face, but Angela had thrown the gauntlet down—I was now on notice; I was to be challenged. Now I had to do things that once seemed impossible. When it was time for a shower, I was now going to wash myself, rinse my body, and finish on my own; as I got stronger and able to stand, there was to be no more sitting in the plastic shower chairs or lying on that moveable table. Most dreadful, I remember, it now was standard practice to make the man-child take off his own gown and figure out how to pull his shirt over his head. I was even expected to find a way to squirm until my arms got into the appropriate holes. This did not end my diaper requirements, but with my knees not bending, it was not natural to expect me to find my way into a Depends. Still, I had to try to do it. Every day it all seemed to get a little bit easier.

The most dreadful incident of my forced physical progress was the day when Angela declared that the man-child would be putting on his own socks. Put on my socks? The Statue of Liberty did not have to attend to her feet! I had not been able to touch my toes in some three years! The toes were foreign to me (you can imagine the length of my toenails that had not been clipped in several years), and now I had to bend enough to put my foot into an open sock? Oh, but Angela was not buying my protests. She produced a tool that allowed me to reach down farther and guide the sock onto my foot. The dang thing actually worked. However, after a few years of having someone lift my foot and guide the socks over my feet, the man-child knew I was losing some real ground as a disabled guy. Before long, the pampered one was no longer just telling my CNA what clothes to take out of my closet and dress me. Instead Angela picked the clothes, tossed them to me on my bed, and told me to get dressed. Ultimately, as my flexibility improved, I was able to reach my own feet and pull on my socks and pants. Once I no longer needed it, I remember passing on my sock tool to another patient who must have been inspired by my progress.

Angela and her CNA partner Jacki became among my favorite friends at the facility. Jacki was totally delightful. She had a wonderful naturally playful attitude. She was not even five feet tall but was afraid of nothing. Jacki and I had great fun pretending that Angela was too tough on me. She would pretend to defy Angela's instructions to make the man-child do it himself. We would laugh as Angela pretended to be disgusted by my pleading for help. It was a special partnership between them that really worked to my benefit—sort of like the good cop, bad cop routine. In any event, the two CNAs began spending some of their break time hanging out in my room. Angela in particular liked the big red lounger Missy had bought me. Midafternoon, she liked to stop and chat for a while. Our banter and my half-hearted protests did not stop, but at least we all laughed.

At Park Strathmoor, the skilled-care facility, eating meals in the community dining room was really more than I (and my guardian sister, Ann) could face. Lots of hands-on feeding was required for the disabled residents. Actual conversations between patients at a table were nearly nonexistent. The issue with eating was getting my food on a fork, guiding it to my mouth, and then actually keeping it there. The scene was not pretty. Being on E-Unit (the highest level of care), where I was, did not even qualify me to eat with the other patients in the communal dining room. My meals were always served in my bed. Initially this started because I was not being fed by mouth but through a tube that hung over my head and went into a hole in my stomach. I lived like this, I believe, for about two and a half years. I somewhat dreaded the milky brown liquid that would drip into my belly. It never varied, and taste was no issue. The good news, I guess, was that I did not taste anything or have the chance to refuse to eat. The slow drip continued. Swallowing anything, including water, was simply not an option.

Eventually during my stay at Park Strathmoor, my feeding tube was pulled out and I was permitted to receive food and liquid by mouth. Now, that might sound like a privilege or good news, but for several months it was anything but. I still was prohibited from drinking anything, as swallowing was considered a big risk. Everyone was scared that I would, in my condition, easily aspirate, and all were pretty sure that when that happened, I would die quickly, coughing to death. What a nice thought—every day, maybe my next swallow would be my last. I also had the nasty habit of failing the special swallowing tests a lab would perform on me from time to time. I never was able to pass one, though over time I quit taking the discouraging tests. My swallowing healed on its own.

Swallowing liquids was never really what bothered me most. Although I eventually was permitted a piece of crushed ice to melt in my mouth (intended to surreptitiously drip down my throat), the first real drag was being told I must drink thickened liquids. No, this did not mean milkshakes or smoothies were now my drink of choice; to the contrary, those were not deemed sufficiently thickened. Instead I was given one or two packages of a thickening powder that looked like powdered creamer for coffee. But this was no such thing. I started by putting the contents of the package into my cup and then added my liquid of choice. After a few moments, the drink thickened into a substance my throat was supposed to be able to accept. Ugh, what that thickener did was disgusting. One more thing to let the man-child bitch about. Over time, it became tolerable with my coffee (think coffee yogurt), and best of all, a beer in a bar. I discovered that I could enjoy thickened beer and fortunately discovered such with my friend Danny, who was not all that certain on our night out at a sports bar together that drinking beers would not, in fact, kill me. I survived, if not thrived.

After my feeding tube was pulled, the worst thing I discovered was my elevation to now eating pureed food. I thought I was now going to get to eat real food. Pork, chicken, eggs, oatmeal, cake, green beans, and potatoes all were finally back in my diet. But pureed? That proved to be about like the chicken allegedly in my dog's canned food. If it was there, I surely couldn't recognize it or prove it ever was part of a chicken. I guess French chefs like to puree vegetables and brains and call it a delicacy, but I assure you no one at Park Strathmoor ever tried to pass off that plate of mushy gelatinous stuff as good food, let alone something to be considered edible. I expected them to have to pay me to eat it. Pureed pork? It had the texture of meringue custard, but it sure did not taste like it had ever even been cooked or been part of a pig. Green beans and spinach? Think of a bowl of green bean or spinach pudding but without the sugar or taste-blunting coolness. Well, it did not take long for the man-child to return to his old ways. I was bitching and, I guess, feeling sorry for myself so much that I was actually losing weight from refusing to eat. I am told my weight dropped to 135 pounds or so, which for a man with a perpetual belly was about a fifty-pound weight loss. In time, management began to either take some pity on me or, more likely, became concerned whether it had adequate liability insurance in place if I were to starve. I do recall on one occasion at lunch, the pureed tuna salad was so dreadfully gelatinous that I insisted the head nurse confirm that there was even tuna flavoring in the blob of mush. Miraculously, this seemed to be the solution, as shortly a real plate of tuna salad was delivered to me. Lesson learned. The man-child now knew that when something did not appear to be food, he could simply ask management or a CNA to taste what the kitchen was trying to pass off. Tuna salad? By its very nature I thought tuna salad was pureed, not something the cook figured he could turn into tasteless mush. Eventually my swallowing got less risky, and more dishes, such as casseroles and pumpkin pie, were deemed pureed satisfactorily for my standards. One morning I nearly choked to oblivion eating a bowl of warm oatmeal. Oatmeal never made it back to my list of approved dishes while I was at Park Strathmoor, though I always thought it was safe.

A pureed dinner. What was it?

Pureed or not, my meals were still served to me in my bed three times per day. A CNA would open my door and bring in my tray. Angela and Jacki were my usual deliverers, since they worked during breakfast and lunch hours. Before long, I was proudly declaring that their room service was every bit as good as any service I ever got at the Four Seasons hotel. After explaining that meant great room service, they soon went their separate ways in carrying it out each day. Jacki thrived on the praise and announced as she entered my room with each meal, "Room service." I proceeded to greet her with great compliments that this truly was the finest room service I had ever experienced. We would laugh and carry on as she placed some nasty plate of pureed eggs or hot dogs on the tray on my lap. Angela, of course, soon thought this was outrageous. She never did really accept that I should be eating in my room instead of the communal dining room. When she delivered my meal, I proclaimed my joy that room service had arrived, and I heaped praise on her, as now I didn't have to do a thing for myself. Angela would scowl and declare that I belonged in the dining room with the others and that this was the last time she would ever be delivering me a meal in bed—at least until the next scheduled meal.

I am reminded by my sister of an incident when I was finally getting my first smartphone. I had done some preliminary investigating and decided that what I wanted was a particular Nokia Windows phone. Well, my sister took it on herself to go buy me a different, slightly cheaper phone made by LG. I guess I was having one of those days on which I did not feel like I was satisfactorily in control. I won't call it self-pity, but I suppose I was a bit childish when I rejected the phone. Angela apparently overheard the conversation, and as soon as my sister started leaving, Angela came into my room and stood at the edge of my bed. "You poor, ungrateful, baby, you. So, the man-child doesn't like his new phone? What are we going to do about that?"

I hope I laughed; I know I was properly put in my place. Sick or not, the message was clear: it was time I act more like a grown-up. I only grew to love and appreciate Angela (and Jacki) even more. She did not have to care; nor was she paid to care. But what a difference she made for me.

CHAPTER 26

SLEEPLESS NIGHTS AND ALL THEIR RAMIFICATIONS

I am not sure why, but one of the constants of my experiences during my adventure was my lying awake at night. I wonder if it was caused by the various drugs. Some suggested that my body clock was so out of line that I really did not appreciate whether it was night or day. I know from my mother's notebook that when I was drugged in the morning, I would often sleep during the day. There were also the reported mini-seizures that I suffered during the first several months, the effects from which may have caused me to sleep for days. The seizures, however, were rare and only seemed to have happened at Morrison Woods up through February 2012. This might explain some of my vivid and weird dreams, but it does not suggest why I spent so many nights awake in bed. I blamed the dreams on being given so much prednisone or other drugs for too many months. But after a while my antiseizure drug was changed to Keppra, in rather large daily doses, and luck has had it that I have never had a reported seizure since.

In any event, sleeplessness has been an ongoing situation, if not a concern. I am in fact writing this entry at 1:30 a.m. on a Thursday in October 2016. I still tend to lie awake, much like I did during my adventure. I seem to hear everything at night (including the large truck that stops 2:00 a.m. most nights, delivering food supplies to The Forum's kitchen). Then there is my problem of needing to piddle seemingly every ninety minutes or so. This is a weird condition, unfortunately, that my urologist attributes more to my turning sixty than my having a curable problem. I wake up needing to go, and I stagger into my dimly lit bathroom and take care of it. In fact, I rarely have much to pass. It has to be psychological. I feel I need to go, but physically I really do not. Whatever the reason, I now am accustomed to being awake at night, and unless I turn my bedside lamp on and read, my mind is often off to the races thinking, planning, or trying to find something to worry about.

The thought of taking my experience and message to interested groups is appealing to me. I have no fear of facing a crowd, because other than having an index card to remember to cover my points, I have so many middle-of-the-night, wide-awake rehearsals of my presentation that I think I could do it on five minutes' notice. Religious groups? I have that angle comfortably covered. My Christian faith is observable and enhanced as a result of my adventure. Fraternal groups or college friends? What I experienced about the unanticipated love, loyalty, and support of old friends is central to my recovery. I will talk about friends coming out of my past and making me proud and feel important. I believe this link is not accidental, but something planned by someone—perhaps a greater force? It's just imperative that I was open to the opportunity. Is having faith equivalent to being open to an opportunity? The Holy Spirit can operate in mysterious ways. What is the role of technology for the infirm or elderly? During my adventure, the quality of my life substantially changed when I got an iPad and was able to use it. Some of my frequent online friends now are people I have not seen in many years, some not since elementary school or my college days. They are important people to me today. What will be the role of nursing and senior facilities in the future? I have lots of ideas and inside observations; I have lived in them for over seven years, a bit prematurely for many in my age group. The next generation of senior retirement living residents is coming quickly. Very few people can afford facilities modeled on a luxury hotel; nor do they even want one. There are lots of life-improving ideas to enhance comfort that require less than a huge budget. Technology is way ahead of current availability in my facilities. The next generation, coming soon, expects far more. Starbucks-type coffee lounges, sports bars, patios, gardens, diners, and bistros are among the expectations today, none of which my facilities offered. Very few formal dining rooms and cafeterias are in commercial use in restaurants today. Even old traditional country clubs are trying new approaches to attract diners. Why no outdoor patio eating when the weather is great? I am inspired by the work undertaken by Michael Graves. While his buildings were often innovative postmodern shrines in American cities, he was very practical in creating attractive products as well. I have a clock hanging in my kitchen and an inexpensive watch I still wear that he designed several years ago. His designs excite. Are Graves's ideas too sophisticated for new nursing facilities? Is practicality sophistication? Graves spent his final years in nursing facilities observing as an elderly man what he desired in a nursing home. I have not seen his notes, but I know they creatively address such mundane subjects as toilets, showers, windows, access, and even flooring. His wheelchair prototype drew national attention. My attitude in moving to The Forum was substantially improved in no small part because of the hardwood floors and interesting configuration of my apartment floor plan. The Forum is the first place I have slept with more than one or two windows in my room since my adventure began. I have twelve windows now, and I look out on the street. Life is good! Think the incapacitated would like to look outside and see action now and then? (That was very popular at Park Strathmoor, where infirm residents spent hours each day staring out the floor-to-ceiling front picture windows in the lobby.)

Most of my ideas probably stem from being awake at night. While not tossing and turning per se, staff often visited me at Park Strathmoor in the wee hours to shift my weight. (I can attest that one cannot lie on one's butt very long without discomfort.) The opportunity to just think about things was an incredible gift. Music and news shows were not distracting my attention at that time of the night. Nor were those constant daytime emails interrupting my thoughts. In short, old folks are known for being awake at night; thinkers and knowers realize that may be a real blessing.

At times, my lying awake at night has taken a toll. While it can be among the best hours to read a good book or write out my thoughts (some of this manuscript poured out during the wee hours), after a few nights in a row I was often getting exhausted. This was fatigue I suppose, but I did not have the energy to get much done during the day. Having the luxury of being forced into my quasi-retirement, afternoons can be both a problem and a solution. Running an errand to Walgreens or perusing the gorgeous shops of NorthPark Mall were too often desired distractions. Since my body had recovered substantially by the time I moved to Dallas, taking long walks could be justified as a daily workout, and coming out of the mall with hot sale items made it a wonderful adventure. Was this my new version of an urban hunting trip? The goal was not shooting critters in the wild but scoring an occasional Crocodile or Penguin brand summer shirt on sale. Rarely did I go out with the intent of finding something, but I would just come upon an unexpected clearance sale and it would be like birds fleeing the brush. For me, my walks around the neighborhood near The Forum took place in fertile ground for unanticipated entertainment.

Being active in the early afternoons had its repercussions. This meant returning from my "workout" a bit more exhausted than when I had left. Especially in the Texas summer heat, I would return pretty wobbly, looking kind of spent. If I was not sweating, my packages (or grocery bags—I did not mention my urban hunting trips also featured weekly stops at nearby grocery stores) tended to tire my shoulders and cause my glasses to slip down my nose. I must have been a sight, but urban hunting takes its toll. When I returned to my room, I usually needed a brief pit stop, and I then found my way to the nearby couch. My intent to catch the news or read the latest book I had just discovered often turned into a nap. I soon justified these naps as good senior living. My fellow residents seemed to relish their own naps as a privilege of retirement or whatever they called their incarceration. Prior to my adventure, naps were completely foreign to me in the working world or when home on weekends with my kids. Now, whether from pleasure or sheer sleepless exhaustion, these were becoming unavoidable. The real trick was waking up in time to make it to dinner before the dining room closed. Naps, of course, are expected routine in hospitals and skilled-care facilities, but I am not sure it is fair to describe my own on-and-off sleeping I experienced while quadriplegic as comparable to the naps I was taking at The Forum due to exhaustion after a workout.

In any event, sleepless nights cause daytime naps and early turning in after dinner. I got used to joking with my dinner companions at The Forum, Bill and Horace, both older than me, about just which of the three of us would first be in their jammies and under the covers shortly after dinner. Hitting the sheets by about 7:30 p.m. was often standard practice in retirement facilities. My last big challenge of the day was not to drift off too quickly and miss that night's coveted ballgame or news show. In any event, sound sleep or not, I think that is why a lot of lights begin popping on in resident's rooms between 4:00 a.m. and 6:00 a.m. each morning. Breakfasts were routinely served by 7:00 a.m.

Lessons I learned from sleepless nights? Melatonin and the like did not have any meaningful effect on me. Being awake was actually a privilege for my mind to explore or read a good book while my brain was still able. Much of my writing is accomplished before a normal workday begins. In future years, maybe lack of sleep will catch up with me; certainly no one considers it healthy. But while in health care facilities, it was a bit of a pleasure.

As I complete this manuscript in what is now 2019, I can report that following more than a year of going to a nearby Life Time Fitness facility in Dallas, working with a physical trainer, and intensifying my walking and lifting weights has improved my health and strength. The process seems slow, but my leg strength and balance are much improved. I still need an occasional nap, and I wake up too early in the morning, but at sixty-three years old, that is probably not going to change. Fortunately, my mind is still full of ideas (at least if I am awake).

CHAPTER 27

DINNERTIME AND WHAT THAT MEANT TO ME

Evening dinners have always been important in my life, though the significance has changed for most of us over the years. We have all seen the change coming. With the advent of more two-parent wage earners and long hours at work, who hasn't noticed a change for many families? Traditionally, dinner for many meant a time of gathering with parents, spouses, siblings, and children, having a square home-cooked meal, and rehashing the experiences of the day. In my childhood, the television was turned off, the only exception being for an occasional moonwalk or Super Bowl game. This was all supposedly very therapeutic and was credited with developing healthy, well-mannered children who, among other things, learned to accept criticism and face up to bullies. Fortunate children learned to keep elbows off the table and not to eat too much salt, and that forks were not for carving meat quite like their knives. Clearly, concepts like "please and thank you" were embedded most effectively at dinner. Parents might have a glass of wine, while children learned that one always wore a shirt and shoes while at the table. When spoken to by adults, you learned to respond, and in no event would you ever read a book while at the table. In short, so much was accomplished in creating an orderly society through a family dinner.

We all know that sounds like a dream from the 1970s and 1980s, and most certainly prior thereto. Dinners now too often seem to be hurried affairs often featuring carry-out or brought-in prepared food. For heaven's sake, let's make sure food is on the table. The goal is to get the kids fed regardless of whether one of the working spouses made it home in time, and soon television and games on cell phones became a necessity. Distractions are a blessing. At least everyone might actually be eating. This sounds kind of jaded, but unfortunately I sense it is often true. If you don't find unresponsive children glued to technology and the act of hopping up from the table unexcused just a bit disheartening, you must be unfamiliar with eating dinner today. For some it may be the end of civilization, at least as we remember it.

Dinners (or "suppers," as assisted-living facilities often refer to them) are nowhere near as aspirational in retirement and health care facilities. Manners have presumably been taught years before, and now dinners are really a necessary mission. Patients must be fed, but preferably in an efficient and timely manner. Profitability is going to be respected, I soon learned, especially in a publicly supported facility. That means a lot of hot dogs and Jell-O on the menus. I do not intend to demean the skilled-care facilities I lived in, as dinners were usually planned with the help of real dietitians, not just staff accountants. The goal was to keep the patients alive and moderately happy. Cakes, pies and breads were often awesome. Besides, having my dinners elevated to hot dogs or the seemingly nightly pork-based dish was a great improvement over that brown liquid that flowed from that suspended bag hanging over my bed and into the hole in my stomach. When my swallowing graduated to pureed meals, it really did not matter what that gelatinous glob on my plate (sometimes multicolored) was alleged to be. Dinners had a distinct purpose, and the sooner served, the sooner the place would quiet for the night.

Unfortunately for me, meals in the skilled-care facilities were not designed to be a social experience I could expect to enjoy. The dining room was often crowded, and patients used to frequent shrieking kept up their shrieking and made things, at best, distracting. Flinging or dropping food on the floor was not generally appreciated but was something to expect. Many patients, if not most, needed physical assistance cutting their food, capturing it on their fork or spoon, and, most importantly, guiding it to their mouths. I was, for a few years, one of those patients. Making sure the food stayed in a patient's mouth was the sign of a great assistant. At Morrison Woods I was frustrated that I could not eat in the main dining room. Despite my protests, I was wheeled past the tables full of independent eaters into a smaller side room. Here, if there was an empty space available, I was put at a table with others. The goal was merely to be fed. Conversations rarely existed, as apparently the task of eating required all the concentration we had to offer. Water and drinks were spilled, and food often seemed to find itself anywhere but the open mouth. Assistants rarely seemed cheery, as one sensed they knew they had been assigned a frustrating and tough duty. Dinners did not last long, and soon after, I was being escorted back through the independent dining area to my room. I don't recall many of my fellow diners at Morrison Woods, other than a man who was described as the father of one of my grade school friends. I never seemed to find out anything about anyone. Nor did I learn why they had disappeared after a week or so. I assume at the time I was every bit as uncommunicative and unattractive to these diners as they were to me. If my mother happened to be there, probably to make sure I ate, she would try so hard to get the diners at my table to talk among each other. I don't remember any actual conversations, so I assume none of us were interested. Very few people in that assisted-living dining room could ever expect to graduate to the independent dining room we passed through for each meal.

When I returned to my room, it seemed as if it took forever to be put back in my bed. The woman who wheeled me back from the dining room was not responsible for transferring patients from their wheelchairs to their beds. Often I would be placed about a foot away, just out of reach of my bed. This was so frustrating for me. Sitting there was tiring and often uncomfortable. Though I would not fall out of my chair (those seat belts worked), my head would drop, my mouth might drool, and my neck would become strained. My mother hated finding me in that position, but usually after dinner she was not there to notice. Certified assistants never seemed to be around after meals, as, appropriately, they likely were serving others. Oh, how it hurt. I was just a foot or so away from my bed. I could unsnap my seat belt, but try as I might, I just could not generate the strength to fling myself onto the bed. Failure to get there meant likely coming up short and falling to the floor, smashed between the steel supporting my mattress and my wheelchair. I wasn't that stupid. Pain is pain, and I might soon be labeled a "fall risk," so there in my chair I remained, seemingly forever—or at least until some assistant finally acknowledged my misery.

At Park Strathmoor, my eating adventures tended to be less interesting. All meals were delivered to my room, and generally I required no individual assistance. I had my ever-present television turned on, and I was stuck lying in my bed anyway. As my strength improved during my stay, I graduated to walking my tray back to the tray cart located somewhere in the hallway outside my room. In fact, it became a distinguishing characteristic of my improving health that I was actually carrying my own tray. This, of course, reflected Angela's "make him do it" success story and led to more of our "room service" banter. (What room service system expects a resident to put away his tray?)

My meals at Crimson Pointe and The Forum were much different. I was now in assisted living but around independent seniors. Not only was the menu more creative, the choices more diverse, and the food much better, but I also always ate in the dining room, usually with others. This was actual independent senior living. The pressure was on the facilities to provide good meals, resulting in a much better resident experience.

CHAPTER 28
A MOST PLEASANT SURPRISE

At some point at Park Strathmoor, soon after I became aware that my brain was now seeming to function more clearly, Missy surprised me one day by bringing in a shopping bag that contained two thick three-hole-punched white binders. Each was jammed with letters, copies of emails, personal letters, and get-well cards that I soon discovered had been sent to me over the past couple of years. All had been received since the worst of my adventure had begun. My mother and Missy had received lots of correspondence addressed to me but had never actually shared much, owing to my mental state at the time. They had carefully preserved the letters, cards, and reprinted emails pretty much in the sequence they had arrived. While both Nan and Missy had occasionally read to me some nice correspondence as it arrived, I had no idea how much additional correspondence had accumulated. Bill Francis, upon learning I now had an email address thanks to my new iPad, quietly spread the word to my FIJI fraternity brothers, former clients, and friends he knew of throughout the country. While I had been truly incapacitated, Bill had served as my sister's de facto link to my outer world. Apparently, concerned friends and acquaintances soon started a flood of emails and letters he then passed on to Missy and Nan. These writings became the binders my family assembled to hold in the event I became mentally aware again. Perhaps it was something to share with my children should I pass.

Despite Missy's words of caution, I spent much of the rest of that day gingerly going through the binders, page by page. I cherish my memories of turning those pages, reading the incredibly kind missives. Page after page, friends and acquaintances uniformly expressed their concern for me and best wishes for how my sister and mother were holding up. Bill had spread the word of my unresponsive condition, my grotesque physical condition, and my emerging ability to read notes from friends. What I read that day was nothing short of what you might hope your family and friends will hear about you at your own funeral. But here I was, experiencing it firsthand and before my own eyes. There were notes from my closest friends, but also notes from many friends I had lost touch with years ago. There were pictures of children and families I had not yet met. There were expressions of love and appreciation. From my years working with the FIJI fraternity house as a graduate adviser to boys some ten to twenty years younger than me, I received the kindest, unexpected notes that really moved me. Several were from onetime fraternity officers and active brothers who were involved with me and with whom I had maintained some contact up until I got so sick. Hearing from now middle-aged guys I remember once being young, including Bryan Ballowe, Ben Caswell, Jeff Eckert, Chris Rowe, Sam Gleason and Jim Brune, was really inspiring to me. What was equally thrilling was hearing from brothers whose letters frequently started out with something to the effect of, "Bill, you probably don't remember me, but I was a FIJI in that class in the 1990s when our fraternity house burned down ..." They then went on to express such kind feelings and concern toward me. I truly was moved; I realized that I was not alone. Several of these acquaintances soon became frequent correspondents and modern-day pen pals, via email. Some I truly did not remember (or barely remembered), but our relationship now developed further. This was all in addition to my own pledge brothers from the class of 1974, SMU friends, and even high school and grade school classmates who were my contemporaries dating back to the 1970s. The effect was overwhelming on my emotions and created exciting optimism for my immediate future. What really struck me was how, in almost every letter, these friends said they were praying for me. They were asking God to please pull me through. This was so important to me, because many of these were old friends with whom we rarely had discussed religion or our personal faith. Friends I remembered from adventuresome rowdy travels and youthful fraternity house capers not to be mentioned more fully here were appearing now to be closer to their God and calling on his support to somehow give me the strength to pull through. The effect was very real on my faith and optimism.

Even though much of the correspondence was one or two years old by the time I read it, it was a day I will remember forever. I realized these were letters and expressions of heartfelt concern that no one in my family assumed I would ever see. I was not going to live long enough to ever hear these sentiments. I thank God that my mother and Missy had the optimism and foresight to save these missives, perhaps in the hope that somehow, despite all medical prognostications, I might have a chance to actually read them. Perhaps they were only saving them as a memorial to be shared someday with my children long after their father died. In either event, I felt it was an act of God that caused Nan and Missy to assemble and retain the two thick binders.

Before Missy left that morning, she warned me that this might be emotionally tough and that maybe I should just proceed gradually so as not to be overcome with emotion. She was right; I soon experienced an afternoon like no other I ever encountered. Of course, I reviewed every page until the binders were complete. My experience that day was as if I were at my own funeral. I have always chosen to assume that after you die, you get the chance to eavesdrop on your funeral service. Why else choose the music, the eulogists, the pallbearers, and the minister? There, likely clad mostly in black, will be the ones you loved in life and, one hopes, a whole cast of others who thought highly enough of you to devote part of their day to fondly wish you farewell. Of course, I also assumed there would probably be a few in attendance who just wanted to confirm that I was truly out of here. But here I was, actually seeing and reading nice things people were saying about me. I was being praised in ways most of us humans rarely express to each other in real life. Try as I might, rarely could I really express the thanks, appreciation, and love to others that I later wished I had taken the opportunity to say. To my great pleasure, nearly everything I read that afternoon was kind, inspirational, and so loving that I really ended up thinking, *No way I am leaving now, Lord; these people really care for me! I have friends, many of whom I did not realize I even had.* Reviewing this correspondence was truly a boost to my determination to survive. Why had it happened, my God? Why did Nan and Missy feel compelled to keep the cards and letters and assemble these binders? Why had so many people written me? Was this happenstance? It was not so in my mind. This enhanced my belief that there was truly a greater power working in my insignificant life that seemed to coincidently make things happen. Friends appeared to pick me up and say they loved me (despite who I was). My mother and sister were to receive unexplainable strength to persist and carry me through my staggering health problems. My doctors and caretakers just got better and better—so it seemed to me anyway. My health was beginning to improve even though no one could say why. My nearly nightly prayer, "Jesus, please allow me to wake up again in the morning," kept getting answered. I truly believe that these things happened for some greater reason I will never understand. Sure, I always hoped for the best in my health, but did I really have faith that it would happen? To me, it was scary to risk being disappointed. In fact, I consciously did not pray that I be fully healed or be spared by God. (I know, Christianity is not about being spared by God to spend a little more time on earth.)

Rather, I prayed, "Please, Lord, do with me what you will." God has a plan for me. It was never a question of whether I deserved to survive. I knew that far more deserving persons than I did not survive or live what I perceived to be a long life. I knew I would not live forever; we all know that. I just hoped it wasn't my time yet. It will of course happen someday, but for now I was not being called to go. Those moments changed my life. I knew I owed something back. I had an enriched faith. I don't know what God has in store for me, but I was changed. I am determined now to take advantage of the moments I have and to try as often as possible, God willing, to be positive, to be faithful, to be supportive of others, and to believe I am in some small way doing God's will. I am far from capable of living up to what I perceive are His expectations; I will and do fall short. So help me, God; let me do my best with what You have given me. Grace and forgiveness, I believe, will make up for wherever I inevitably fall short. Thank you, Lord, for giving me this chance.

The correspondence I read that day frequently did drive me to tears. My door was shut, and I wanted it to stay that way. Several letters, simple in scope, confirmed that I was in some way touching people—I was making a difference in some lives. Of course, I had never consciously tried to take such a step. Circumstances just happened. I believe people had been placed in my life, often at unanticipated times, who would go on to affect me forever. I cover the scope of this elsewhere in my story. I believe it and am acutely aware that it's true. Now here was evidence, expressed in cards, letters and emails, that I, too, was making a difference in some people's lives. I loved it. I knew others had done it for me and were continuing to do so. All I can say to readers is that you should be aware and look for it. You are making it happen for others (whether you fully appreciate it or not), and they are definitely making it happen for you. This is a true gift of God.

CHAPTER 29
A MOST UNEXPECTED VISITOR

As I worked my way through the many pages of letters, emails, and cards in my big binders, I came across one note card that particularly caught my attention. It was a two-sided handwritten note from an old friend with whom I had not been in touch for several years. Dan Freiburger had been a freshman on the first Forrest Gregg–coached football team that SMU fielded following its infamous NCAA death penalty suffered in 1987. I had become a casual acquaintance with Dan when Coach Gregg had asked members of the SMU booster club to get to know his young (mostly freshmen) players and provide them with some moral support during what was likely to be a very difficult experience on the field that year competing against fully stocked Southwest Conference schools. Well, it was a difficult year despite SMU shocking us all with two wins that season. (The University of Houston, not being one of the losers to SMU, passed its way to 95 points against the outmatched Mustangs in its one particularly ignominious game.) At a preseason mixer between the young players and a group of us modest booster-donors to the program, I met Danny. I was some fifteen years older than the eighteen-year-old, and not surprisingly, it was always a bit awkward for the kids to try to mingle with adults they never had met. Coach Gregg wanted his boys to become comfortable with adults as part of their growing experience at SMU. I had vaguely become familiar with Dan when I happened to see Peter Jennings and ABC News run a feature on the young Ohio boy choosing to play football for the startup Mustangs. Dan was a sharp-looking boy clad in a navy blazer and tie speaking up confidently about his decision as Jennings asked him questions. So, at the gathering, I introduced myself to Dan and broke the ice by complimenting him on his television exposure. Dan laughed, clearly embarrassed that he had been singled out.

We went on to develop whatever friendship a bright, confident, eighteen-year-old quarterback can have with a corporate lawyer who never played football outside his family's side yard. Shortly it became easy to become friends, as Danny's very involved dad, who was a lawyer in Columbus, discovered that a couple of my partners and I were also lawyers. Over the next few seasons, a few of the principals in my firm and I would have a Monday-morning conference call with Chuck Freiburger to discuss how the Mustangs (and more importantly, Dan) had played in that last football game. Chuck became a real friend, and it became logical for me to check in now and then with Dan. Over time, we developed a nice friendship. We both liked an occasional Rangers baseball and Mavericks basketball game. On the golf course, he was tolerant of my poor play, while he could often murder the ball with long, high drives, some of which even landed in the same zip code. Generally, it was just a nice relationship ... I would get some (very valuable) insider tips on the football team, and I, in turn, was an occasional source of a good steak cooked in my backyard. After Dan graduated following a nice career as a two-year starter for SMU (I believe he, at one point, completed more consecutive passes than any prior Mustang quarterback), he moved away to Memphis and Ohio. We basically lost touch.

When I came upon Dan's note to me, I was pleased and surprised and very touched. It was dated a year or two before I ever was shown it. Dan had apparently learned from someone in the SMU grapevine that I was mysteriously ill. He had no idea what I was facing, but he wished me well. What moved me was how he went on to express how much it meant to him that I had befriended him, a mere eighteen-year-old coming from Ohio to the world of SMU in Dallas. Although I knew he had no problem making friends, certainly not with the coeds and football players on campus, I did not appreciate that our very occasional encounters actually had an effect on him. In the card, he bravely expressed how he had been so homesick that first year and really intended to return to Ohio. He said that but for my kindness in showing him some of Dallas outside the campus, he would not have stayed. This, of course, was an exaggeration; I knew so because this big blond athlete quite easily fit the definition of "big man on campus"— especially, I presumed, in the sorority houses. But how incredibly kind to say that to me so many years later. It reminded me of the special occasions in my younger days when someone unexpectedly came into my life and had an actual impact on me. Needless to say, this expression of gratitude really hit me. It was so unexpected considering my current situation.

Dan was the first person I actually wrote to with my newly discovered functioning right hand. Everything to date had always been communicated via email, as I had lost all my handwriting ability while being quadriplegic. I wrote back to Dan, scribbling out a two-page letter telling him how happy I was to hear from him, especially at this late date. I could not email him, as I had no contact information on him other than that I had last heard he was living in Columbus. After several days of trying to locate him online, I finally found his parents' home—or at least I assumed it was, as they were living on a street with an exotic French name. That sounded appropriate to me for one of Ohio's best lawyers. Fortunately, I guessed correctly, and his parents gave Dan my letter. I had laid out all the gory details of my adventure and how I was somehow improving despite my ALS. I guess I hit an accord with Dan. Shortly he was calling me at Park Strathmoor and insisting that he wanted to come to Rockford to visit as soon as possible. I warned him that he might not be prepared for the condition he would find me in, but he would not, to my silent joy, take no for an answer. Within ten days, Dan appeared at the door of my skilled-care room. I hope I was at least dressed, as there he was. His darling girlfriend Suzanne had come with him, driving all the way from Columbus, Ohio (in a snowstorm), bringing along a colorful throw she had stitched and was now presenting for my bed. We talked and reminisced on past old times. They had their two dogs in a hotel room. (Why do football players so often seem to end up with strange little dogs once they get a girlfriend?). We planned dinner that night and a Swedish breakfast the next morning. I was so charged up from the visit. I had rarely been out of the facility. I told the afternoon staff that evening that I was going out to watch NFL championships with my old friend. "Don't expect me back early," I said, as there were two games scheduled that night. What fun I had! We were in a real sports bar, being real male friends, just like all the normal people sprinkled through the bar were experiencing. When our sports talk eventually bored sweet Suzanne, she soon discovered that Illinois allowed slot machines in bars and quickly wanted to go play. Dan and I emptied the change in our pockets, and off she went. Dan and I talked and talked. Yes, we had some drinks, though I at least tried to limit my intake to beers I filled with that nasty thickening powder I brought along. Before long, the evening continued; our visiting let time pass. At 10:00 p.m., Dan suddenly realized, "Hey, this is late! Park Strathmoor will be locked up. We need to get you home." We left the table, me with my walker. Suzanne said, "I will get the car." Dan said he needed to use the loo (not his exact words).

I told Dan that would be fine and said, "I will just stand here and wait for you until we get the car." Off they went, with me standing there alone in the bar, leaning on my walker. As soon as they disappeared, in came my nurse Joe Quayson, directly from Park Strathmoor. Joe was a delightful experienced nurse who must have been a workout fanatic (big upper body build, originally from Ghana, and one of my favorite people at Park Strathmoor; we joked constantly, and I will always appreciate his positive words and encouragement). Joe on more than one occasion had seriously reprimanded me when he sensed that I was losing my determination to fight for my survival. It was Joe who once said, "You will walk out of this place someday." But this time, Joe was not smiling. "There you are; we have been looking all over for you!" Oh my God, he had not gotten the word from the afternoon crew that I was going to be out late. Confused by my absence, he had gone out searching for me, guessing correctly (fortunately) that I was at this sports bar. I could see Joe was skeptical; could his skilled-care patient living near the dementia wing truly have wandered out to a sports bar on his own? Fortunately, Dan returned and assured Joe that I was in good hands. I kept warning Dan that the authorities would not be happy knowing someone had taken me out for my first beer since arriving at Park Strathmoor. I loved it. There were no repercussions. They even let me go out with Dan and Suzanne the next morning for our Swedish breakfast at the venerable Stockholm Inn. My emerging independence and improving health were starting to be noticed.

Our relationship restored, Dan, during this time of my illness, became one of my closest friends. We still correspond and speak frequently to this day. I could not be prouder or more blessed. I consider it one of those strange seeds being planted in our lives for a long-term, though distant, relationship.

My story with Dan is just one of several encounters I had with old friends while I was in the skilled-care and rehabilitation facilities. My friend and onetime roommate Rob Topping was a persistent guest coming up from his office in Evanston. Eventually Rob and his wife would invite me for weekend getaways to see Big Ten football, as Northwestern hosted both Stanford and, later, Penn State. I was still

Together with Dan Freiburger at the sports bar in Rockford.

wobbly, but taking the bus from Rockford into Chicago and spending a few days away from my facility was a total treat for me. On one trip to Chicago, my law school buddy (and Bracewell partner) Glenn Ballard came in from Houston, and the two of us spent a memorable day at Wrigley Field watching the Cubs play baseball. Friends Lloyd, from California; Bill and Kristi, from Dallas; Sam, from Houston; Bryan, Doug, and Jeff, from Dallas (while on business trips in Chicago); Tom, from Milwaukee; Kimm, from Chicago; Jim, from Charlotte; my wonderful client friends, Bob and Andrea at Fidelity National Title in New York all found time to visit while I was at RIC. At no time was I pleasant to look at, but none of them expressed shock. What these visits from them and others meant to me was immeasurable for my attitude.

Lloyd Rowland on a visit to see me in Rockford.

*Kindly friend Lloyd takes me to local Rockford Mall.
Very funny? Parks and leaves me in my wheelchair
before the big picture window at Victoria Secret.*

CHAPTER 30
SATISFYING DAY

Memorial Day weekend has always been special to me. It's the traditional start of summer, good weather is often in the air, and it's time to release yourself to the joys of the forthcoming season. Also, it's a time for solemn reflection for those whose lives ended too early.

There is a certain sadness when you realize and accept that you truly are getting older. You experience memories of your lost ones, memories of those who preceded you in your family's passing generations, and memories of friends you once loved or cared for. You experience memories of courage and bravery and of all losses that seemed so sudden and unfair. Such memories confirm that, one way or another, life, for all its greatness, unavoidably includes sad events, broken hearts, and the realization that we are privileged to be here now. That being said, yesterday, the Sunday before the actual Memorial Day Monday, was a particularly satisfying day for me. It was full of activities I enjoyed.

The morning started with waking up at 6:00 a.m. after a typically restless night in my room at Park Strathmoor. Being up early on this Sunday meant that I could catch Pastor Joel Osteen broadcasting his message about experiencing life as taped from his megachurch in Houston, Texas. I got in the habit of watching Pastor Joel partially because he was easily accessible on my Rockford cable television system. In fact, he was broadcast for thirty minutes on three different channels each Sunday morning, one after another, beginning at 6:30 a.m. For me, Pastor Joel was a welcome alternative to choices like Teletubbies, endless "get-fit" infomercials that ran on other channels, and those doom-and-gloom TV evangelists who seem to assure me I am inadequate in God's eyes because I can't be just like they say I should be. As I watched more often, I started getting hooked. While I was a Methodist by tradition and accustomed to worshipping in high church sanctuary settings, going to a Rockford church (especially early in the morning) was not an option. Pastor Joel was right there, in my room—actually three times that morning. Pastor Joel became my norm; if you listened, he was nothing but a source of good news and Christian hope for whoever tuned in. There was no scolding or calling me a sinner; Pastor Joel had his unique style just for those seeking optimism in life. This morning, Pastor Joel did not disappoint. Most every—no, maybe every—week, Pastor Joel did not fail to speak a Christian message directly to me—at least so it seemed to me. It is nothing short of bizarre. It drove my sister to more than once inquire whether I tell the pastor just what to say for me each week.

That morning, Pastor Joel was assuring me that Jesus and God were standing behind my every challenge. No matter how daunting, he said, as long as you are breathing, you will overcome if you have faith in God through Jesus Christ. No matter how sick, how financially challenged, or how disappointed you may be in lost relationships, Pastor Joel assures me that God has a greater plan. His plan for me is one that is far stronger than the forces working against me. *Wow*, I thought. *You are talking to me!*

My recollection is that Pastor Joel did not like to address the unfairness of death. Instead he prepared me to be satisfied that if I try my best and have faith in the Lord and, equally significant, have a great attitude, I will have most all I ever need to prosper in life. That, of course, does not say nor assure me that I won't be dying, but I was not looking to discuss that anyway. To me, Pastor Joel dwells on solutions for the living. He specializes in providing answers for how to cope, how to face challenges, and how to keep your head high through it all. Did I seem like someone who could appreciate a steady dose of that? Granted, I was lying on my back with nowhere to go. I was not about to switch the channel back to that infomercial on hearing aids just yet.

Pastor Joel does not preach much about sin. His message did not criticize me or make me feel inadequate. God is there to forgive you and show you unconditional grace, so he said. By tuning in, I grew more certain that my behavior and situation may be part of God's plan. Could I do better? Have faith, he said, and you will have the tools to overcome your challenges, no matter how daunting they may seem. There is something liberating about knowing that your inadequacies are part of a plan—not authorized by God, but nevertheless somewhat unavoidable and with a purpose you can maybe address. God's grace will be there. I always knew free will is part of the human equation. Sure, I will come up short. But keep trying. For me, he was preaching to the choir. I never felt bad or depressed after hearing one of Pastor Joel's messages. Critics might call his message "Christian light"; I prefer to see it as Christian optimism.

The second part of my satisfying day included watching, as I always do on Memorial Day weekend, the Indianapolis 500. As a native Hoosier, the event seems larger than life. As a child, I listened to the race with neighborhood friends, riding our Schwinn bikes with our little transistor radios blaring every word. Back then, Indianapolis prepared for the annual race with a month of coverage, both on television and in the papers. Drivers were household names in Indiana. For us, drivers were colorful heroes. A. J. Foyt, the irascible Texan, was mine, probably more so than almost any athlete, and I had many—Sandy Koufax and Don Meredith among them. A. J. was my May Hero. He was tough, plain talking, often annoying, and, best of all, a winner. He was not ever going to be overly successful in a commercial sense (he loved to piss people off), but when he won, I loved it. His winning was sort of like sticking up his middle finger at the racing establishment. There was a reason he was probably the most loved and hated Indy racer ever. If you were an A. J. fan, Indy knew it. Today Indy tends not to be the same, but neither is much in life. Most of the one-name wonders are gone. A. J., Mario, Parnelli, Rick, Al, Bobby, Little Al, Johnny, and Emerson needed no other explanation. They were all heroes—for the ages, in my world.

On this Sunday, Indy is still exciting to me even if the names of the drivers seem to change frequently. The two hundred twenty-five thousand fans still show up in the grandstands (plus even more in the speedway infield). I went to the race every year since high school, even later attending from Dallas. I was one of many who made this pilgrimage. It continued until I somehow managed to agree to get married on a Memorial Day weekend, thereby establishing our anniversary date. I had not been back to the 500 since. Nevertheless, I never missed catching the race on television or radio and would not now. I could not wait to hear, "Gentlemen, start your engines" just after Jim Nabors finished singing "Back Home Again in Indiana."

Yesterday the race was good, if not spectacular. It had a few too many yellow flags, meaning there were some wrecks and engine blowouts, causing time delays. Still, it had its intense feeling to me. I remembered sitting on the edge of my seat at the track as the rocket machines blasted by at up to 230 miles per hour. This was the same intensity I felt when A. J. was racing years earlier at an average speed of 160 miles per hour. This year a Brazilian in a Penske-owned (very racing establishment) Chevrolet won the race. Juan Pablo Montoya wasn't a household name or a local hero. In fact, he has raced at Indy only three times, the first being fifteen years ago when he won the race as a rookie. Juan went on to chase Formula One and NASCAR money but was never as successful as he was at the oval racing at Indy.

Rich, yes, but as happy as he would have been staying at Indy? For me, watching the race was great fun.

After a rare late afternoon nap following the race, I was on my way with my sister, Ann, to see Gordon Lightfoot perform in an old theatre in downtown Rockford. I think the last concert I had attended prior to my adventure was U2 in the massive AT&T (Cowboys) Stadium in Dallas before some 85,000 people. There was a somewhat different feeling this time. But Gordon represented something special to me. I liked some of Gordon's hits over the years: "Sundown," "Wreck of the Edmund Fitzgerald," "Carefree Highway," and others. More importantly, I saw Gordon in one of the first concerts I ever attended live. Forty-two years ago, my high school friend Doug Miller and I visited our college friend Kevin Smith at Miami University in Oxford, Ohio. This was forty-two years, but the memory is still fresh in my mind.

Gordon was seventy-six now. The concert may not have been quite the same, but neither am I or the rest of the audience. Gordon somehow rattled off some twenty-five songs, and he didn't fall off his stool or fall asleep while performing, or lose his voice. He entertained a crowd of some two thousand, most all of whom were nearly his age. The audience had canes, frequent bathroom breaks, and a distinctly absent smell of pot. I am sure there were lots of drugs being used, but they were likely prescribed and legal. A makeshift Walgreens pharmacy on site would have sold more product than the bar at the concert hall. The Coronado Theatre, where Gordon played, came from an era far earlier than even Gordon. Rockford has too few remnants of past wealth and glory, but this beautifully restored theater is one.

What a day! Pastor Joel, Indy and Gordon Lightfoot—that's a very satisfying day for a guy in assisted living ... my adventure style.

CHAPTER 31

NATURE AS I LEARNED TO KNOW IT

I do not think anyone can very be happy if he or she must be inside all day long. My mother never for even a minute believed my being inside all day was healthy. Shortly after my time in the ICU at Ball Hospital in Muncie, I became aware that there was something out there—something besides the four walls of my hospital room. Lying there, unable to move, I don't specifically recall wanting to be anywhere else, as moving at all was simply too daunting. In time, it became apparent to others, especially my mother, that it was not acceptable for me to spend all day on my back in my room. Indeed, my back and bottom quickly developed sores if I wasn't physically repositioned in my bed. The repositioning soon graduated to being lifted out of bed and placed in a wheelchair.

As a quadriplegic, it was not so much that my body was necessarily stiff, but there was nothing my brain could tell me to do that would make any part of my body move. At my worst, I remember the sensation of concentrating on making some part of my body, usually my right arm or an ankle, twist or rise up. It simply would not happen. I don't recall the attempts causing any pain; there was just unresponsiveness. However, my body moved if someone else moved me. Several times a day, I was lifted onto my wheelchair. My body obviously was being reframed into a seated position. I don't know why that would happen other than that it just did. Clearly my brain was sending signals that my body was incapable of receiving. I was moveable, I just could not make it happen on my own. My head would droop, and my arms would fall. Gravity could move me. I sat in my chair but could not reach for anything or intentionally cause my hands to rest on my thighs. The big battle soon became trying to hold my head up. Try as I might, my head, for the longest time, insisted on dropping toward a shoulder or facedown toward my belly. My mother was aghast; she moved my head into a straight position looking forward. She also gave me various support pillows and braces designed to hold my head in a stationary position. I found these pillows and braces annoying. I, of course, could not reach or adjust the brace with my hands. I remember her encouraging me to keep my head up, but too frequently it would just droop to one side or the other. This often upset my mother, as it was visual evidence of just how little control I had over my body. Keeping my head up was hard, and it took considerable concentration to even try. I guess I was getting a little more successful with time. Maybe I still could not hold something large in my hand, but I could move just enough so that my head either stayed up or, with oncoming muscular fatigue, collapsed forward or to one side or the other. The important thing was not my struggle to maintain my position but that my head actually moved at all. This and the act of moving my ankles were to become significant over time, indicating that maybe I was repairable and not developing further muscular disintegration. This improvement did not happen overnight but gradually, day to day. Little did I know at the time that this was to become a potential clue that maybe I was suffering from something other than ALS.

Now that my body was malleable, wheelchair living became an important part of my day. Sitting up led to looking out my window and seeing there was a world outside my room. My mother soon insisted that I get outside. I don't actually recall how quickly this started, but my mother considered it a requirement that I get out of bed. Weather permitting, nearly every day she would push me down the hall, through the double doors, and out onto the parking lot pavement. This was incredible. How long had it been? Here I was, looking at cars and the sky, and watching people come and go, even feeling the sunlight or drizzle.

Our initial journeys were relatively simple. Being outside, I was now fully aware that I was in Muncie on an asphalt parking lot that surrounded some three-quarters of the sprawling Morrison Woods facility. Why being there did not compute during many of my strange dreams was never to be clear to me. No, this was not some Waco, Texas, nursing home with an adjacent golf course; nor was it a ship docked in a Perth, Australia, dockyard (each of which I was certain of through specific dreams). The apartments across fields on the edge of the parking lot indicated I was in Muncie. My mother was tenacious. Even at her advanced age, her afternoon walks pushing me in my chair were not the only vigorous walks she had. There was the little dog Emma she lived with that required a couple of walks each day. My mother craved her brisk neighborhood jaunts, and she slowed down only when Emma paused to take care of its business, usually in the park. She was just as spirited as she pushed my chair into the lot and began our walk around the exterior of the building. People parking or going to their car in the lot would often stop and visit with us. "My, isn't it good to see you out? You look good [despite my drooping head] and so happy to be out." I have no idea if I really was capable of smiling, but I assume I was happy to be seen. "Look at these pretty plants," my mother might say. They usually looked rather sparse to me, but my mother insisted that they were still beautiful in their own way. Maybe that was her allegory for how I and other battle-worn residents actually appeared—beauty despite our ravished physical struggle.

When we were not dodging an occasional moving car, we did try to make the walk interesting. Muncie had no commercial airplanes flying overhead, but we had a lot of birds. The nearby field behind the back of the facility was home for several ducks. For part of the year, the fields collected water in small ponds—wetlands I guess they were actually. Ducks, coming and going or swimming with their baby ducklings, were a source of interest for me. Ducks, yes, but for me they were something free and alive. Unlike me, they could come and go whenever they wanted. I loved watching them. As we completed our walk, we returned to the front door of the facility, sitting on a bench watching my world go by. Soon my mother would have us chatting with others. She knew no strangers; quickly we were learning all about our new friend, whether a longtime Muncie schoolteacher or maybe a Delaware County area farmer. She made everyone feel interesting. This was usually the only way I developed new friends at Morrison Woods. Perhaps I would sit with the now familiar face at dinner tonight?

Nature walks were much different after I was transferred to facilities in Rockford. Although the old Illinois town had lovely big trees all around (it did refer to itself as the Forest City), the grounds surrounding Park Strathmoor were much more compact. We had a narrow sidewalk trail carved around the five-wing facility. I could go all the way around until I came to a locked gate in back. If the gate was unlocked, I could complete the circle around the building. However, I was to learn that the gate was never supposed to be unlocked, as that was where the more severe dementia patients spent time outside on nice days. Patients in my condition did not mingle with that crowd. Turning around at the gate actually allowed my wheelchair excursions, usually with my sister, to be twice as long, since we had to retrace our steps to complete the loop. Wheelchair walks were not that easy, as cracks in the old sidewalk were not very conducive to the wheels on a chair. My sister was good about getting me over a curb or navigating around potholes which later proved difficult once I became strong enough to go by myself. My prized electric wheelchair was no fan of curbs or potholes that might inadvertently steer me off course. By the time I was walking with my walker several months later, curbs and uneven walkways made for a good obstacle course.

Alden Park Strathmoor, Rockford, Illinois.

Although the Park Strathmoor facility was set in an urban medical office area, the old grounds were interesting. On one side there was a thick ravine. It was mysterious to me. Some sort of nasty wire fence ran through the creek, which was thick with growth. No one was getting through or across that ravine. It might as well have been the Atlantic Ocean, as there was no way I was crossing that. Most frustrating to me, just a few feet beyond was the back of an old shopping center. Driving required taking twisty roads to the shopping center, which was maybe two miles away. To my consternation, this was to become maybe my favorite shopping center in Rockford. Right across that ravine, maybe one hundred yards away, sat my Walgreens and Culver's, home of frozen custard and those great fried walleye sandwiches. It was right next door, as the squirrel scurries though the thick brush, yet so physically far away in a car. It reminded me of the frustration I sensed at Checkpoint Charlie in Berlin many years before; the East Berliners on the east side of the wall could only gaze at the freedom in West Berlin. My deprivation was really only ice cream and a fish sandwich, not a lifetime of personal freedom. I am not sure that was really a factor to me, as I had no expectation at the time of ever leaving Park Strathmoor.

Despite its limited size, Park Strathmoor proved to become an exciting nature preserve. With my sister pushing me along, we soon started noticing a few rabbits. In fact, there were two rabbits, one bolder seeming than the other. My challenge was to see just how close I could come to it before it hopped back into the brush. Two rabbits usually turn into more rabbits. We all know what rabbits like to do. Soon we discovered a baby rabbit, and this rabbit soon became my third rabbit I searched for on my walks. Fortunately, no predators for the longest time seemed to get one of my rabbits. As I recall, by the time I finally left Park Strathmoor in August 2015, now fully walking without aide, I saw that my rabbits were still there.

One species I often encountered was the bold Canada goose. These beautiful birds seemed to love Rockford for much of the year. They were everywhere. True to form, they traveled in large flocks and seemed to clearly have a leader. The term "honking goose" was ever so true. Together they would keep a banter going among themselves, and it soon became apparent that they were communicating, especially when I approached too close. In addition to the many ponds and waterways around the city, these geese were amazingly comfortable around people and would think nothing of hanging out around the Park Strathmoor facility. In truth, they became a bit of a deterrent during my walks, as I was never sure they would move from my path. Pigeons would scurry as I approached, but these large birds often required encouragement to move on. The patients sitting in the front lounge, staring out the Park Strathmoor front windows, found the Canada Goose a constant form of intrigue. Would that goose make way? Would it attack back? Would the car moving through the parking lot stop to let the flock walk across the road? There was just enough intrigue to keep things interesting. These big birds were stouter than a duck. My sister hated them, as once when out jogging, apparently too close to a nest, she was attacked by one that hit her from behind and scared her nearly to death. Missy kept her distance on our walks, though I did enjoy seeing how close I could get to a few. I was, of course, unprepared for an attack, so the game was partially to see how brave I was approaching one. Fortunately, the goose would usually just waddle away. By the way, the sidewalks often reflected that geese do, in fact, "shit like a goose." Initially I thought it might be deer droppings, but there were no deer around the place.

In addition to geese and rabbits, I soon noticed many interesting species of birds making an occasional visit to our bird feeder outside the front window. This made for much excitement for residents who seemed to spend most of the day looking out the lobby windows. In time I eventually discovered a large brown muskrat that chose to live by the ravine. Its hole was deep and right on the edge of my walkway out back. It became a game to see if I could sneak up and discover him coming out of the deep hole. Sometimes only its black head was peeking out of the hole, but not infrequently the muskrat might be on the lawn. On seeing me, it would run and dive into the hole, safe from my gaze. I wonder if the little fellow is still in that hole?

Rockford had some surprisingly beautiful Midwest terrain. The forests were thick and engrossing on Rockford's often rolling terrain. State parks nearby became a favorite for my walks with my sister. The gorgeous Anderson Gardens in Rockford is billed as one of the most extraordinary Japanese gardens in America. We spent many days exploring its pathways, dating back from when I was pushed in a wheelchair up through when I was walking without assistance. The gardens were my favorite place to play with my Leica camera. Nature was such an inspiration for me after spending way too long on my back in bed. Yes, my mother was right, patients are blessed if they can get outside.

CHAPTER 32
ROARING THUNDER

They arrived one Friday afternoon with a piercing roar—literally a roaring, gritty noise. It peaked as they revved up their engines. There were shouts, but mostly deafening masculine noise.

How many of them were there? Maybe, by my quick guesstimate, forty? They looked rough; they had chains and wore the black vests that had become familiar to me following the biker assaults in Waco shown on TV earlier that week. The black t-shirts, faded dirty jeans, and occasional biker chick on the back of a motorcycle seat left no doubt that this was the real thing. A gang or a club? Their hair was often long, and unkempt from the wind; the sunburned skin and thick beards added to the intimidation. Several had stitched "the Goons Gang" on their leather vests.

Mostly, they seemed out of place at the Park Strathmoor skilled-care nursing home. We rarely had unusual visitors of this sort—certainly not noisy ones. Once an old hippie-looking country Christian band appeared, but I found out later that they were there to entertain their aged mother and her country and religious friends. To the contrary, this particular group was so noticeable that the staff, patients, and administrators all came to see.

It turned out that late the night before, an ambulance had delivered a very sick patient to that back entry at E-Unit. The red glow from the ambulance lights and the beeping as it backed up to the delivery door woke me up. I listened. Soon a man on a gurney was shuttled by my room and placed in a vacant room two doors away from me. There was lots of staff activity in the halls but little I could figure out. Sick people often were sent to Park Strathmoor late at night. The next morning I might wake up and have a new floor mate.

This particular next morning was busy. Word spread that our new guest was very ill; in fact, he was not expected to survive a week. Skin cancer reportedly was killing the forty-one-year-old man. The staff was very attentive as his family checked him in. What family members I saw appeared a little tough and not what most call attractive. They rarely smiled or acknowledged hellos. But they were clearly very concerned that the sick man be comfortable.

The roar of motorcycle club members started later that afternoon. Word got out that the sick man had a last wish. He wanted to go fishing one last time with his buddies—his gang, his club. Within minutes, a fire department ambulance appeared, and in front of his entire troop he was loaded into the ambulance. Motorcyclists gathered, and soon, with a huge collective roar, they led the ambulance away. I am told they were going fishing one last time.

After a few hours, later that day, the roar reappeared. I got out of bed to see the commotion outside my window. This time even more cyclists and their chicks had joined. The ambulance pulled up, and the doors opened. As the man was wheeled out, the crowd soon gathered around. Members of the seemingly tough gang were there to see their buddy off. Rough men cried. Many shook his hand and kissed him on the cheek. Others could hardly keep their composure. They walked aimlessly around the bikes, hugged each other, and kissed their women. Many could not hold back their sobbing. Finally the group reassembled around their friend. Propped up, the stricken man stared ahead. Pictures were taken as if they were members of a football or rugby team. Everyone wanted in.

A few days later, the man remained alive but very sick. Family members, some looking tough and some not, appeared to be keeping a vigil, waiting for the inevitable. The staff was attentive, but nothing seemed to be improving. The crowd was long gone. But most poignant to me was that several times per day I heard the roar of one or two motorcycles outside my window. I realized friends were driving up to his window and revving their engines in salute before heading off. It was touching. It showed loyalty. It was love expressed in a way unfamiliar to me, but it was love nevertheless. When the man finally passed, silence returned. The motorcycles went away, although I am certain the hurt remained for many.

There was a lot to learn about life and death here at my nursing home.

CHAPTER 33
"I WANT TO BE OUT OF HERE ..."

During spring and summer in 2015, my life at Park Strathmoor was beginning to get me down. Even with the good friends on staff and the help of my prescribed daily dose of my "happy pill," Prozac, I was feeling as if I was outgrowing my need for the facility. I was walking, I was active, and I was getting restless. I pestered Missy to take me out, pretty much anywhere. Our trips around Rockford included going for my beloved Culver's frozen custard, visiting Walgreens for developing photographs, going to Marshalls for any clothes, as I was no longer spending my day in a gown, hitting up the Stockholm Inn for Swedish pancakes, and shopping at the local Valli Produce grocery store for its exotic foods. Next to my bed, I kept boxes of food, such as cereals, crackers, cookies—whatever moved me but did not require refrigeration. No one else on the E-Wing had these privileges. My closet starting filling with new clothes, and my nightstand with books from Barnes & Noble or a local discount store. Everything seemed new and exciting for me. Over the past several years, I had forgotten how fun it was to shop. Possessions I had accumulated in my prior life were all in storage in Dallas or in Missy's basement or had been disbursed during my illness. More importantly, I was now physically much stronger. I wanted to do things. I was strong, though not by the standards of a truly healthy person, but I was getting to feel as if skilled care was too restrictive. After my time at the RIC the previous spring, I was beginning to get some serious follow-up physical rehab in Rockford several hours per week. Progress seemed slow, but over several weeks I was becoming mobile. More importantly, my attitude was good. ALS was no longer hanging over my head.

My six weeks at RIC were an amazing experience. I was with some other very physically impaired patients. I describe the experience as in some ways reminiscent of my years at summer camp while a boy. My schedule was planned by doctors and was filled all day, just as they keep children at a camp busy. I felt constantly on the move, going from one activity to another. After an early breakfast in my room, I was soon in a sophisticated therapy room, ready to be twisted, turned, stretched, and otherwise challenged. After a bout on the mat, I was usually given an hour to rest or otherwise vegetate. Then some other therapist would pop in and announce it was time to practice swallowing or organizing blocks or trying to write words. One time they had me paint a birdhouse. I remember being proud of the decor I painted, which I modeled on the Swedish, Norwegian, and Danish flags. None of the other painters that day were so inspired. I felt there was some creative life left in me. Within another hour or two, I was put in my wheelchair and taken down the winding hall to a very modern fitness room. The room was packed with one-of-a-kind treadmills, workout machines, and other progressive machines. I was frequently placed in a leather saddle that allowed my feet to stand on the treadmill as I hung from the ceiling. I would work my feet, starting to walk as I hung suspended in the air. The sensation of walking was incredible, although it did not take long before my groin got sore. I remember commenting more than once that clearly no man who was even marginally endowed had invented that contraption. As I got more efficient at the exercise, I graduated to a treadmill that operated with me in a weightless box. Walking never felt so good. When I was finally discharged from RIC, I was by no means self-sufficient; nor had I even stood under my own power. Nevertheless, I was discharged with specific instructions on how to continue to improve. My return to Rockford found me physically advancing and with a positive attitude, but I was certainly still facing lots of challenges, as I was essentially still a quadriplegic.

The remainder of 2014 and much of spring 2015 found me in daily physical rehabilitation either in Park Strathmoor or at an advanced therapy facility in Rockford named Van Matre. Initially we worked on standing or seating myself in my now-treasured electric wheelchair. The chair was loaned to me by the Chicago ALS Foundation. I soon loved the chair and its ability to allow me to zip around the facility. My hands worked well enough to change the controls and steer the machine around the halls. Best of all, I figured out how to elevate the speed controls despite the frequent attempts by staff to slow me down. The only time they really took over control was the day I plowed my chair into the front door and nearly broke my foot. Damned thing kept going forward while I thought I was backing up.

One day in the Park Strathmoor physical therapy room, Brian, one of the assistant therapists, announced that we were going to try something new. My chair was directed to one end of the parallel bars. The bars served as a ten-yard track on which patients learned to walk. I remember being challenged to pull myself up from my chair and try to stand as I held on to the two bars on either side of me. I was skeptical, but as I pulled myself up the trainers and patients in the therapy room began to clap and offer encouraging words. I managed to take one step while, I am sure, filled with pride. After pausing a few seconds, I plopped back down on my chair. For the first time since my grand mal seizure in September 2011, I was actually standing without assistance. Sure, it was one small step for a man, but I felt as if it were a miracle for mankind as I knew it. (Cool thought; wonder where I got that?) Taking a step never felt so good to me. The following afternoon, we repeated the process. This time Brian did not offer to help me up. Standing was easier than it was the day before; I remember taking a few steps—maybe three or four. Now this really felt like an accomplishment, as I could actually boast that I was walking a bit under my own power. The next day, I walked the full ten yards, turned, and came back the ten yards to my chair. I was not scared, but I must admit to feeling cocky. The next week, I practiced with my own walker—a four-legged stand that challenged people to keep their balance. Nothing, however, exceeded the day I did not just walk the ten or so yards to Brian but also stepped past him and out into the hall. People who had never seen me stand up now saw me actually pushing along behind my walker. Although a trainer or two stood behind me holding a chair I could drop into if I tired, I remember that day being determined to walk out into the lobby. There was a large reception desk area that I frequently used to take my wheelchair around, sort of reminiscent of a traffic round-about. This time I walked out and circled it before returning to my base. Patients and CNAs seemed to be shocked. This was at least four times the distance I had ever tried to walk. As I received cheers and encouragement from my friends, I was so proud. Only later did I reflect on how difficult the scene must have seemed to many of the patients; I was to come to realize that very few patients ever had any realistic hope of standing or walking again. That was sobering, but it was still wonderful to be able to provide some inspiration for others. What seemed like a natural progression for me was to many at Park Strathmoor an unimaginable achievement.

Soon walking with my walker was a given to me. I was mobile now. I lost the use of my cherished electrical wheelchair, but a new world was opening. At Van Matre, where the physical therapy was more advanced and taxing on my body, they soon had me walking without the walker. It could seem tenuous at times, but my progress was rapid. Within days I was increasing my distance and showing I could find my way around the multi-roomed complex. Occupational therapy included such tasks as using the bathroom (both ways!) alone, showing I could pour a bowl of cereal, and showing I could make macaroni and cheese from a dry mix. (I am not sure I had ever bothered to make that in my whole life. I would have preferred to make some blackened redfish or something else.) Before long, my progress was considered impressive. My simple walking tasks had turned into walking straight lines and hitting golf balls. By now I was feeling too advanced for what Park Strathmoor could provide. Although I was still an occasional fall risk (and still heavily on prescribed drugs), I was now mobile enough to go places. When I could, I jumped at the chance to go with Missy on any errand she was willing to make. Walgreens and Marshalls were my favorites; I would come back to the facility loaded with snacks and cereals from Walgreens and new inexpensive clothes off the designer racks at Marshalls. The trips to Valli Produce were my favorite, as I was soon loading up on Italian cookies, good sandwiches, fruit, foreign bottled water like Evian, and even a steady supply of bottled Swedish lingonberries for my breakfast pancakes and cereal. If I was being well behaved in my sister's sole and exclusive opinion, we might go to Culver's for fried walleye sandwiches, Stockholm Inn for Swedish pancakes, or to Starbucks for something expensive if not exotic.

In time, this privileged lifestyle began to take a toll. Patients at the home were usually very aware (if, in fact, they had the capacity to be) of what was going on around them. While we consciously tried not to be obvious about my excursions or purchases, it became apparent to many that this seemed unfair. While there was generally a lot of goodwill between patients, it soon became a topic of conversation about what I was getting to do next. These were truly struggling people, many of whom were rarely, if ever, getting to leave Park Strathmoor by any means other than the ambulance. Nearly all were on public assistance, as rumor had it that I was one of very few full-pay patients. While some had family visiting, many did not. Their whole world centered around a routine that included subpar meals in the assisted-living dining room; light, if any, physical therapy; and a whole lot of time sitting in their wheelchairs while staring out the large front windows of the lobby. They saw nearly everyone who came and went. The mailman and FedEx drivers were their friends. Family members seeking out a select few were often kind to all but were certainly not there to see the patient who was necessarily alone. Indeed, the delivery of a flower vase; the arrival of an entertainer, such as an aspiring pianist taking advantage of the grand piano in the lobby; or even the once per week church service leaders were cause for notice and discussion. You can imagine the stir that was caused by the elderly Czech couple who showed up once per month and performed old country waltzes to music playing on a small CD player in the lobby. Many enjoyed the sounds and any attention.

As my physical mobility advanced, it became a daily occurrence for me to go outside and walk the grounds surrounding the facility. I needed exercise. As long as I promised to stay on the pathway, I could go whenever I wanted. I came back with stories of my adventures, such as seeing geese on the grounds. I reported the good news that we still had three rabbits hopping around. Others were also permitted to take a walk, but they had to be escorted by staff or family. Even this was not possible for many of the patients. Between my excursions and my walks around the grounds, I sensed I was becoming a source for understandable envy. This was increasingly uncomfortable for me. I found I was shading the truth to my friends about what I was doing. Trips to Walgreens were reportedly made to get medicine, when usually they were often made to get food, have photographs developed, or buy magazines. My morning excursions were to get therapy at Van Matre (poor me), even though half the time was spent for lunch or a visit to Marshalls. All of these are things I grew to crave, but these wonderful folks could not experience them. I did not like not being fully honest to my friends. The crowning blow for me came on the day the executive director called me in to say that she was receiving complaints from residents that I was free to go walking outside while they were forced to stay inside. She asked that I discontinue my frequent walks around the grounds. Suddenly I felt as if a noose were around my neck; my cherished taste of freedom was being deprived. (Ultimately, my friends on the staff let me sneak out a back door and walk around, provided I did not walk by the big lobby window in the front.)

While my impatience grew as I became more self-reliant, the real factor was my frustration with being left alone. I had no Rockford outside friends. My sister and her son Peter were extraordinary about visiting me when she was in town (and when we were not spatting over one of my silly demands), but no one can visit a disabled patient often enough when he or she is confined to a private room. Jack was kind to take me to movies at the local AMC, but that, of course, was on a limited basis. Ann and her family loved to travel and made frequent trips to fascinating places like New Mexico, often with little or no prior warning to me. This was certainly within their rights, especially considering how much time and attention they were giving to me. But to me, the patient, this meant no trips around town, no Walgreens, and no walleye sandwiches while they were gone. In short, they were long, boring days. From my perspective, the cup overflowed when I counted seventeen days (most consecutive) in the month of July in which I had no outside visitors and no chance to get out. Taste a little freedom and you want it daily. Back while I was not conscious or capable of getting out of bed on my own, this was no big deal. Poor me. I am sure my CNA Angela saw it as "You poor, spoiled baby; so, your sister wants to have some fun being away, and here you are, all stuck here … my, my, my." Big help she was, but I was not about to say anything to her that might piss her off or give her incentive to also leave me alone.

By August I was determined to get out of Park Strathmoor. I began insisting we begin looking for a less restrictive care facility—one where I got an actual room with a kitchenette and was free to come and go. Most importantly, I really wanted to live somewhere that provided ESPN. Ann started scouting for places around Rockford that qualified for my disability insurance requirements and was affordable. Though it probably took only a few weeks for her to research this, it seemed like forever to me. I was so ready to get out of there.

CHAPTER 34
AUGUST 24 MOVE DATE

August 24, 2015, could not come soon enough. Finally, after twenty-three months, I was cleared by my neurologist and ready to move from my skilled-care facility at Park Strathmoor. I was excited but also sad to be leaving the familiar surroundings of my nursing facility, my home for several years. I was now physically leaving, moving, with the help of Jack and Missy, to an assisted-living center a few miles away, Crimson Pointe.

Moving to an assisted-living center was a big step up for me, at least conceptually. For most elderly, it is a hard adjustment. Usually it indicates the presence of health or mobility issues that need frequent attention. This means serious doubts about one's ability to live alone or care for a spouse. Help is needed on a daily basis. It also involves a likely inescapable realization that you, as a fortunate one who has lived so long, are now entering the last phase of your life. Most who move to Crimson Pointe never leave, or they have only one final hospital or hospice stay.

Approaching inevitable death is strange in a positive way. I have observed that while few assisted-living patients are happy about being in an assisted-living facility, most don't seem to fight it or resent it. Having a nurse's assistant on hand means that you will not forget to take your medicine. That pill that drops on the floor will be picked up. Meals aren't much of a challenge any longer. You will be bathed, and you probably don't even have to leave the facility to get your hair done. Some allow friendships to be fostered and encouragement to reign, and they enjoy a perspective that allows you to want to eat your meals at an early hour, likely before your family and coworkers ever would be willing. If you wake up at 4:00 a.m. every morning, getting in line at the dining room by 6:45 a.m. for a good breakfast is not so strange. If you have breakfast so early, why not join the rest of the residents lined up at 10:30 a.m. for your primary meal, dinner, at 11:00 a.m.? Everyone seemed to be there early even though all meals had a two-hour window. Supper line at 3:45 p.m.—why not? The food is hot then. It sure seems to make being in bed for the night by 6:30 p.m. or so all the more plausible.

Moving to Crimson Pointe was not, surprisingly, a big adjustment for me. Early on I did not do what most everyone else did at the facility. Park Strathmoor served meals at 8:00 a.m., 12:00 p.m., and close to 6:00 p.m. in the evening. I, of course, had the added luxury of being served all meals in my room. "Room Service!" was the gleeful pronouncement Jacki would greet me with most mornings as my tray was brought in. It became such an annoyance to dear Angela as I got better physically that it soon became a wonderful point of contention each morning. Her dedication to my becoming in all ways independent was greatly fostered by her desire to send me to the dining room and make me take care of myself. So here I was, moving into a new facility with no personal experience of eating in a dining room during the last several years. Admittedly, at Park Strathmoor, where so many residents were in really bad physical shape, I realized that some powers that be were intentionally sparing me the experience of sharing tables with the disabled or those who needed spoon-feeding attention from aides. That experience, I think, would have been very tough for me psychologically as I sought to be more independent.

My eating travails never materialized at Crimson Pointe. I was used to eating late, so I came into the dining room fifteen or thirty minutes before closing time. For me this usually meant having most meals with only two or three other stragglers in the entire room. While not very sociable, this was not an intentional snub of others but a way to think positively and know that better days were ahead for me. Rather than some of the natural depression that comes with feeling trapped in a no-way-out atmosphere, I soon became happy with being substantially on my own, keeping an eye on my future.

One of my favorite aspects of meals at both Park Strathmoor and Crimson Pointe was my supplementation of my institutional dining with my own favorite foods Missy and I could buy at local grocery stores. I now had my first in-room refrigerator. The institution's cereals tasted a lot better with my fresh blueberries or scoops of lingonberry jam from Stockholm Inn. I added my own granola products, cider, apple butter, or pumpkin butter to spruce up breakfasts. Nearly every sandwich or pizza slice the place served received my added dose of the special Chicago hot peppers I discovered on Rockford-area Italian beef sandwiches.

All of this is primarily to admit that I was very conscious that I was getting much better. The residents at the assisted-living center were often older than those at the skilled-care facility, Park Strathmoor. I met at least one resident that first week at Crimson Pointe who was a sprightly one hundred! She was a joy to talk to. Interests varied depending on patients' ages and points in life. Both Park Strathmoor and Crimson Pointe were proud of their daily activity schedules. Fortunately, my mind came back sufficiently so that reading and watching cable news and the endless sporting events kept me away from a weekly proffered diet of bingo, crafts, and trivia games. These things were inspiring and necessary for some, but they were not my scene as I got better. My gap in age was beginning to show.

After a few months at Crimson Pointe, I was able to realize an active lifestyle far in excess of that of my fellow residents. Most mornings, I liked walking around in the adjacent neighborhoods (yes, even on those seemingly endless zero-degree winter mornings), riding the rarely used stationary bicycle I discovered in an activity room, and especially using Uber to venture out on my own to other parts of Rockford. Hitting golf balls at the Golf Shack driving range became frequent "therapy" for my balance, though this was maybe questionable when I followed it up with an occasional pint of Guinness at the tavern next door. Generally, I hated to sit still in my room if there was not otherwise a Dodgers, Cowboys, Northwestern, or SMU game to be seen or heard. Biggest thing? I believed I was now truly on my way back to an independent life, maybe like the one I used to know. No more wheelchairs, no more walkers, no cane—just independence in what I wanted to do.

One of my fondest memories of my newfound freedom at Crimson Pointe was making an occasional trip to Chicago. Although some residents were occasionally taken out by family for overnights, few, if any, seemed to want to make a habit of this. After my time the summer before at the RIC in downtown Chicago, my infatuation with that enchanting city only grew. I was raised to consider Chicago (along with Dallas in a different sense) the most dynamic and colorful place a Midwestern boy from central Indiana could imagine. My father had spent much of my teenage years making regular sales-related trips to the city for his Muncie-based advertising agency. I always assumed, "Poor Will, he has to go to Chicago again. I sure bet he would rather be home with us." One weekend in the fall of my junior year in high school, my father took me to visit Northwestern University. As we checked into the stately Drake Hotel, located on Michigan Avenue in the heart of downtown Chicago, I soon learned the truth of my father's love of the city as the registration clerk greeted him with "Welcome back, Mr. Millard, we show that this is your two hundred twenty-fifth night staying with us." I was awed. In those days, Chicago was to me exotic, muscular, and full of unique urban life. I had been quietly indoctrinated in it, reading the *Chicago Tribune* whenever I could, loving the city's brawny tales, ethnic flavor, and massive skyscrapers. I enjoyed Mike Royko's book *Boss*, about Mayor Daley, which completely captivated my high school–aged imagination as to how this very different place functioned. My introductions to the city included the magic of The Berghoff Restaurant, the Billy Goat Tavern, the *Chicago Tribune* building, the Chicago River boat architectural tours, and the (mostly mediocre) football of Northwestern University, where my parents had gone to college. But for a bad impression at the Northwestern student admissions office and a subsequently gorgeous Texas weather day at friendly SMU in Dallas, I probably would have tried to go to Northwestern with the aim of moving to Chicago for my career. (Unfortunately for me, the Northwestern admissions officer on that visit spent much of my meeting and campus tour espousing the virtues of the school's overwhelming support for George McGovern and the student-led protests against our government that had shut down an Evanston street.) This rock-ribbed small-town Indiana Republican high-schooler was subsequently swayed by the unusually conservative (and happy) bent of SMU students, the on-campus beauty and sunshine, and the outdoor swimming pool, not to mention Texas's eighteen-year-old drinking age. It may have been an omen that my father took me that day in Chicago to see SMU play a rare football game against Northwestern. The Mustangs beat the Wildcats 21–20. I found myself secretly rooting for SMU. Chicago, nevertheless, was important and enthralling to me, and I returned every time I could in the subsequent years.

Northwestern stayed my second favorite college football team, and being far from Texas, I was now watching and listening to every Northwestern game possible while lying in my quasi-paralyzed condition at Park Strathmoor. Even at Park Strathmoor I spent Saturday afternoons alone listening on radio and imagining the flavor of the fall afternoons in the purple-draped Wildcats' stadium. Northwestern football was actually pretty good at the time, not infrequently knocking off big state schools (and even Notre Dame!), and I loved its team feistiness. It was not without my notice that my onetime Dallas friend, Rob, and his family were now living in Evanston, only a few blocks from campus. Now that I was relatively free to travel, I soon was bugging Rob to let me make my first out-of-town and all alone weekend venture to a Northwestern Big Ten game.

With Missy's consent, I was soon planning my first out-of-Rockford weekend escape. Rob probably was wary of whether this was realistic or not, and I am sure his wife was concerned about what they were getting into with hosting an invalid overnight. Missy asked, "Billy, is this wise? Really? How are you going to get there? Jack can't take you; he is working." Rockford was some ninety miles west of Chicago, being nearer to Wisconsin and Iowa. All it seemed I had been hearing about previously from my sister's family was how easy it was to take the special bus service that ran each day from Rockford's tawdry Clock Tower highway resort motel. (Mostly well past its time, the Clock Tower was still labeled a resort because it had indoor recreational facilities including a few empty bars, a Hooters-like sports restaurant, a conference room, and an old swimming pool with a waterslide.) That was the solution! I would Uber over to the bus stop at Clock Tower and take the bus to Chicago! The bus route not only went to downtown Chicago but also made an interim stop at the Chicago airport. In fact, given Chicago's traffic snarls and expensive parking facilities, many Rockford residents routinely took the bus instead of driving a car. Rob said that it would be easier for him to pick me up outside the international terminal at O'Hare Airport, as Evanston was a suburb somewhat north of downtown. The deal was done; nothing would stop me. I was going to see Northwestern play its first game of the new 2015 football season. To the somewhat muted dismay of the Crimson Pointe administrators, I announced my plans and asked to have my pills packaged in advance so I could take them on the two-day trip. One of the principles of assisted living is that patients are never trusted to manage their own pill taking. You can imagine the notion of my being trusted with this responsibility (even though I had been taking the same pills for several years and knew them well), but their policy was not to restrict an assisted-living resident's ability to come and go. A more pronounced objection, of course, came from my dear mother, "Oh, Billy [I was now fifty-nine years old], is this really a good idea? Be sure to take your medicine with you. Be careful." This coming from the loving, concerned mother who put me alone on planes bound for Far East Asia the day after I graduated from high school. How perceptions of me had changed.

The trip went fine. Uber picked me up at Crimson Pointe and delivered me to the bus on time. My ride was a wonderful adventure in my mind: *Were those deer crossing that farmland we were passing by?* I was all alone! Rob found me on the curb outside the upper deck of the international terminal (thank God for cell phones), and soon we were off to a very Chicago authentic local breakfast diner. After reacquainting with Rob's wife and now incredibly active two high school daughters, we went to the game. I felt sure I was now in heaven. Big Ten football, a band playing, the color purple everywhere … what had I been missing these several years? Best, Northwestern was playing Stanford that day, which was the third-ranked team in the nation in the preseason polls. Going to a Northwestern game in these circumstances with my friends was a special feeling, one I had not experienced in many years. At the game, Rob had prime fifty-yard-line seats, up-front parking, and halftime access to the big stadium club. I felt as if I were being treated like royalty: drinks in the stadium club were free to me, game day food was plentiful, and seemingly every big hitter in Chicago business was up there. The Wildcats even pulled the upset that day, drawing national attention and general glee all over Evanston. I had not been to a Northwestern game in several years (when Rob hosted my then little son and me), but I never felt so "back." In my mind, I was free again, independently doing what I loved most. Give me a sporting event, some beers, and a day with a close friend; for me, nothing can be much better.

Without seeking prior approval, Rob and I spent that evening hitting what I call some of the cool bars of Northside Chicago. His wife, Alice, and the girls had left for her family's beach house following the game. It was Labor Day weekend, and that's what some big city people get to do. How cool. After our postgame naps (me in a lounge chair outside under a big tree that dropped small nuts) on this perfect early fall day, we headed off to some of the area's new bars—no chains or franchises, of course, just the innovative and creative spots that were now occupying every cool old storefront building on many of the backstreets. Bars were crowded, and the people looked big-city sophisticated. Women looked like potential models, and the men dressed as if they shopped somewhere more cutting-edge than Brooks Brothers. Style was everywhere in that urban casual sort of way. I was there proudly wearing one of my favorite new Euro-hip Moods of Norway shirts I had recently bought on Amazon. The rest of me was undoubtedly in "cool" clothes I had bought on trips with my sister to Marshalls of Rockford. (Hey, don't knock Rockford's finest; look carefully enough and great designer stuff occasionally sneaks in there. Buy it now or you likely won't see it again until you find a Nordstrom's in a big city.) I missed my Texas-made Nocona western boots, but alas they were probably in storage someplace back home.

We did our part to blow it out that night. What started with a nice scotch and water at the first bar changed to a beer at the next bars so I could seem to show some sense of self-control and caution. As we moved from bars to increasingly cool cocktail lounges, my adventurous spirit grew. Soon we were thinking up drinks I had not even thought of for several years. "Manhattan ... what's in that again?" The next place, which was an old speakeasy supposedly dating back to prohibition days, reminded me of those Old Fashioneds I used to like. These cocktails, which were alarmingly multicolored, came with one block of ice, bigger than a cube but definitely fashionable. As I hadn't spent a great deal of time recently in sophisticated cocktail lounges, I realized maybe this use of one block of ice wasn't really innovative, but it was to me. Like Uber, mini iPads, and many other contemporary things I never foresaw before my adventure began, I was always on the watch for things that were new to me.

Before too late in the evening, Rob announced it was time to go home. By now I was no longer caring much about being responsible, and I wanted more fun. When would I ever be free to do this again? For whatever reason, God (assuming he was even on duty that night) seemed to forgive me for my behavior. After a stop at an all-night news stand, which I don't think either of us knew at the time why we were there (we have a history together of finding quirky, colorful bookstores), Rob managed to get us home by way of tiny backstreets. I was a bit wobbly, I recall, as we got to the house. I hoped there was nothing odd about that, as I was always kind of wobbly back then, with or without alcohol. Poor Rob. I think he was probably thinking he might be killing me. I had been assigned the third-floor guest room up in the attic, and I remember his steadying hand pressed on my back as I climbed the steep and narrow staircase, wobbling back and forth. Once up, I promised to be up early in the morning, as we were both meeting my old law school friend Glenn for breakfast at my favorite Chicago-area Swedish diner the next morning. I had enough wits to know that under no condition would I be walking near those stairs that night. What I did not expect was how soundly I would sleep that night, way up high in that attic loft. When I finally woke up, it was nearly 9:00 a.m. Curses! My poor buddy had arrived much earlier at the restaurant, having come all the way from South Bend. After a classic Swedish breakfast, Glenn and I headed for Wrigley Field and a colorful Cubs game. We had more beers and a bratwurst, of course— good times. What a great weekend away from my assisted-living facility! I was exhausted for the next week. Somehow, much to my good fortune, I did not die; nor I am dead yet.

CHAPTER 35
CRIMSON POINTE

Anytime I live someplace for a few years, I think it is always exciting to make a move. The only way I knew how to really clean out my house full of things was to move. This forthcoming move did not necessarily involve clearing out too many things; instead it meant having a place to now put my things that had been in storage in Missy's basement in Rockford. My health was improving in the spring of 2015, and Park Strathmoor no longer satisfied my needs. I made it clear to my sister/guardian that I needed to do something soon. I pushed to return to Dallas, but she had legitimate concerns that, physically and mentally, it was too big of a move for me at this time. Indeed, my latest psychiatrist's evaluation (prepared in June 2015) concluded that while I was significantly better and certainly not suffering from dementia, I still had impulsivity issues. To me that just meant I wanted to move on in life. I often felt, lying there in skilled care, that I was literally wasting another day of precious life each day I did not progress to getting out. If that was too impulsive, so be it, but that seemed to mean to the psychiatrist that I was not fully recovered. I believe the doctor said I was maybe about 85 percent recovered, but that missing 15 percent, she projected, was going to cause me much frustration over the next few months and even years.

Missy came up with the reasonable suggestion that maybe I should consider moving out of my skilled-care facility and into an actual Rockford-based assisted-living facility. This, for me, would be a big step on my journey to return to society, while not so radical as abandoning family.

Assisted-living facilities serve a real purpose. However, for most residents this meant things were getting worse or at least more difficult in their daily lives. Assisted living provided on-site care but with limited supervision. Patients who could no longer keep their drugs straight, cook their own food, or needed bathing help were perfect for assistance in living. Often, residents had walking or eating problems, frequently being in danger of falling or choking. Fortunately, this level of care was still covered by my disability insurance and government benefits. Because this was a step up from skilled care for me and neither my guardian nor neurologists were ready to give me a totally clean bill of health, we turned our search to Rockford assisted-living facilities rather than the more aggressive independent senior living.

I know I was no longer fully satisfied with my situation at Park Strathmoor and my attitude could be frustrating for my sister and her family. I was initially angry that I would not be returning to Dallas, especially by the end of the year. It had been my goal once I realized that my health was starting to improve. I wanted to reconnect with my children who were still in Dallas. I knew I still had lots of friends and Dallas was my definition of home. As I became more impatient and irritable, Missy finally gave up her caution and sped up the process of finding a new facility for me in Rockford.

It is amusing to look back and see what the process entailed. There were several nice assisted-living facilities around Rockford. However, some seemed to have more elderly people that required lots more attention than others. I was clear that I viewed the move as improving my situation so that my next move would be to independent senior living or an actual adult apartment. As I saw it, the less time spent in assisted care, the better. Most people going into assisted living are not expecting to move on to more independence (other than the few placed for rehabilitation to recover from a temporary problem such as surgery or a broken bone). For many, family had moved them out of their home for safety reasons or they required too much attention for standard senior living. Not surprisingly, moving into assisted living is often very depressing for the elderly (indeed, anyone) as they may sense they are nearing the last stop. My selfish fear was that I would not have enough upbeat friends, or even friends with whom I who could effectively communicate.

As we visited various facilities, it was apparent that my priorities for a new home were not always the same as Missy's. We both agreed that we could not pursue an expensive facility or one that required a nonrefundable buy-in or hefty deposit. Missy knew this because she knew I was essentially broke. I had not received a paycheck for some four or five years, and I was coming out of a divorce settlement that included substantial legal fees. To me the primary issues were how long I would have to be in the place and whether I could freely come and go. We identified three or four facilities that seemed to fit. While Missy favored the classier-looking facilities, I decided that the most important concern was whether I could come and go and whether the facility was situated on wide multilane streets that would put me at risk when trying to cross. Rockford obviously had a habit of spending tax dollars on constructing wide avenues that commercial and residential development was nowhere near yet requiring. In fact, Rockford's economy at the time was so poor that for every new commercial development aimed to serve consumers, there seemed to be another that had closed down and remained vacant. I never saw a place with more new age Christian churches innovatively occupying failed shopping centers and warehouses. I narrowed our search for a new home to a couple of modest facilities that had some commercial development. (Okay, Lowes and Chick-fil-A being nearby won me over.) Without having to venture across any seven- to eight-lane roadways, Crimson Pointe proved most acceptable. The physical location played a big role in my decision. I soon learned how to order Uber rides and found a great walking trail through some quiet neighborhoods, past a few medical office buildings, past the Lowes warehouse, and, best of all, through a Porsche dealership. More than once, my heart became set on a used red Porsche sports car. I tried to sell the idea to Missy that one would be a nice investment, but that idea failed since I did not have a driver's license, let alone clearance to drive.

My little one-room apartment at Crimson Pointe was not much bigger than my hospital-style room at Park Strathmoor. It did have a small kitchenette that gave me access to my first microwave in four years, a modest walk-in closet, and a clean bathroom with shower. Crimson Pointe had a nice, formal dining room downstairs and even a small coffee room (cleverly labeled a "bistro"). With freedom to come and go, I felt as if I had checked into a Four Seasons hotel.

The residents at Crimson Pointe were elderly—in fact more so than many patients at Park Strathmoor. I was easily the youngest person there, as rather than suffering from some significant disability these folks in assisted living were just getting feeble. At Park Strathmoor, this was not often the case. While we had several patients in their nineties, many were younger but had suffered a stroke, disease, or accident. Many were not expected to live very long. At Crimson Pointe, the residents tended to be active; many of them occupied their days playing card games. For me, playing games was not my idea of fun, as I was ready for more physical action.

My daily routine soon began with a slightly delayed appearance for breakfast. In fact, for nearly every meal at Crimson Pointe, I timed my arrival in the dining room close to closing time. Only later did I come to realize that showing up late was probably unfair to the kindly wait staff who wanted to go home. Crimson Pointe residents liked to line up in their wheelchairs fifteen minutes before service began for breakfast, lunch, and dinner. They reminded me of airplanes lined up and waiting to take off at O'Hare. With their early eating schedules, I didn't meet many of the diners. As a frequent late diner, I discovered my selfish luxury of getting to eat alone. If I went early, I had to share a table, which meant making conversation. It had been some three years since I had last shared tables with others. At Morrison Woods, eating with people who could not communicate or serve themselves was very depressing. The fact that I was also one of those noncommunicative people did not seem to bother me. Sitting alone and facing a wall in the dining room at Crimson Pointe undoubtedly made me appear unfriendly to those diners who could discern such a thing. Not to be rude, but I was not there to make friends but just to get healthy and leave.

Winter day at Crimson Pointe.

My time at Crimson Pointe was usually pleasant. The staff and residents were friendly and tolerant of my ways. My long walks were not discouraged; nor did anyone seem to object to my use of Uber to escape occasionally from the facility. I think I was just seen as a friendly but strange guy who liked to disappear. When the weather was mild, I enjoyed going to the nearby driving range to work on my balance by swinging a golf club. At Van Matre, my physical progression had reached the point where hitting golf balls was considered prescribed therapy to improve my balance. The golf range is something I miss the most about my Crimson Pointe experience. I did not ask about prescribing the post-range beer, but I suppose it was a form of occupational therapy. After all, one has to master lifting that cold mug to his mouth.

One of the benefits of moving into my one-room apartment at Crimson Pointe was that Missy soon began letting me open some of my boxes of stuff that had been stored in her basement since I had left Dallas. There had been no room at Park Strathmoor. This meant reacquainting with my boxes of Lord Nelson stuff. Each box I opened was like Christmas morning for me. Pictures were retrieved and soon were being hung on most every open space on my walls. Boxes of books were emptied, and my personal library started coming back to life. Am I the only person who thinks it is perfectly logical to have collected some 125 books and publications about the life of Lord Nelson?

Besides creating a wonderful form of clutter, my books and Nelson items seemingly everywhere, it soon created a possible mental health issue. My things came out of boxes but—shortly, I hoped—would need to be repacked for when I moved out of Crimson Pointe. Residents of nursing facilities are not expected to have much stuff; indeed, none of my facilities provided onsite storage outside my own room. Where would I ever locate replacement boxes? Well, to the staff's horror, I kept every box I had opened. While Nelson paraphernalia was seemingly everywhere in my room, whatever free spaces I still had were soon full of empty boxes. These boxes were stacked and created artificial barriers throughout my room, including in my entrance hall and bathroom access. No one understood me, and while it was admittedly inconvenient, I was a happy hermit. I finally had my stuff, and no longer was it in some hidden place.

My five months at Crimson Pointe were very satisfying. The staff was kind and diligent. The food was a significant improvement in my mind, and the menus more diverse than I had experienced at Park Strathmoor. I, of course, thrived on my newfound sense of emerging independence. Taking an Uber ride all alone with a driver I did not know felt like freedom. With the necessary caution of a disabled man, the boundaries of where I could walk were gradually expanding. I could walk around downtown, go to a museum, or even see a movie at the mall. Of course I even went to Chicago on a few occasions. To some extent, my newfound freedom only hastened my desire to return to Dallas.

CHAPTER 36
TIME TO MOVE TO DALLAS

The story of my adventure would not be complete without reflecting on my experiences during 2016 when I moved from Rockford and returned to my true home, Dallas, Texas. For many it may seem strange for me to declare Dallas as my favorite place, but if you live there long enough and allow yourself to become enamored by the Texas and Dallas culture, you will just have to assume that I am onto something. Dallas is a very welcoming city. I am unavoidably a Texan by birth. Although my formative childhood years were as a Midwesterner growing up in a moderately sized town—Muncie, Indiana—my perceptions were always that Texas was a special place. When I was a child, my family returned often to visit, usually around Easter. I am proud to consider myself a Hoosier through and through. Most Americans have no idea what that really means, but Hoosiers from Indiana implicitly understand. The term "Hoosier values" is good to us—something special. Indiana may be a flyover state to many East and West Coasters, but it proudly refers to itself as the "Crossroads of America," as trucks and travelers headed from north to south and east to west, and vice versa, inevitably cross Indiana on one of its interstate highways. Indeed, if Muncie in the twentieth century was famous for anything other than the production of Ball mason jars (and occasional state high school basketball championships), it was its designation, through anthropological studies by a couple of eastern sociologists (the Lynds), as "Middletown America." In all our supposed ordinariness, there is plenty of societal good as well as bad that fascinated these Ivy Leaguers. Muncie, of course, is full of highly successful, hard-working, interesting, educated, caring, and religious people. The fact that some of its youth moved on to bigger or more interesting places throughout the world is a tribute to the core good values it instilled in many of its people. For me, despite traveling to forty-nine of the fifty American states (sorry, North Dakota) and some twenty-seven foreign countries, Dallas, Texas captured my imagination as a child, and ever since it is where I have enjoyed living.

Dallas is deep in my roots. I was of course born there prior to my parents moving to Muncie when I was two years old. My grandparents lived in Dallas, and as a child I visited frequently. Possibly equally importantly, it was the home of the Dallas Cowboys. If Sandy Koufax was not, in fact, my first hero ever, Cowboy quarterback Don Meredith certainly was. Something about Coach Tom Landry in his signature fedora and the Cowboys winning was bigger than life for me. Best of all, Meredith, an SMU graduate, lived close to my grandparents, and my granddad always had to slow down as we traveled down Preston Road so I could twist my head as we drove by and see if Meredith happened to be out in driveway. My grandparents' unabated pressure turned me into a fan of the SMU Mustangs. Before long, SMU was my choice for college. I liked my time at SMU as I went on to earn all my graduate and postgraduate degrees at the Dallas campus. I never actually was to live farther than a few miles from the campus until my adventure sent me to Indiana and Illinois.

When I moved in August 2015, from skilled care at Park Strathmoor to my new assisted-living facility at Crimson Pointe in Rockford, I was determined not to lose sight of my goal to move to

Dallas. I intended to live at Crimson Pointe only on a temporary basis, but with a spur from Rockford's nasty, snowy, subzero winter weather, my determination became resolute. While I still required medical and physical assistance, I became increasingly committed to getting physically stronger and more self-sufficient. I was still wobbly even on my better days, but I was a regular at my physical therapist, and I made a point of taking long walks in the neighboring area at least twice a day. Few of the patients or staff at Crimson Pointe seemed to understand why I was doing that, but I never lost sight of my goal. I suppose staff had an inkling of my intent, because I never threw away the empty packaging that I acquired from moving my stuff from Park Strathmoor to my new place. "What do you need these empty boxes for? We can barely move around in here" was a common refrain of the medical staff. *Exactly*, I thought. I liked to think I was living in a temporary storage facility that had a bed and bath.

In November I became increasingly insistent that I wanted to go to Dallas as soon as possible—irritatingly insistent, I am sure. After trying to convince me (likely very appropriately) that I was not physically ready to move to Texas, my guardians (sister and mother) finally consented to allowing me to go because, I argued, I wanted the chance to reconnect with my two children. Having not seen my children in several years, my insistence must have been compelling. I really believed being in Dallas was the only way possible. I wanted to go to Dallas that next month, December, and pick a place to move. The compromise was that I had to return to Rockford in time for Christmas, which seemed fair, because while I got to Dallas, it was not likely I would get to spend Christmas with my children anyway. Fortune had it that my good friend Bill Francis went scouting some assisted-living places and among them discovered The Forum at Park Lane, which just so happened to be operated by Five Star Properties, the same company that operated Crimson Pointe. Arrangements were easy, and soon I was off for my coveted three weeks in Dallas.

The Forum at Park Lane, my new home in Dallas, Texas.

My trip was great. Bill and Kristi hosted a welcome-back party, and soon I was visiting with friends, colleagues, and clients I had not seen in some six years. Bill had saved emails he had received from those inquiring of me from time to time regarding my condition. He used these to create the guest list for the reception. We had nearly fifty people show up. In Dallas it is common for many to greet each other with a southern twang, saying, "It's so good to seeee you ..." My response soon tired, as I typically replied, "Thank you, it's so much better to be seen than viewed ..." I was happy to be seen again. I admit I was not fully prepared for how several of my friends and the city had changed in the five plus years I had been away. This was no fault of theirs, but five years can change a person when you are moving from, say, fifty-five to sixty years old or so. A little bit of gray here, a little more belly there—we looked different. The changes were likely due to prosperity and a dose of stress, I assumed. Houses were bigger, kids were off to college, and many personal corporate titles had become more impressive. Besides, I was one to talk; my body had been through five years of a kind of hell during my adventure. I knew I looked very different. The considerate folk tended not to gasp or act shocked. Those who had visited me in Muncie and Rockford were generally very complimentary, noting that my condition had improved greatly from the skinny quadriplegic mess they had seen before. No longer did I look like the bullfrog that previously horrified me in a mirror. I certainly was on an emotional high. At the reception, we exchanged many business cards, and the rest of my Dallas visit was filled with lunches, dinners, and attendance at every SMU basketball game played at home that month. I found it amusing that several people I recognized at games or my church were not aware I had even been gone. I tried to be judicious in explaining the reason for my absence. When I did try to explain my absence, my story became much more abridged and less dramatic. Usually the descriptions all ended with how much happier I was now to be seen and not viewed.

My return to Rockford for Christmas was generally uneventful. I had chosen to move to The Forum, and now it was just a matter of time. I had a nice Christmas holiday with my sister, her family, and my mother. I was, however, given plenty of opportunity to once again experience Rockford's subzero winter days. My determination to finalize my permanent move to Dallas only grew more desperate for me.

CHAPTER 37
THE MOVE TO DALLAS

Picking up and moving back to Dallas in early February 2016 sounded a lot easier than it actually was. Packing up the many boxes filled with my stuff that we had emptied from storage in Missy's basement did not seem to take just hours but weeks. Of course, there were my clothes, art, and artifacts unpacked when I moved into Crimson Pointe, but also that Nelson library and other books I was maybe a bit premature to pull out of her basement. My excess boxes soon started filling once again, and the light stacks of empty boxes in my apartment turned into heavy makeshift walls that, if tipped over, created all new messes. Then I discovered that there were, in fact, many more boxes of my stuff from my previous life that had never been removed from the basement. Soon the stacks grew. My collections included many pieces of art, framed prints and paintings, and even things I had long forgotten about, including some furniture, pots and pans, kitchen items, and sporting equipment. These all had to be sifted through, and much was designated for donation to Goodwill in Rockford. Missy had quite rightly taken a number of my better things, such as the Southwest Indian pots and some paintings, and intermingled them among her beautiful collections in her house. These had to be recaptured, and most required careful packing into yet more boxes when all was said and done. Finally my life possessions were ready to be placed in a Rockford storage unit for temporary holding to be sent back to Dallas once I was settled. I had a storage unit with chairs, lamps, and over thirty boxes filled with my stuff. All would ultimately be in one pod for shipment to The Forum in Dallas.

I arrived at The Forum on Park Lane in early February. I could not have been more excited. I moved into a two-and-a-half-bedroom apartment in the Healthcare Center, which felt like living in a mansion to me. The Forum is located in what might be the most prestigious and diversified retail shopping and restaurant area of Dallas. NorthPark Mall, probably one of the older and finest such facilities in America, complete with its own contemporary art collection, a movie complex, and every high-end market retail store ranging from Neiman Marcus to Tiffany and Nordstrom, was right across Park Lane from my apartment. I was in affordable retail heaven, as T. J. Maxx, Barnes & Noble, a Bloomingdale's and Saks outlet store, Whole Foods, Trader Joe's, Best Buy, and countless restaurants were all in easy walking distance of my apartment. The SMU campus, with its football and basketball, its continuing education art classes (I renewed my interest in drypoint printmaking), was a short Lyft ride away. Highland Park Methodist Church, my longstanding home church, which I once again frequented, sits on a corner of the SMU campus. I even joined a leading gymnasium club, Lifetime Fitness, which was right across from the SMU campus, to continue my therapeutic workouts.

Even as I was still facing real health issues, I was fortunate to get most of my medical attention from doctors at the magnificent University of Texas Southwestern Medical Center, where I was treated by the neurology, gastroenterology and general medical departments. Best of all, I soon discovered that visits to the massive medical complex could always be planned around lunch at Mike Anderson's BBQ, which is my favorite barbecue restaurant in Dallas. Resisting a piece of

Mike's homemade bourbon pecan pie after devouring one of his huge beef brisket sandwiches was usually my biggest challenge in visiting the medical center.

My first concern in moving to The Forum was seeing what, if anything, of value remained in the storage facility where my share of worldly possessions was being stored since my leaving Dallas in 2011. I knew I had some things I would need for an apartment, but I had little idea of what was there. All my share of household things had been sent to Abel's storage after I had left for Muncie in 2011, and I was not part of knowing what was there. I was very fortunate that my old friend Pete Gleason stepped forward and offered to help me clean out the facility. Pete is an innovative redesigner of existing houses in Dallas and seemed to be working from 6:00 a.m. until midnight every day. He nevertheless took it upon himself to help get my life in some semblance of order. What a great and caring man! Pete would squeeze me into his incredibly busy schedule (he was a contractor overseeing many renovations each day), fit me in the backseat of his old truck, which was usually filled to the brim with his construction materials, and off we would go to the distant storage unit deep in the warehouse district of Dallas. Stuff? Yes, there was tons, I decided—a large pallet three shelves high. It was dusty, even dirty, as nothing had been touched in at least four years. There was some good stuff I could use now, including some furnishings I might need in the future. I had no use for the classy iron double-bed frame we had bought in Taos, but maybe I would someday when not in an assisted-living facility. Lots of the stuff was junk and even trash. I was to make several trips to Abel's to sort things out. Some was delivered to my apartment at The Forum, much was trashed, and the reminder was left on a smaller pallet at Abel's. A few months later, Missy arranged for my storage pod to be shipped from Rockford to my apartment at The Forum; it included thirty boxes of stuff and a few furnishings. No wonder I began referring to my once spacious two-room, two-bath apartment as

"my new storage facility with room for my bed, television and shower."
Unsettled living? Not to me. How privileged could I be?

I was very fortunate to reconnect with a nucleus of good friends
in Dallas. My buddies were so welcoming, and I had more fun getting reconnected. If I did not take Lyft or Uber cars to get around
the city, friends were willing to pick me up as we went out for lunch
or an evening to a ballgame or big-time concert in the Dallas area.
Whether I was fully recovering physically or not, I made sure we got
to see U2, Bruce Springsteen, and Coldplay at big stadiums, as well
as college sports at SMU. I enjoyed excursions downtown and to the
Deep Ellum entertainment district. There was a DART train station
only a few blocks' walking distance from The Forum, so distant ventures were very possible. The Forum offered three drivers and cars,
which would take me to medical appointments and pretty much any
daytime activity I wanted to undertake. Life was back again, though
my conditions were so different. I was living in assisted living and had
access to familiar haunts (including my longtime and beloved barber
Sandy Goodwin ("Where have you been? You disappeared.")), but I
did not have my family, my old neighborhood, or my legal career. I
was excited but was learning to be a retired fellow concentrating on
restoring my health.

Little did I know when I moved into The Forum that it and its
residents and tremendous staff would have such a great impact on me
and what is now appearing to be a successful recovery from the illness.
The friends I made at The Forum, even though all older than me,
often by a full generation, were to be so supportive and influential in
my success. They befriended me, advised me, and, most importantly,
showed me how to face our most elderly years with class and dignity.
Some were to pass during my three plus years at The Forum, but I saw
dignity, support, optimism, and appreciation for life at every turn.
They loved visits from their families (especially on Sundays for the
big formal brunch in the dining room), but I sensed that many were
more involved with their new friends who were fellow residents. Few

of these people had ever met prior to moving into the facility, but all were quick to welcome and often befriend a new resident. Very few of these people were at The Forum to rot, complain, or just waste away. You don't go to exercise class and yoga and Wii bowling sessions to stop living life. You don't start your morning reading the *Wall Street Journal* in the library and later attending a concert in the activity room after dinner if you have lost your lust for life. Near daily happy hours were overflowing with friends, and wine was often included at very social dinners. They soon knew your business and health status, and you soon knew theirs. If someone might be missing at a meal, the inquiries went out quickly. Not everyone seemed to like his or her station in life, but you would not know it, as you were greeted warmly when walking the halls.

As I arrived at The Forum and into my latest new world, my biggest challenge, just as I expect it is for most everyone, was determining how to fit into the flow. The traffic was moving, and fortunately for me I soon discovered I could just merge into the flow. A good attitude, participation, and time would take care of the rest. My experience at The Forum exceeded my expectations. How privileged is that?

CHAPTER 38

BREAKFAST AT THE FORUM AND OTHER ADVENTURES THAT MAYBE SHOW I HAVE GROWN UP

Shortly after my arrival at The Forum in Dallas in February 2016, I was soon settled into my strangely shaped two-bedroom, two-bath apartment on the first floor. I say it was strangely shaped because my ground floor unit was obviously at one time two separate rooms each with its own bath. Somewhere along the line it was consolidated into one and connected by a pleasant little kitchenette in between the two rooms. The kitchenette had big windows and room for my table desk and file cabinets. I loved the space because it felt so big after my years in one-room facilities. My initial view was out onto a parking lot and across to a Panera Bread, my dry cleaner, and my bank. There was a lot of light and much commercial activity in sight. Although my view was soon interrupted with the placement of a big green Waste Management brand trash dumpster, I still loved my location and the chance to watch street activity. Because of insurance coverage

requirements because I was disabled, I was in the assisted-living com-
ponent of The Forum facility, which fortunately offered multiroom
apartment living as well as on-site medical attention.

I chose The Forum over some other higher-end Dallas facilities
because, while also very nice, it allowed me to live in assisted living
while still having full access to its much larger senior independent living areas. I could eat and participate with the independent folk. These
people were not there because they may have had health problems but
really just to simplify life and maybe allow them to be nearer to family.
The senior living had a nice, large dining room area, activities, game
rooms, and, most importantly to me, four large buildings full of active
seniors. Other than receiving medical assistance and some therapy
provided in assisted care, I soon focused all my attention on mingling
with these fun-loving interesting seniors. I was once again likely the
youngest resident, often by as much as thirty years, but I soon was
making friends with some of the most special people I have ever met.
I was a bit of a curiosity for most, as many had children visiting them
who were older than me. I seemed too young to be there, let alone
retired. As the story of my adventure became known, I was never
more appreciative of how these kind and interesting people chose to
become my friends.

One of the standard rituals for many of us at The Forum was
getting up before 8:00 a.m. and heading off to the breakfast room to
secure a favorite table and save room for our friends. My goal was to
be showered first and grab my special fruit, cereal, yogurt cup, and
flavored coffee grounds (in my French press) and hustle down to the
independent-living auxiliary breakfast room. If I got there on time, I
would find a big spread of food and goodies to pick from. Each day,
the buffet table offered fresh melons (and prunes—not my choice),
milk, oatmeal (porridge to some), dry cereals, muffins, danish, mini
scones, bagels, and English muffins. There was a hot dispenser for coffee and tea, with cups and saucers nearby. Best of all, covered serving
trays featured the special breakfast item of the day. Early morning at

The Forum was not so much known as the day of the week but for the special dish of the day. "Don't forget tomorrow is pancake day; will I see you there?" one resident might ask another. Monday was renamed Spanish egg dish (lots of cheese and peppers) day; Tuesday, pancake day; Wednesday, scrambled eggs and bacon day; and Thursday, home-made biscuits and creamy, thick gravy day. Friday, the wimpy day, featured a limp version of French toast. Making it timely to breakfast was greatly influenced by the item of the day.

At 7:45 a.m. or so (I never seemed to get there earlier) a regular breakfast crowd began shuffling in. These actually represented the second shift, as I discovered another whole group arrived at 7:00 a.m. to get the fixings at their freshest. At the big round table there sat six mostly white-haired women whom I soon learned we affectionately labeled the board of directors. These five or six women were prompt and regular. One seat was saved for Ellis, the eminently popular staff member who was director of activities. On Fridays, Ellis could be counted on to bring a bag or two of donut holes and some mini pigs in a blanket. Ellis knew how to stay in good stead with the power base and patiently listened to their complaints, observations, and sugges-tions. I decided that this table was the real seat of resident power at The Forum. Each lady was proudly in her nineties (except for Eleanor, who had recently celebrated her one hundredth birthday with a nice cock-tail party in the activity room), and if someone was absent that day, the absence was certain to be the initial topic of conversation. Should a regular, God forbid, not show up one day, word would quickly get to Ellis or the executive director, who would dispatch staff to check on the missing person.

My preferred table was next to the board's table. The ladies, who usually spoke in a stage whisper, were often fascinating and fun to hear. This group reported on the results of the previous night's bingo ("I don't how she does it, but she usually wins ... can you cheat at bingo?"). They liked to discuss politics but usually agreed this presi-dential election between Trump and Clinton was just too disgusting to talk about much longer. Fridays meant figuring what college football games each intended to watch that forthcoming weekend. I knew when it was Friday because Jimmie (the true power in the group, I was soon to decide) was all decked out in one or two shades of purple to celebrate her beloved TCU Horned Frogs. Others were very conversant about OU, Texas, and even SMU football. They often knew the betting lines and scoffed when they felt their team was being underappreciated. On Mondays their moods changed depending how their teams fared. If they lost, they knew the play that cost their team the win. Fortunately the Dallas Cowboys pro team was off to an uncharacteristic good start that season of 2016, so attention was easily diverted from complaints about the coaches.

The directors had very little time for the men, maybe with the exception of an occasional widower. They were always kind in greeting me each morning, but men were on their own or at least needed to find their own group to sit with. Even when The Forum's Residence Council had a rare male president (which we did that year), the women's coalition kept control. After all, it was only last fall, I was told, that the dress code for dinner was reluctantly changed; men no longer had to wear coats and ties at every dinner—a longstanding tradition at The Forum. Apparently men, being the significant minority at The Forum, threatened to stop coming to dinner if the rules on ties were not loosened. "I just so miss seeing those handsome men in a starched dress shirt and nice coat and tie," I overheard Jimmie say one morning. "They complained that it was just too hot in Dallas and threatened not to come." Serving as council treasurer, Jimmie knew the risk to the food budget if the place lost diners. "At least we still banned wearing T-shirts, caps, and shorts at any meal. I think we won overall."

My breakfast team usually came together about 8:00 a.m. There was an implicit agreement that four of us would sit at the four-top near the food and coffee. At least four days each week, my buddy Bill Fuqua, possibly the kindest man I encountered at The Forum, would bring his big SMU plastic coffee cup and save me my spot. Bill was a remarkably spry ninety-one, and he only recently had lost his beloved wife of sixty-three years, Gerry. It was my pleasure to have a chance to join him at any meal, and we were soon referred to as "the Bills." Bill liked to qualify that by pointing out that by no means were we a couple, like, say, "the Smiths" or "the Cochrans." He preferred we be referred to as "Old Bill" and "Young Bill." Ashley, the dining room manager, preferred to call Old Bill the "Love Bug." Simultaneously with Bill's arrival, I could pretty much count on the arrival of two of our favorite gals at The Forum. Jane Porter was a tiny Scot who at ninety-one was still a ball of energy. She had been a longtime resident of Santa Monica, California (after spending time in her youth in a convent in Scotland) and had only recently lost her husband, Bill. She likely had the best attitude of anyone at The Forum. She would fetch her daily porridge, salt it lightly, and begin considering her day. I got into the habit of getting her hot tea (later changed to my strong New Orleans coffee in my French press), which she seemed to appreciate, though she probably considered my actions a bit condescending. "You know you don't have to do that. I can get it myself, of course; I just happen to choose to let you do it." I enjoyed seeing her let me get it.

Phyllis Baker, also Jane's age, was our fourth friend. I became friends with the two when they sat as a couple at breakfast after each of their husbands passed. They noticed me as a newcomer and invited me to sit with them. Little did we expect we would become daily breakfast buddies throughout my stay at The Forum. Phyllis was still Jane's close friend, and Bill and I were initially mostly just tolerated. I rarely saw them at any meal that year when they were not together. Phyllis was a proud Methodist from a small town in Iowa. "You know Herbert Hoover grew up only twenty miles away from my hometown." That particular day, I happened to be reading a new biography on Hoover, whom many called probably the greatest Republican Party figure (other than Reagan) in the twentieth century. Whatever interest Phyllis had in the Quaker Hoover was quickly dispelled by her liberal Democrat views. Phyllis arrived each morning with her little bag (to collect fruit or muffins) and greeted Jane like a familiar sister. As she came to the table, she often had her cell phone playing music sung by an opera tenor. She liked to hold the phone up to Jane's ear and let her guess the music. In addition to both being ninety-one, Phyllis and Jane were, to me, true peas in a pod. They loved Old Bill and secretly grew to tolerate, if not even enjoy, me. I know they actually liked me, though I was constantly on thin ice. Phyllis and Jane were huge Hillary supporters. In fact, they so hated Trump that they could not begin to ever accept that the "vulgar man" had a single redeeming factor. They would get a bit angry if Old Bill or I criticized Hillary for anything. We knew we just could not go there. Hillary was their favorite, and nothing was going to change that. Of course, once it became apparent that I really liked Jane and Phyllis, we got pretty good about talking about more pleasant things. I, of course, would tease Jane that I still had several days yet until the election, and I was confident I would convert her. I even promised to pay for a full day for her to be pampered at a woman's spa, provided it be on Election Day and she not have time to vote. At one point, I brought in my new Trump bobblehead doll and, after her expression of outrage, I caught her in a little grin. Jane and Phyllis soon had us Bills going to the daily exercise class that Jane led twice each week in the activity room. They were very pleased that I also joined them for yoga on Mondays and Wednesdays. They remind me every week, and I had fun being not only the only class member attending who was male but also the only person under ninety. At breakfast we talked of many things, including travel, music, arts, the brain, and forthcoming programs at The Forum. However, we walked a tightrope each breakfast; one comment on Hillary or Trump and things might well become tense. To date we are doing brilliantly. Since I promised to get Old Bill to the polling place on Election Day, we know we all are canceling each other's votes out. Why argue? That makes for a nice peace.

Since Trump's successful election, Jane, Phyllis, Bill, and I have handled the matter brilliantly. We simply never discuss it. How I wish all Americans and the media could be more like the four of us. Smile and try to find common ground.

CHAPTER 39
PLEASANT DISCOVERY AT THE FORUM

One of the pleasant discoveries I encountered while living at The Forum with the many independent retirement residents emerged as, frankly, an unexpected surprise. We all know the situation when an elderly person begins nearing the emotional and physical end of life. Frequently, mere inevitable physical deterioration causes the individual to lose the fight for life. Humans do that, of course; our bodies inevitably wear out, and we die. This is a gift of God, I suppose, whether one becomes terminally ill or simply reaches the point where his or her system no longer can function. There is a point for all of us where enough is enough. We have also all seen the situation when losing a good relationship, such as in a long marriage, is enough to hasten the immediate death of the surviving spouse. The emotional loss is just too great. The assumed reason for living seems to be gone. Now I am alone; what to do? What purpose do I have? The subsequent death of the surviving spouse is often seen as a beautiful thing; the couple is thought of as so dependent and committed to each other that the thought of one going on without the other is too much. We see them as one, no longer separated in death. However, at The Forum that is not always the case. A surviving spouse or loved one who may also be very elderly somehow seems meant to live on. The survivor may just be physically healthier and have more life to lead. It may not be easy to want to live on, but it is a God-given benefit of life. Better yet, I find that continuing to live even several years after the loss of a spouse or companion is far from uncommon at The Forum. The place is full of these people, most often widows but certainly widowers as well. I saw it with my friend Bill Fuqua, who at ninety-one lost his wife of sixty-three years. Life is precious if one can recognize all its beauty and be open to support from friends, extended family, and colleagues. One may find oneself open to new friends, bingo, bridge, Wii bowling, and happy hours in the lounge—activities one had not considered in years. Couples often move into an independent living facility together fully aware they no longer need or want the house that previously served their family so well, or the inconveniences associated with such. What forever seemed an accepted part of having a house, whether it be maintaining a yard, keeping the air-conditioning operational, paying utility bills, or driving a car, naturally becomes far less important for many as they age. An alternative form of relief from these responsibilities, I discovered, is really what The Forum and other senior-living facilities are all about. Indeed now, the trend is to attract an even younger age group to good senior living. Think of it as an apartment building for the active but with the added benefit of a new community of friends, services, and extraordinary benefits, such as good, healthy dining.

When one spouse dies before the other, even if both are in their nineties, it is invigorating to see how frequently the surviving spouse seems to rebound and appear as a somewhat different person. It is as if many have come out of their shell. Perhaps this change may often be tied to the loss of a spouse who suffered illness or decline for quite some time. Watching a spouse or loved one fighting to survive is, of course, physically and emotionally draining. Chances are that attending to them, feeling depressed, and, as a consequence, not going out into society should be anticipated. That, for some, was their purpose—to be there with an ailing spouse. Those destined to survive often find a situation such as that at The Forum inspiring. Many other residents have been through the same experience. It is amazing how so many are quick to rally around the surviving spouse, welcome him or her to their dining table, and invite him or her to participate in various activities. Seeing an elderly surviving spouse become active and live for several years thereafter is very impressive. It's a built-in support system I did not expect to discover. No one exhibited this more beautifully than my friends Bill Fuqua, Jane, and Phyllis.

CHAPTER 40
RISE UP AND SLAM

The sensation was awful. I hardly knew it was happening, and just as I began to realize it, I had no time to do anything. My arms and hands reached out, but it was too late. The concrete seemed to rise up, completely unexpectedly, and brush aside whatever resistance I offered. My face and the right side of my body took it straight on, slamming, crashing, and scraping as I came to a stop. The rest of my body, indeed including my brain, wanted to push on, only making matters worse. As I physically came to a stop, there I was, very briefly stunned, feeling nothing but the sensation that I was done moving. In this state, my first thought was, *What is broken? Careful now, move a little. You can ... that's surely good.* Then the adrenaline took over. Momentarily I felt nothing ... then the sensation. Massive hurt. It might be anywhere, but it was initially concentrated where I took the blow. I had slipped off a curb and crashed onto the concrete parking lot, leading with my right shoulder.

"Oh ... ouch, oh." I could not breathe; then, slowly, among gasps, I did breathe. Then came the tears, brief but welling. When I fell, slamming my shoulder straight into the concrete, the pain started to become intense. It grew. This was no place to be. I tasted grunge, concrete, dirt, and particles—whatever was there. My tongue tried to dispel the grit from my lips. A new sensation arose; I felt my companion's hands, likely around my stomach or waist. I was being pulled up and brought to my feet. My feet were useless. I immediately began to fall forward. My buddy Jason, who was with me, was horrified, but he was strong. He held me up until I could get some balance. I was bent over, gasping for air, but I was not all that much in danger.

"Bill, what did you do? You fell, man; that had to hurt. Steady now, let me hold you up." I felt the strength of Jason's body holding on to me. It felt strange. But this transcended normal feelings. I was being supported, feeling the care. "All right, I am okay ... really," I managed to mumble. "The curb [or was it a hole?], I did not see it." I took stock of my pain as he held me against the weight of his body. What hurt most? Where was the pain? "Oh, my hand, it hurts." I wriggled fingers, closed my palm. It stung, but I hoped nothing was broken.

"My shoulder, my face. Oh, that hurts ... give me a moment ... am I bleeding? Do you see any blood?"

"No, but you look scraped up."

Tomorrow or the next day, surely, I would know, as the scraped spots on my hands, face, thigh, and shoulder would begin to turn into a gruesome gray, then darker. Man, I was hurting. Black and dark gray my skin did become. I had always easily bruised. The bruises developed around the edges of my direct wound covering my chest, my arm, and my right hip. Within a couple of days, portions of my skin turned an ugly brown, then yellow. It was too ugly to look at but very present.

Back to the scene of the fall: I could move now. My injury wasn't too severe; I could move most everything. Slowly I began taking stock of the parts of my body that seemed to be working. *Feel. Move.* Was anything broken? Maybe not. Oh, but the pain. One time several years earlier, when a wall at the side of the basketball court we were playing on at the YMCA had slammed into me, Rob, my friend who was there to pick me up, discovered my left arm broken in half. It was a compound break; we even had a glimpse of my gray arm bones peeking out of two holes, exposed to the air for the first time ever. That was gross; I pushed my twisted, mangled arm back into a straight position so the bone was no longer exposed. Adrenaline immediately took over that time. It was certainly not comfortable but I didn't experience the searing pain I had expected. Rob and I even chatted as he drove me to the hospital emergency room. I say we chatted; actually, I was in shock, but we spoke nevertheless. But this time the pain seemed different. It began to throb. It was a slow sort of pain, not intense but very present. I realized that probably meant something was fractured, if not broken. The few beers I drank before I slipped off that curb probably helped dull this pain. At least for the moment.

My accident falling off a curb occurred in October 2016, about eight months after I had moved into The Forum. I was, up until that night, feeling so much stronger and independent. I walked all over The Forum neighborhood, which included the NorthPark Mall and a number of interesting retail establishments. I had reconnected with friends in Dallas, including Jason, and was slowly feeling close to normal again. I went out with buddies to occasional ballgames, concerts, bars, and restaurants, always with a recognition that I had to be careful, drink modestly (if at all), and not push my body too hard. The fact that I slipped (or tripped?) off that curb that night was really bad luck. We were not out very late that night, but balance was always a big issue in my recovery. Indeed, I was receiving intense balance therapy from the rehabilitation group at The Forum. Most of my near daily exercises involved improving my balance.

The prior year, while still in Illinois, I had a nasty face-first crash, tripping on one of the cracked sidewalks in Evanston. Rob and I were walking to a Northwestern basketball game when I stumbled so quickly neither I nor Rob could prevent it. As ugly as it was, I was fortunate not to break anything, and we went on to the game. I was sore the next few days, mainly on my right thigh. It underscored to me that my balance was very much an issue, especially as I got more independent and quit using a cane or walker. That is why I underwent the balance therapy at The Forum. A year later, this ugly crash occurred, which did actually result in a broken bone in my shoulder.

When my buddies returned me to my apartment in assisted living at The Forum, I was put to bed, as nothing seemed very bad. Needless to say, that night was hell for me, and early the next morning, the nurses sent me by ambulance to nearby Presbyterian Hospital. Yes, I did have a break, deep in the ball of my right shoulder. I was put in a sling and sent back to The Forum, and I spent five very uncomfortable days waiting for my appointment with an orthopedic surgeon. I spent much of that week telling my elderly friends in the dining room what had happened. They, of course, could not have been kinder, but I did have a sense that it shook up several. Very little is more feared among the elderly than having a dangerous fall. Avoiding falls is the reason many are in assisted living and use wheelchairs and walkers. Here I was, the seemingly mobile young guy, suffering a dreaded fall.

I would like for this story of breaking my shoulder to get better, but unfortunately it does not. While my competent doctor decided that I could recover without surgery, it did mean I needed a nasty brace and had to cut back on physical activities. Nights were no fun, because once again I had to sleep on my back, my arm propped up on a pillow. Movement to one side or another resulted in pain that awakened me immediately. Projected recovery and use of the brace were expected to take at least three months, well into January. That's not the bad part of this story. Actually, my recovery went quite well, much as the doctor had projected. It seemed slow to me, but repeated X-rays showed good progress. I started increasing my physical activities, especially my long walks around the area. I was even using light weights while I walked to help strengthen my shoulder. One early January morning I was walking one of my favorite courses, which happened to pass a shopping center a couple of blocks from The Forum. Of course, there are curbs in shopping centers. I was careful, but wouldn't you know it, I missed this one. Down I went, fast, face and shoulder first! *Oh no.* The pain was immediate. My right arm quivered; I had no control. I was lying on a sidewalk hurt again. Fortunately, a young fellow in a Ford Mustang saw me and got out of his car to help. The nice guy took me to the Presbyterian Hospital emergency room. *Do they remember me?* I thought. I had more X-rays, which showed more evidence of another break. Same shoulder, same bone. Same doctor, fortunately no surgery. Same big brace. At least three months more to recover. That's a total of six consecutive months having little use of my right arm. I am not the first at The Forum who has fallen more than once. It was scary. I did recover, and I did join a good gym with a great trainer to further develop my strength and balance. So far, I'm all good. No more falls have occurred to date. I have, however, become quite accustomed to walking with my eyes staring at the pavement. Every curb I cross, I think of my shoulder. I just hope I don't walk into a clothesline that is level with my head.

CHAPTER 41

RANDOM OBSERVATIONS FROM LIVING AT THE FORUM

One morning I noticed immediately that my friend Jane had an impassive expression on her face as I sat down at our favorite table in the breakfast room at The Forum. When I asked what was up, Jane said, "Barbara looked so good last week. Did you hear? She died last night." Jane really did not appear particularly shaken or distressed as my Scottish friend went on preparing her bowl of porridge, something she steadfastly ate every morning. Barbara was a lovely, dignified lady who usually at breakfast sat at a table next to ours with a group of ladies we referred to as the de facto board of directors. Today, of course, her chair at the table was empty, though we all knew that would change shortly.

Barbara was a veteran resident at The Forum and, at ninety-four years old, one of the most appreciated in the place. She was an active participant at The Forum's twice-per-week yoga class, and in fact she fit in quite nicely with the other participants (and me), all of whom were in their nineties. That December she had fallen in her apartment and broken her ankle, which resulted in her absence from the class. She had originally moved into The Forum with her husband in an independent-living apartment on the second floor. Prior to her husband dying, they transferred over to The Forum's assisted-living facility to share a tidy first-floor apartment with a view of the street. When her husband died, Barbara transferred to a smaller independent-living apartment on the third floor. There she lived out several remarkably active years participating in events and acting as an elected member of the residents' council at The Forum. Those couples fortunate enough to survive for several years in independent living often ended up seeing a spouse moved into assisted living during those last few months or weeks of his or her life. Whether the healthy spouse joined his or her ill mate in assisted living or chose to remain in the independent-living apartment really did not matter much; the assisted-living facility was an easy walk just down a hall into the next building. That's one of the selling points for a facility like The Forum.

Within a few days, we noticed several young men show up with a truck and their dollies to start removing Barbara's stuff. This was not particularly noteworthy, because it was necessarily a frequent occurrence at The Forum. In a few days, Barbara's apartment would be repainted and probably recarpeted as it was prepared for a new resident. Maybe even the refrigerator would be replaced. Everything about the apartment would look fresh and new and inviting to the next resident. Within a week or so, Barbara's nameplate would come down and a fresh tag would be in place for a "Joe Smith" or whoever rented the place. Joe would become relevant now, and Barbara would progress to a fond memory for her friends remaining in independent living. I asked Jane who had lived in Barbara's apartment prior to Barbara. Jane did not remember; nor, likely, did anyone else in the breakfast room that morning. Whoever may have lived there belonged to another era's time and experiences. That's how it had to be at The Forum and at every such facility. Time passed, and one had one's time there. We all knew someone would someday succeed each of us. I suppose only the walls really knew the history, and I never heard the walls talking.

Jane had last seen Barbara at breakfast a few weeks prior. When she asked Barbara how she was doing, she was struck by Barbara's apparent indifference. The usually vivacious Barbara said that she would be going to the health care unit in assisted living for a few days. "Nothing to worry about; it's just temporary until I feel stronger. I will be back in my apartment by the weekend." Barbara's responses were not that coherent; they seemed to be affected by a haze of unawareness. Barbara did ultimately get to move back to her familiar surroundings, but this time her family had arranged a twenty-four-hour on-site assistant. Jane looked at me and said, "I never really expected her to come back. She was so confused. It's nice she lasted another week really." Jane faced the news not with an outward expression of sadness but more with a clinical matter of twist in fate. This is how it is at The Forum. People come; people go. While here, they contribute to the vibrancy of life at The Forum; when it's time to pass, they fade into memory.

In February 2019 I observed another such instance. Several months prior, I had developed a friendship with a man named Arnold. He was somewhat unusual, as he had only recently moved into the independent senior-living facility despite the fact that he was ninety-six years old. He instantly became the oldest man living at The Forum. Arnold had trouble expressing himself, as he was on some sort of oxygen tank and his voice was muffled. Arnold also depended on his self-operated electric wheelchair to get around, even though he managed to get out of it and walk into the dining room. (No wheelchairs were allowed in senior independent living dining rooms.) I began to notice that even though he usually sat alone, Arnold always said hello and asked what I was doing. Arnold spent an hour after every breakfast reading the entire *Wall Street Journal*. Soon we were often dining together, and I found Arnold had an unusually inquisitive mind. He wanted to know lots about me—especially my recent travels and unusual collections. Arnold was born in New York City and lived much of his working life in Southern California. He had made many trips to China, which was pretty interesting since it had been many years since he had last worked. I began helping Arnold pick out books in the library; he especially enjoyed World War II spy novels and biographies. What an inspiration! The last time I was to see Arnold, he was in his electric wheelchair up on my third-floor hallway in assisted living, quite far from his own building. I asked Arnold, "What are you doing here, my friend?" Arnold said he had come to see my new apartment and all that Lord Nelson stuff I had told him about. He drove his chair in, complimented my extensive collection, and then noticed my Hopi Indian artwork. Arnold knew all about the Hopis and seemed excited to hear about my visit the previous year to the reservation. Arnold was so interesting.

A few days later, I heard through the hallway grapevine that Arnold had fallen while trying to get out of his wheelchair. I had not seen him that day, but he was rushed to the hospital. Arnold spent several days there but was finally returned to The Forum's dedicated health care center, which was located at the far end of the five-building complex from where I lived. He was not in his senior-living apartment. His condition was not good, so I was told, and visitors were asked to stay away. This went on for a few weeks, and I felt bad that I kept forgetting to drop by to see if he was awake. Finally, on the night of the Super Bowl, I was told that Arnold had just been wheeled into the big watching party The Forum was hosting for its residents. I had missed the first quarter of the game and was running late. I was told Arnold had in fact just paid a visit, greeted his friends, and consumed a beer and two bratwurst sandwiches! He was happy but got tired. I was so sorry to miss him, but fortunately I could go see him tomorrow. I felt Arnold must be getting better indeed. He died that night sometime after the game was played. Maybe the beer and brats were not good for him, but what a wonderful way to go! That was the consensus among The Forum residents left behind.

I found it invigorating to see how so many residents seemed to accept this real inevitability. Few appeared to dwell on, at least in front of me, what was in the long term ahead for them. "Who does SMU play next?" my friend Horace Mitchell would ask. "I got my football season tickets, you know, and I need to be sure I get to the game." Horace is in his mid-eighties and will get to a game daytime or night. After his friend Sarah moved out and no longer could go with him, he would get his loyal friend and caretaker Melissa to take him. And she would in fact do so. Horace is completely blind, but he can hear a pin drop. He walks with a cane but amazingly finds his way around the hallways, even to the fitness room down on the first floor some four hallways from his elevator. Horace counts the steps he takes and knows when to turn. He makes this trek five days a week, finds the treadmill, which is preset to his liking, gets on it, and walks for thirty minutes. He says he passes the time singing old Methodist hymns he knows by heart. Horace is an SMU grad from the early 1950s and a big SMU fan. His family has its name on one of SMU's tennis courts at its fancy new stadium on what use to be the Mrs. Baird's Bread bakery site. As a former SMU football team student trainer, Horace is a lifetime member of the Mustang Club athletic foundation, and he is completely up to date on the team. Melissa does take him. She is his devoted paid assistant who, among other things, keeps his iPhone operating, his apartment spotless, and his dignified Brooks Brothers outfits color coordinated. Melissa uses Uber to get the two of them to the stadium. SMU sends a golf cart to meet them and escort them to his seats on the handicapped row. Horace listens patiently as the crowd cheers and boos. The next day, he can tell me exactly what happened in the game. The Forum is great for Horace. It's close to SMU and his daughter in nearby Highland Park. His charm is non-stop, especially with the ladies. Horace is phenomenal with recognizing voices; he rarely needs to be told a woman's name more than twice. When he senses a woman approaching, he gets a big smile, extends his warm hands, embraces her hands, and usually asks, "And who is this lovely lady?" The women smile, chuckle, and often give Horace a hug. "Will you have a seat for a moment with us?" Horace usually does not realize that there is not a vacant seat at his table, because he can't see the table. The ladies move on, flattered and chuckling. I remind Horace at our frequent dinners together that he gets (and earns) more hugs in an evening than I receive in a month. He is a complete inspiration to me. He is kind and wise. His attitude about life is nothing but positive. We still attend church together nearly every week. The ushers seat Horace in the front row of the big traditional sanctuary. He does not miss a thing. On our drive back after church in a Forum-driven car with our friendly driver, he recounts details of the service he just sat through. I then guide him back into The Forum's entry area. After a brief stop for him at the men's room (I make sure he is facing the correct way, turn on water in the sink, and get him his paper towels), Horace often reminds me I could ask for a dollar tip, as I am a mighty fine restroom attendant. Our Sunday lunches in The Forum's dining room, with its multi-table buffet ("You want the lamb or tenderloin today? The crab salad and an omelet?"), become lively discussions joined in by others. He is full of fun jokes he seems to dredge up from his past. I often get him a to-go pack for his dinner that night. I walked with Horace back to his second-floor apartment and made sure his dinner made the refrigerator. He often says, "You know you don't have to take me back here; I know my way." Each time, I respond, "Of course I know you do, Horace, but this is my joy, because look at all the fun we have visiting." It's the truth; Horace and his kind determination are special to me. Like me and most everyone else, he is as human as can be. What a God-planted friend he is for me.

Jane is also an inspiration. She is small in stature, a former dancer, and now at ninety-two a present fitness fanatic. Light as a feather, she scurries around the facility, walking faster and with more resolute purpose than anyone in the place, including staff. To know her (and everyone does) is to marvel. Our near daily breakfasts joined by her longtime friend Phyllis are always interesting and unexpectedly

My great friend Horace Mitchell joining me for dinner at The Forum.

conversational. Once we learned during the 2016 presidential campaign that politics simply have to be off limits, our morning discussions became incredible. We talk arts (her daughter runs a major dance studio in Dallas); opera (Phyllis's love); movies and books; my art and photography, which they patiently review; culture; travel (Jane took a six-week trip in the summer of 2017 to great European capitals and in 2018 to China); computers (and why they are so hard to work); people; and even sports. Jane did not know a Dodger from a tomato. With my patient prompting, she can now identify our local teams, Cowboys, Rangers, Mavericks, and SMU. She now knows that

I am a Dodgers fan, that they do in fact play baseball in Los Angeles (a city she lived near for many years), and that the Dodgers had my full attention during the World Series of 2017 and 2018. Yes, my mood swung from day to day depending on the outcome of the game the prior day, but fortunately the Dodgers won a lot of playoff games. Yankees, Packers, Celtics? That might require more study for her to be sure, but I'll bet she now knows that Houston has the Astros, because they played my Dodgers in the World Series during two weeks of our breakfasts. At 9:00 a.m. we would all laugh and wish each other a good day. Jane would rush off to exercise class, and they would both remind me on Mondays and Wednesdays to come to yoga class. They are two of the regulars.

Since no one at The Forum is a stranger to Jane, I found her reflections on Barbara's passing quite intriguing. Yes, there was an element of sadness at the loss of a friend. But more, I sensed, there was a resignation that this is part of the process of being here. Barbara was a lovely person, but Jane and the others will get over it—actually quite quickly, I sense. Jane fixed her eyes on mine one day. "This is such a lovely place. So many interesting and wonderful people come through here, you know? I am just sorry it's so late in our lives. I would have loved to know these wonderful people when they were young and vibrant. We could have shared so much."

After my close friend Bill Fuqua died in October 2017, I really was sad. I knew it was inevitable; he was ninety-three. But he was in such good shape and such fun to be with. The elderly Texas wildcatter, onetime backup running back at SMU to the great Doak Walker, was the former short time owner of a bar on Greenville Avenue, which he won ownership of playing craps with the prior owner. At the time, Bill was only a sophomore at SMU. His stories of a life well led were so colorful to me and his friends at The Forum. It was hard for me to accept that this kindly man, with his contagious good attitude, had now passed from my life. What a special eighteen months our friendship had been. He was good to Horace too. He was good to me. We miss him, but our journey moves on. His vacancy at our dinner table was soon filled by Ed Collins, a new man at The Forum, who liked to sit with us. Ed turned out to be a highly-educated and interesting man. He is a career educator and former president of both the College of Charleston and Millsaps College. More intriguing to me, I soon discovered he had spent two years in Muncie, where he was brought in as an experienced heavyweight consultant to help carry out a major fundraising campaign at Ball State University. I grew up basically on the Ball State campus. I knew of the people he said he met during the campaign. We totally hit it off. Ed is now one of my good friends. Of course, I miss Bill Fuqua, but the orderly flow of life at The Forum goes on. Ed may be fifteen years older than me (Bill was thirty years older), and we likely are not destined to be friends for a high number of years, but however long it may turn out to be, it is great for the present. When one leaves The Forum for whatever reason, his or her apartment will be emptied by a moving company, the carpet changed, and maybe a new refrigerator installed, and most certainly a new name will appear on the door. Life at The Forum will go on.

CHAPTER 42
THE JOY OF UNANTICIPATED FRIENDSHIPS

As I bring my story to a close, I reflect on a number of things that are life-changing events for me. Without question, one that will always be with me for the rest of my life was discovering and gaining so many new and unexpected friends. To say I never anticipated making so many new friends may be true, but I find it a joy of life, regardless of one's situation. Be open to it; you will treasure the experiences and memories. Throughout my stay in skilled-care and assisted-care nursing facilities during my adventure, including up through my residency beginning in February 2016 at The Forum in Dallas, I experienced important but admittedly unanticipated friendships with many of my fellow resident patients. I refer to it as "unanticipated" because I certainly did not enter these facilities with any expectation of making meaningful friendships.

Entering Morrison Woods and then Park Strathmoor, I was a physical and something of an emotional mess. I was far from pleasant to look at (yes, that prednisone made me swell up like a bullfrog), and frankly neither were many of my fellow residents. We were all fighting something, most significant of which was our battle for our continued existence on this earth. If our personal concern each day was not necessarily worrying about surviving the day or week, it was, oddly, a form of immediate comfort. We could worry instead about things that at that moment seemed so important: When will I be fed? Why is lunch fifteen minutes late today? Will my soiled gown be changed? Why can't my hand hold anything? Do I have someone visiting today? Does the nurse have the right channel set on my television set? All pretty simple stuff, but for most of us in our personally undesirable situation, it seemed to dominate our concerns at that moment in a day.

When you are very ill or otherwise impaired, friendships with heretofore strangers, whether in the hallway or lobby, are not seemingly important. Likely these people had no more interest in me than I had in them. A nice comment and a smile from one or more of your attendants was sufficient. Whether another patient acknowledged you was rarely important. This of course was especially true during hospital stays. There you rarely get a glimpse of another patient even if he or she shares your room. This is not so much the case as the period required for recovery extends, especially in a long-term care facility. At Morrison Woods, I frequently shared my room with another man. CNAs might treat us as friends, but one, if not both, of us was usually so out of it mentally that we took little interest in the other. The exception was my roommate Lyle, whom I described earlier. But how close were we? I erroneously thought the whole time that his foot had been cut off. (In fact, it never had been.) My mind was in this state of confusion for much of my time in Muncie. Lyle and I sort of became friends as we became able to talk, although I found him hard to understand. The fact that I learned later that during this particular time I could hardly speak at all obviously means I was more difficult for Lyle to communicate with than he was for me. Lyle had a delightful, kind wife, Beverley. She visited our room frequently and was always nice to me. She developed a strong relationship with my mother, and soon each was looking out for the two of us. Lyle at some point was moved to another room that was large enough to let his wife move in too. I don't really recall having another roommate at Morrison Woods, but Lyle made the most lasting impact on me. As my time continued at the facility, I would often see Lyle and his wife as I was being wheeled around the hallways by my mother. They were always friendly, and I know that, among the four of us, we stayed up to date with each other's respective health situations. Strangely, while Lyle and Beverley were my favorite residents, Lyle became an active and significant part of my bizarre, irrational, and vivid dreams which I began experiencing (most likely due to my high doses of prednisone or whatever drugs I was on) while at Morrison Woods. I was convinced that the facility had cut off Lyle's foot at some point, for which I remember feeling strangely responsible. Another vivid dream involved an FBI sting operation trying to establish medical fraud at the facility. I remember being surprised by a call from an FBI agent who asked for my cooperation in a pending investigation. I was instructed to keep all of this secret, of course, but shortly I was asked to come over to the FBI office, which, ironically and conveniently, was just across the street from where I was living. Flattered, I went to the meeting. I have no idea how I got there, but even more strangely, the secret office was located behind a restaurant in Highland Park Village Shopping Center. Highland Park is a village within Dallas, Texas, and the center of a place where I frequently shopped in my prior life in Dallas. Obviously I should have known that there was no FBI office across the street and that I was not currently living in Dallas. I was so excited to be part of an investigation that I went eagerly. I remember that the place was dark and mysterious to me. I recognized one of my legal partners at Bracewell who was there, apparently volunteering to help. This was surprising but made sense, as he was formerly in the military. Because everything was secret and confidential at the FBI office, both of us knew not to acknowledge the other. The meeting did, however, verify to me the authenticity of the FBI's requests to me. Most surprising of all, my friend Lyle was there. He was working. I worked out in my mind that this all made sense; Lyle must be an undercover agent assigned to my health facility. It must have added to his effectiveness that someone had cut off his foot. As my roommate, he had apparently scouted me out and told his superiors at the FBI to interview me. For whatever reason, following my interview the FBI did not pursue using me. My mind at this time may have been severely delusional, but it was certainly not dull.

I had other acquaintances at Morrison Woods, but my favorites were usually CNAs or other staff members. The only patients I seem to recall were very elderly and not anticipated to remain there very long. I remember having an occasional dinner with a quiet elderly man who I was told was the father of one of my boyhood friends. I vaguely remember him as an active dad involved with my boyhood Boy Scouts troop. He did not like to talk, and shortly he passed away, so I was told. Disappearances were not uncommon in that world.

Relationships radically changed for me when I was moved to Park Strathmoor in Rockford, Illinois. Most significantly, the facility served a different purpose than the (mostly) assisted living provided at Morrison Woods. As it was a skilled-care center, the patients at Park Strathmoor tended to vary in age and in the scope of the problems they faced. Several were, in fact, younger than my fifty-seven years and often were not as mobile. Wheelchairs seemed more common among the Park Strathmoor patients, and many patients were rarely out of their rooms. The B-Unit was a memory care center with residents so severely impaired that they did not mingle with the patients in units C and D. I was placed on the E-Unit hallway, which generally housed the most severely impaired residents (including those of us needing respiratory assistance), many of whom had short life expectancies. I was placed there on purpose, as my sister soon learned that the staff and attendants did not expect me to survive that initial week. I was fortunate to have a private room that my sister and some friends had decorated with a floating balloon and other cheery knickknacks that obscured the cold cinder-block walls. For the next several weeks, I was rarely out of my bed. I was bathed and moved and had my gowns and diapers changed all while I was prone on my back. My meals were served in my room, and I basically had no contact with other patients. My need for respiratory care was constant, and nurse Linda attended to me throughout the day. The drooling from my mouth grew worse. Everyone who approached me seemed to wipe off my mouth, chin, and neck. Socially, I was little more than a nameplate on my door. The only friends that I seemed to make were the kindly staff CNAs and nurses who truly bore the worst of what I had to offer. Merrie O'Brien, Mary Kemp, Brad Hayes, Angela Shaw, and Jacki and Joe, among others, will forever be treasured memories for me.

In time I was put in a wheelchair, and Missy would wheel me out for my first big adventure—a trip to the large entry lobby down my hallway. The lobby was full of patients, most of whom were just sitting in their wheelchairs and staring out the big picture windows. This was initially a weird feeling. Faces were strange to me, all of them being new. The faces were often old, tired, and sculptured. Few—except for maybe Screaming Johnny, who sat folded up in in a corner—said anything at all. Those who could focus simply stared at me, presumably thinking, "Who is this messed-up new guy?" I am sure I was quite the sight. Missy, friendly to all, was pushing her older brother, who, with his head cocked, was staring right back. Among the group was the really elderly Italian couple, Gino in his wheelchair, who was pushing his wife in her wheelchair. I saw the extremely obese middle-aged woman lodged behind a table, looking up at me over her tattered paperback novel. She was much younger than me but could not stand up. A chiseled-faced lady well into her nineties seemed to stare at me with some interest. Little did I know that Katherine would soon become one of my favorite ladies at Park Strathmoor. On days when she was talking, she could be heard greeting me across the lobby with a hearty "Hi, honey … let's go do something." Katherine's sheer joy at seeing a younger man, no matter his appearance and condition, was a constant pick-me-up for me. Over time, as my mobility improved, I would go find Katherine in her room on A-Unit, where I would often have to wake her up or distract her from staring at her television some twelve inches away. Only then would I receive her great smile of recognition. It became a race between us to be first to proclaim, "Hi, honey, what do you want to do today?" Katherine's suggestions usually amused me, as I could tell she once really liked the younger men. I can only imagine what was going through her once fertile imagination. Most staff considered Katherine a bit moody, as she was often fine with telling others what was on her mind. I figured out that maybe because she found her life challenging at times, she just had no time for pushy people—especially women, it seemed—whether a staffer or a spouse of another man. She could snap an insulting "You just go away" with the best of them. Toward the male patients, her charm and desire to hold hands would return almost immediately. When my good buddy from SMU, Dan Freiburger, came to visit from Ohio, he said a nice hello to Katherine as he passed by her in the lobby on his way to my room. I asked Dan if he had seen my friend Katherine on his way to find me. With a big smile on his face, he responded, "Why yes, she just told me I was a piece of shit." My loving friend Katherine …

Others in the lobby grew to become daily close friends. There was kind Stephen, a former pharmacist who had suffered too many recent strokes. Sitting in his wheelchair, he could usually be found with his sweet wife who patiently came to see him at least five days a week, and with his friend and fellow patient Bill (whom Missy and I would soon come to call "Massachusetts Bill"), who came from New England. Stephen would strain to greet us with his faint whisper and tell us a joke we would all laugh at regardless of whether we could really hear what he had said. Massachusetts Bill had suffered severe-seeming strokes as well. He had no apparent family in the area but loved the four of us. It truly broke Missy's (and my) heart when he would mumble some kind greeting as the drool leaked out the corner of his mouth. He would show such happiness when Missy came to visit me that soon she was spending time each visit greeting Bill and Stephen before finding my room. As I got stronger and more mobile after a few years

in Park Strathmoor, it was very tough on Missy and me to go out the
front door for our excursions around Rockford and see the two of
them watching at the window as we left. "Where are you going this
time?" they might say. Neither had likely been out of the facility in
several years; we were quietly ashamed when I would suggest it was
to see a doctor rather than admit I was really getting a frozen custard
and fried walleye sandwich at the Culver's up the street.

There was also NASCAR Nellie. She would wheel herself out into
the lobby each day and visit with the three of us. Nellie was a proud
woman, likely in her early forties. We called her NASCAR because she
loved to recount the latest NASCAR motor race that she had watched
on television that weekend or prepare us for the next forthcoming
race. Shame on me, was it Dale Earnhardt who was her favorite? I
forget, but likely it was. Nellie was working hard to learn to stand up,
and though she reported some success, I never actually saw it happen.
She joined her two buddies, Bill and Stephen, in attending our exercise
class I began leading at ten thirty each morning. She was always optimistic; her daughter would visit soon, surely? Nellie was concerned
about her house she had "temporarily" left and her several cats. Nearly
every week, she would tell us how she would be moving back to her
home and cats soon, at least in the next month or so. All she had to
do was get a little stronger. This went on for several years, even while
I visited her some twelve months after I had left Park Strathmoor.
"Yeah, just a little stronger ... when I stand up."

There were other patient friends I began to encounter, but
none were nearly as close to me as these four and my pal Katherine.
Attitudes were surprisingly (to me) good among these naturally optimistic folk. I like to think the witnessing of my improving health was
positive for them. That day, after over a year living with them, when
I first walked with a walker into the lobby was shocking to all. That
kind of improvement rarely happened at Park Strathmoor. I was a bit
self-conscious that my success would depress some for whom no such
improvement was really possible. A few residents quietly complained

later about my unattended daily walks outside the building, but only a few. Most were visibly inspired and happy for me. The group's increasing willingness to participate, to the extent they physically could, in our new, now nearly daily, exercise class was inspiring. We sometimes got up to thirty participants, which was surprising seeing as how there had not previously even been an exercise class until we asked to start one. After encouraging patients to leave their rooms and join us, wheelchairs and walkers would crowd the lobby. We would ask each participant to select his or her favorite exercise and take his or her turn leading the group. Some had to be reminded what to suggest, and others awakened and reminded to try. Favorite exercise choices included "rock the baby" (shoulders rocking back and forth), "kick the ball" (an imaginary ball, of course), "reach up for the money on the money tree," "throw a pitch," and "wave your arms and wiggle your fingers." On Katherine's good days, she would lead us and count aloud to ten or fifteen as we went through the motions. Some participants had no functioning feet; nevertheless, they would move their legs or fidget and squirm with the best of us. As CNAs and a now walking me would wheel residents back to their rooms, it was uplifting to see attitudes picking up and patients acting as if they were worn out. Often a family member or other visitor or favored staff member would occasionally participate, and it was always great fun to ask them to introduce us to a new exercise of their choice.

My time at Park Strathmoor eventually reached an end as my health and prognoses no longer required highly attentive skilled care. After relocating to Crimson Pointe Assisted Living in August 2015 (which I recount more fully elsewhere in this book), I never really developed any noticeable friendships. Except for the sports-loving staff marketing director, Mike, these residents were actually somewhat different from those I had previously encountered elsewhere. Generally, they were much more elderly. Most had active minds (the card games were constant), but in my view seemed to be accepting that this was probably an inevitable last stop. Most, of course, might never be destined to move out alive. They were kind and socialized with each other. I never really tried to know many, other than some familiar faces I grew to recognize at breakfast. One colorful breakfast buddy used to constantly comment that I was looking better than ever and that I soon would surely be out of there. She would claim that she was getting worse. I did not really see evidence of that. My daily walks, infrequent excursions by train to Chicago, and trips around town with Missy and Uber obviously contributed to that perception. I was, in fact, doing much better physically, and unlike probably anyone else at Crimson Pointe, I anticipated my stay to be brief. I of course left the facility and moved back to Dallas in February 2016.

On my return to Dallas and my taking up residence at The Forum at Park Lane, my relationship with fellow residents changed significantly. On moving into the health care facility (a.k.a. assisted living), it was a condition of mine that I had to be able to eat with people who did not require assistance. Mixing freely with the independent senior-living residents was an entirely different experience for me. For the most part, these were active, lively people. Most were there to simplify and celebrate life, taking advantage of The Forum's many conveniences. Likely they had family in Dallas. Most were very energetic and up to date on current affairs. With well-attended morning exercise classes and daily afternoon 4:00 p.m. happy hour gatherings, I found a near unanimous appreciation of life among the residents.

I really believe that while at The Forum, I began to appreciate that God had given me a new important purpose for my life. I had spent some time during my recovery trying to understand why I was so fortunate to be able to recover. Yes, I prayed for restoration of my health (or, more accurately, for continued survival in whatever form), but I consciously did not want to jeopardize possible good fortune by expecting my prayers to be answered. It was fair to say that I was cautiously optimistic that my faith in Jesus, my restrained prayers for forgiveness and God's grace, and the collective prayers and words of encouragement I received from others would all work out for my best, whatever "best" might mean. I had no doubt I was nowhere near worthy of special treatment and fortune. I knew my sins were very real and that I am so imperfect as a person that special treatment from God was out of the question. For all I know, that remains very true today. (How far does God's grace truly extend? No one living absolutely knows.) Nevertheless, that did not mean that I did not hope at all times to be so fortunate. I like to think I was consciously trying to clean up my act, though I still had a strong presumption that as an imperfect being, I could never truly meet such a standard. Hey, experience teaches me that everyone but Jesus has been and will be imperfect. There is something to this free-will thing that I cannot come near to fully understanding. But here I was, slowly getting shockingly better. After the first couple of years, some of my doctors referred to it as a miracle that I had not died. My Rockford neurologist even took to calling me the "Miracle Man." Further, it was a type of miracle to me that my quadriplegic state was so significantly improving. Some even credited my fortune to certain "good" characteristics that I was showing: faith, optimism, trust in my caretakers, good nature toward others, and a high degree of patience. I believe to some degree that these may have been contributing factors, but it was God's grace that made these characteristics, if at all true, even possible. I was never determined to fight my illness by employing these traits as a disciplined strategy. This was not preplanned like some Bill Belichick game plan for the Patriots. Was this the presence of the Holy Spirit in my life? I tend to think God just let all good traits be possible. To the extent they contributed to my recovery, I praise God for allowing me to be receptive. In whatever manner I may have gotten to this point of recovery, it was, I know, all due to the grace of God.

So, in my new home here at The Forum, it was nagging at me that I have real responsibilities to carry out God's will to the extent he lets me figure it out. Again, I am no special man in my eyes or, certainly, God's. I am not privileged to have millions of dollars to spend helping the disadvantaged or a great podium from which to change the lives of others. I do, however, believe my second chance means I must contribute to the benefit of others. I believe I am not still here to make significant money, become the world's most talented lawyer, or change the world through politics. I am, instead, such an insignificant, minor figure on this earth that I must concentrate on affecting those to whom I can contribute who are within my reach. That reach, to my knowledge, is not far. I sense I reach to those who come into or—more accurately, I believe—have been placed in my path. Of course, millions of people could be placed in our paths (for example, a person who passes by you in a mall or airport and whom you never notice or see again), but I take this to mean those that I, for some reason, seek out, and more significantly, those who seek me out. We can quietly become so important to each other. Secretly, I come to even love some people. My recovery is so dependent on feeling the love and commitment of others. Of course this means my immediate family, mother, and siblings, but it also means the special handful of friends who seem to give me attention. Beyond the ones I refer to throughout this narrative, I came to realize that some were right there under my nose at The Forum. As I said, most of the residents were significantly older than me. When their children came to visit, those kids were often older than me. More than once, new staff at The Forum inquired as to what parent patient I was there to visit. My favorite outside-The-Forum friends, most of whom assuredly know who they are, and a few others are mostly younger than me. While by no means exclusive, these are incredibly important people in my well-being and recovery. I do know that all of them, while being so-called accomplished people, have their own very human issues. They too need help, and I hope I can provide inspiration to them in some form or another. I don't suggest to anyone that they follow me or look to me as an example of some sort (I will let you down in one way or another); just see what God maybe has let me share with you should you desire so you might learn something from my experience. I am acutely aware of many past friends that have provided that for me, and it only serves to make me more committed to offer the same.

What I never anticipated when I moved into The Forum was that some particular persons would become so greatly important to me. The fact that a number of them were over ninety years old only made the experience more gratifying. I like to think I have a calling from God to help elderly people in some way, even if my impact will necessarily be very small. Most are people who have had tremendous blessed and happy lives. I know that; I hear their stories. I realize mine is completely blessed as well. As I expressed earlier, I am privileged. I believe I was comfortable knowing that my death was imminent during my adventure. Now I might expect to live longer. If I do, I know (and they know as well) that I will likely outlive them, certainly if I should live the same number of years as they have. But these people have become such a significant part, even if only for a brief period, of my entire life. What I have learned from some is invaluable. My life has such a different perspective now. We are all living day-to-day. That sounds cold, but I mean it in a positive way. While they still have their health, they are enjoying themselves even though age is taking its inevitable toll. It's the same toll taken on anyone who ever lived. Of course, we all have regrets, and the thought of death and an afterlife may be beyond true comprehension at times. My friends at The Forum come from different worldwide faiths as well as Christian denominations. I don't believe my role is to evangelize in some public sense of the word, but I hope to provide encouragement through positive attitude and works. The fact that I admit I am a Christian and choose to go to church many Sundays is the most I choose to exhibit. However, if I show as much care and respect to others, and especially these friends, it must be positive in some way—at least, so I hope. Only time will tell.

CHAPTER 43

WRAP IT UP

I am tempted to admit that now, as I finish this manuscript in the spring of 2019, the story of my adventure has had a pleasant outcome. I am no longer living in a senior facility, having moved in May 2019 into an apartment building not far from The Forum. To a great extent, this is a pleasant outcome. Some might say "Congratulations, you survived. You won; you defied the odds." My Rockford neurologist still tells my sister that I am a "miracle man" because of my unanticipated recovery. To this day, none of my neurologists are certain what I was suffering from, though one neurologist says it might have been one of twelve hundred neurological viruses, the exact one of which probably can't be identified even following an autopsy. I suggested that if that is the case, I certainly don't see any reason to pursue the autopsy very soon in hopes of finding an answer. Another neurologist suspects it all arose probably because of my ulcerative colitis greatly weakening my immune system, resulting in a propensity for severe illness. For a while my case was even presented to Duke University Medical Center and its neurological disorders clinic, which, led by Dr. Richard Bedlock, is doing incredible work trying to establish some link among the few patients who have recovered from ALS. It's an extraordinary undertaking that would have involved my participation in frequent visits to and analysis by Duke doctors to see if there is some explainable gene or the like that some of us may share. After reviewing my Mayo Clinic and Rockford medical records, I was not included as a participant in the program, as Duke doctors decided I indeed probably never did really have ALS. Along the way, a few of my doctors doubted the diagnosis, but only Dr. Rezania at the University of Chicago actually concluded I did not have ALS.

Frankly, it's never been important to me to know or understand what I was suffering from. You may have noticed this manuscript makes very little attempt to explain or define my illness. All I ever focused on (to the extent I could focus at all while under heavy drugs and in a frequently unconscious state) was receiving the next treatment and getting to the next day. That's no hero; it's merely a fortunate survivor. Yes, I admit I lived. At sixty-three years old, I am free of ALS, never actually suffered from creeping dementia, and to date have no apparent life-threatening medical issues lingering before me. My mind seems to be fully restored (some say "The old Bill is back again"), though that may not be pleasing to everyone, such as those who don't like this book, don't like some of my opinions, or disagree with me about President Trump. I am free of most outward signs of having been quadriplegic for several years, although I have yet to hit a tennis ball. I do hit golf balls, and yes, I am still the bad player I have always been. I am careful about my walking; I did trip on curbs twice back in late 2016—a time when I felt I was completely functional again—and broke that bone in my shoulder. I have not tripped or fallen since, but I do think about avoiding falling more often than ever. I am careful, I am cautious, and I move slower than I used to. How much of that is in part because I am sixty-three and not fifty-five any longer? Today I feel as good as I ever hoped I could.

My adventure changed my life; that's why experiences like mine are called "life-changing events." I feel settled, and I am pursuing things I want to do. In the past couple of years since returning to Dallas, I have been enjoying friends, working out with a trainer at a local gymnasium, getting stronger, following my sports teams, and reading books on subjects I never had time to pursue in the past. I have written this manuscript. I have accumulated some seven thousand photographs using my little Leica camera and pursuing my obsession with picture-taking. I have produced over forty drypoint prints on copper plates since going to evening art classes at SMU. (Whether my prints are any good or not does not matter, as I enjoy creating them.) I finally got my Texas driver's license back in April 2019 after being fully cleared by my neurologist to drive once again. I bought a "mature" low-mileage 2009 Volvo—something I equate to me, as we both have some special traits and a life left in us despite our advancing age. I even take an occasional trip out of Dallas, having gone to fun American places with or to see friends, including New York, Chicago, Miami, Detroit, and the Hopi Indian Reservation in northeastern Arizona. Best of all was an extraordinary trip in 2016 with my college buddy, Lloyd, when we traversed the western states, traveling from Chicago to Seattle. Lloyd rented a sharp new RV, and we had a ten-day adventure that included the South Dakota Badlands, Mount Rushmore, Deadwood, South Dakota casinos, the Little Big Horn Battlefield, Yellowstone National Park, Mount Olympia, the Washington state Pacific Ocean coast, and finally downtown Seattle. It was an amazing trip, although we did not cover as many miles as the two of us put on his mother's station wagon driving to Alaska as twenty-year-old college boys back in 1976. These are all good things, but they are, I admit, rather shallow in the scheme of things. My life has changed in so many ways that I think are far more important.

I can't exactly define my calling, but I sense I have one. I have learned so much since the advent of my adventure. I am fascinated with elderly people in ways I never before appreciated or realized. I know my ease with elderly people is in no small part because of the relationship my sister and I had as children with my grandparents

Charles and Agatha Howes, who taught us respect, wisdom, family, and love. These experiences I have had during my adventure are in a sense the experiences of every one of us, whether now or in our inevitable futures, though our stories will differ. So many live such rich and special lives no matter their present physical and even mental conditions. I have learned much about aging by witnessing and living among so many. More importantly, I witness the sanctity of life and just how special it is to be us. I am full of ideas about my future, but it is beyond the purpose of this book to speculate where I might go. I can only be excited to discover where my life goes, as I feel that I am on the way to being healthy again.

AFTERWARDS

Wednesday, October 16, 2019, some three and one-half months since I moved out of The Forum assisted living facility. By now, I have my own car (a mature 2009 Volvo – ironically, the last year I was doing much safe driving, with less than 50,000 miles on it), my new Texas Driver's license, my own apartment on the 5th floor of an apartment building not far from The Forum, and no one overseeing my medicine disbursement any longer. While still a disabled man to some extent, I am a free man in my mind. But on this day, I have a new experience, one I deem worthy of this *Afterwards*.

Bill Francis, ostensibly and most generously in celebration of my newfound independence, arranges an October guy's weekend trip for us to a Green Bay Packers game at Lambeau Field. A Bucket List item. I quickly manage to turn this into us joining old friends Rob Topping and Mack Findley (and wives) in Evanston a few days before the pro game to see Big Ten football when Northwestern hosts Ohio State. A reunion of four of my best friends! Why stop there? I arrange to fly up to Chicago early this Wednesday morning and, of course, the bus to Rockford, a mere 90 minutes away. Missy, Jack

The great reunion, Evanston, October 13, 2019. (L to R):
Bill Francis, Mack Findley, Rob Topping and Author.

and Peter are there and a 24-hour visit sounds great. I arrive in time
for lunch at a new Norwegian restaurant. Then, we hit some of our
favorite spots including a picture-taking walk among the fall colors
at the Anderson Japanese Gardens and, of course, Swedish pancakes
at Stockholm Inn. My perfect day in Rockford! But is it? Can I really
skip returning to the place in which we all think my life was saved?
The Park Strathmoor skilled care facility is too nearby. Do we dare?
It's been some four years since I last lived there. Who could still be
there? So many friends, yet most were in such tough situations. Many
were very elderly five years ago. What now? I felt the tug, frankly the
need; we must stop by.

Park Strathmoor looks the same on this October afternoon, just as
I remembered it. Entering, we do find a newly renovated lobby (*what,*
no giant picture window we patients spent much of our long days gazing
out?) and a new receptionist who could not possibly know us. We suggest a name we want to visit, doubting seriously anyone we suggested

was probably still there. No Angela Shaw or Jacki, she said. They had new jobs at another facility. Sorry, she says, the nurses are all in a staff meeting so no one is available right now. Then I spot a familiar face; my first therapist, the delightful lady who first had me trying to lift a one-pound weight with my lifeless arms. She recognized Missy, not so much me initially. Big hugs, warm smiles. We walk into the newly refurbished sitting area, I scan the scene. Anyone we know? Then a shout, giant smiles, his arms wide open! Joe Quayson, my great floor nurse comes out of the staff meeting. "I can't believe it's you," he says. "I just told your story just two days ago, and now you're here." Joe is no longer in his white floor nurse's uniform, but a nice sweater befitting the boss. Joe has deservedly been promoted to head of all nursing. I am brought into the staff meeting, only a few familiar faces among the dozen or so nurses. There is my last executive director, Nina Kuljanin-Thompson, still in charge and friendly as ever. "Please come in and tell our nurses about your recovery here." What a special time for me; nothing rehearsed, just from the heart. Tears of joy were hard to hold off. Soon, we are asking about my friends, the patients I spent so many days with and grew to love. Surely, not? No lie. Incredibly, one after another, still there. Massachusetts Bill, Stephen the former pharmacist, Nascar Nellie, even Gino. We go room to room to find them. Except for a couple in deep sleep, we find them awake in their rooms. Warm greetings as they hold our hands and smile in apparent recognition. One more. Katherine? I look where I remembered she had last been. Incredibly, Katherine is still there, asleep in her wheelchair, a foot from her little television, just as I found her many afternoons years ago. I go in alone. I gently stroke her exposed arm. "Katherine...you there?" Slowly her eyes open. Would she focus on me? That was not always guaranteed, I recalled. I say, "Hi, Honey. What we going to do today?" A smile comes to her beautiful face. She takes my hand, "Hi, Honey," she responds. All smiles, she awakens. She notices Missy, no objection this time to a woman there interrupting her moments with a younger man. Katherine insists on following us out in the hallway. Did she really know me or was it a smile for just a new unexpected visitor? More smiles, a hug, Nina assures me Katherine knows me. Yes, there was a tear or two. Too beautiful.

The Author reuniting with super nurse and friend, Joe Quayson, Park Strathmoor, October 13, 2019.

Not much had changed at Park Strathmoor. The great facility was still patiently performing miracles. Patients were living lives far beyond what some of us may have presumed possible. What a place! What a great wrap up to my adventure. I could not have scripted it better.